Xolela Mangcu is an internationa..., ...,....
commentator. He is based at the University of Cape Town and is also a Senior Fellow at the Brookings Institution in Washington D.C.

To the memory
of
Mrs Alice Nokuzola Biko – MamCethe
for giving up her beloved son so we could be free

Xolela Mangcu

BIKO
A Life

I.B. TAURIS
LONDON · NEW YORK

Published in 2014 by I.B.Tauris & Co. Ltd
6 Salem Road, London W2 4BU
175 Fifth Avenue, New York NY 10010
www.ibtauris.com

Distributed in the United States and Canada Exclusively by Palgrave Macmillan
175 Fifth Avenue, New York NY 10010

Copyright © Xolela Mangcu 2012, 2014

Published by agreement with NB Publishers, a division of Media24 Boeke (Pty) Ltd. Originally published by Tafelberg, an imprint of NB Publishers, Cape Town, South Africa in 2012.

The right of Xolela Mangcu to be identified as the author of this work has been asserted by the author in accordance with the Copyright, Designs and Patents Act 1988.

All rights reserved. Except for brief quotations in a review, this book, or any part thereof, may not be reproduced, stored in or introduced into a retrieval system, or transmitted, in any form or by any means, electronic, mechanical, photocopying, recording or otherwise, without the prior written permission of the publisher.

ISBN: 978 1 78076 785 7

A full CIP record for this book is available from the British Library
A full CIP record is available from the Library of Congress

Library of Congress catalog card: available

Printed and bound in Great Britain by Page Bros, Norwich.

Contents

	A Tribute to Stephen Bantu Biko by Nelson Mandela	7
	Preface	11
1	In My Mind's Eye	23
2	Steve Biko in the Intellectual History of the Eastern Cape: The African Elite and European Modernity	33
3	Formative Years in Ginsberg Location, King William's Town	79
4	Leaving Home: Lovedale, St Francis College	105
5	The Trouble(s) with NUSAS	113
6	Steve Biko and the Making of SASO	150
7	Strategic Leadership and "Losing Grip": The Black People's Convention	176
8	Banishment and Homecoming	204
9	How Steve was Killed	243
10	Steve Biko's "Extraordinary Gift of Leadership"	267
	Epilogue: Coming Full Circle	311
	Select Bibliography	325
	Acknowledgements	329
	About the Author	333
	Index	334

A Tribute to Stephen Bantu Biko
BY NELSON MANDELA[1]

On 12 September 25 years ago, the 31-year-old Steve Biko's life came to an end. His life was extinguished with more callousness and casualness than a person snuffing out a candle flame between calloused thumb and forefinger.

Living, he was the spark that lit a veld fire across South Africa. His message to the youth and students was simple and clear: Black is Beautiful! Be proud of your Blackness! And with that he inspired our youth to shed themselves of the sense of inferiority they were born into as a result of more than three centuries of white rule.

Assert yourselves and be self-reliant! With that he ignited a passion in the youth and they walked tall.

I never had the opportunity to meet him. From prison we followed his exploits and closely followed the emergence of the Black Consciousness Movement.

Well before they murdered him in detention, I realised that his stride was leaving indelible footprints in the struggles of

---

1 Reprinted with permission from the Nelson Mandela Foundation. An edited version was published in 2002 as part of a Steve Biko supplement that Xolela Mangcu edited for the Steve Biko Foundation.

our people against apartheid rule. In his short life he achieved what many would need a lifetime to accomplish.

We know today that when, in the life of a nation, the time comes for an idea, nothing – not even murder – can kill the idea.

All the information we collected about Steve pointed in one direction: he was an engaging young man who thought deeply and acted with conviction. He lived for freedom and was infused with a zest for life.

He understood that an enslaved people through their actions make freedom. He was focused on how to get our people into action, on how we could achieve freedom.

He forged a space in the midst of repression and saw the inexorable logic that the forces he was helping mobilise had to become part of the liberation forces.

He was arrested while he was busy going around the country consulting with a broad spectrum of people, gathered in different pockets of resistance. He was quietly preparing for a clandestine meeting he was due to hold with Oliver Tambo, the President of the ANC.

It now appears certain that the apartheid regime got wind of this. Whether his death came from an accidental blow or not, they had to kill him to prolong the life of apartheid. The very thought of a link-up between the ANC and the Black Consciousness Movement was unthinkable to the apartheid government.

As he grappled with the question of how to achieve freedom, he showed one of his strongest qualities – an ability to confront reality, to grow and develop ideas and continually broaden his outlook.

Today there are those who claim validity for their ideas by claiming a lineage to Steve Biko. To live with Steve's ideas they need to live out this singular ability of Steve, to adapt and grow and display the courage that belongs to leadership.

Steve lives on in the galaxy of brave and courageous leaders who helped shape democratic South Africa. May we never cease celebrating his life!

NELSON MANDELA

Preface

As I write this book there is a raging debate between two leading South African political commentators, Moeletsi Mbeki and Zubeida Jaffer. Mbeki stirred the hornet's nest when, at the 2012 Franschhoek Literary Festival, he described Steve Biko as a Xhosa prophet. Jaffer found this characterisation of Biko objectionable, given the Black Consciousness Movement's (BCM's) non-ethnic politics. The approach taken in this book is that this is an unhelpful dualism. Steve Biko was as much a product of South Africa's multi-ethnic political heritage as he was a child of the Xhosa people of the Eastern Cape. **Chapter 2** locates Steve within a long trajectory that goes back to the wars of resistance by the Khoi-Khoi and San people in the Northern Cape frontier in the 17th and 18th centuries, right up to the anti-colonial resistance of the Xhosa people on the Eastern Cape frontier throughout the 19th century.

I have provided an approximate periodisation of frontiers – if only to demonstrate the length of time it took to resist colonial rule, which is almost 150 years in each case. The third period, which is taken up in later chapters, would be that of the almost 100 years of nationalist struggle since the formation of the African National Congress (ANC), and later the Pan Africanist Congress, the Unity Movement, and the Black Consciousness Movement. This adds up to almost 400 years of political action and intellectual thought. Years are not a substitute for intensity of struggle, and there are great degrees of overlap, which is exactly the point of this chapter – the intercultural solidarities that were forged by different groups over time, culminating in Black Consciousness in the 1970s.

I use the term "frontier" for ease of reference to the literature. Roger Levine argues that "to describe the Eastern Cape in the early to mid-nineteenth century as a frontier is to underplay the long-term presence of Africans in the region". Levine uses the term "border region"[2] to signal the degree of intercultural contact among the Xhosa, the Khoi, the San and the European colonists and missionaries. This idea of intercultural contact is central to Steve Biko's attempt to reframe European modernity into a progressive African modernity through the philosophy of Black Consciousness, resulting in what he called a "joint culture".

There is indeed more than a superficial relationship between the Khoi and the San on the one hand and the Xhosa on the other. The clicks in isiXhosa come from the languages of the Khoi and San people. Roger Levine observes that "the Xhosa have incorporated three click consonants from the Khoisan into their language – the explosive plop produced by the tongue rocketing from the top of the mouth [q], the gentle tut from the front of the mouth [c] and the cluck from the side [x]".[3]

---

2   Roger Levine (2011). *A Living Man from Africa* (New Haven: Yale University Press), 4.
3   Levine, *A Living Man from Africa*, 13. Indeed, my name has at least two of those clicks: the x in my first name and the c in my last name, but when pronounced with a g it assumes a heavier sound.

Jeff Peires similarly notes that one sixth of all Xhosa words have clicks in them, attributing this to "the influence of the Khoi and San languages on Xhosa".[4] The BCM's definition of Blackness to include Coloureds and Indians is a supreme example of the centuries-old construction of hybrid identities. Aelred Stubbs describes Steve's unique contribution to the solidarity that developed among Coloureds, Indians and Africans as follows:

> ... it was a special strength of the Black Consciousness Movement that from the beginning in the 1960s SASO [South African Students Organisation] had been open to Coloureds and Indians. I am not sure that the importance of this achievement, in the given social structures of South Africa, has been emphasised ... but the way in which SASO managed to overcome traditional barriers between Africans and Coloureds ... was not only indicative of a new mood in the Coloured community, but a significant achievement of non-ethnic solidarity.[5]

Recognition of this hybrid heritage does not mean we cannot trace specific political themes of Black Consciousness to 19th-century Xhosa chiefs and intellectuals, who took up the resistance after the Khoi and the San were defeated and almost

---

4   Jeff Peires (2003). *The House of Phalo: A History of the Xhosa People in the Days of their Independence* (Cape Town: Jonathan Ball), 28.

5   Aelred Stubbs, "Martyr of Hope: A Personal Memoir," in Steve Biko (2004). *I Write What I Like* (Johannesburg: Picador Africa), 220. Stubbs had come to South Africa as a representative of the Community of the Resurrection first at St Peter's College in Rosettenville, and later at the Federal Seminary of Theology in Alice, where he first made contact with the Biko family and later with Steve, Barney Pityana and other SASO activists.

decimated at the end of the 18th century. By this time the Khoi and the San had been reduced to "a servant class on European farms and with European livestock ranchers under a quasi-legal situation that amounts to forced labour at worst and indentured servitude at best".[6] In this chapter I pay particular attention to the crucial role played by two Xhosa chiefs, Ndlambe and Ngqika, and their respective allies as prophet-intellectuals, Nxele and Ntsikana. Through their contrasting responses, these chiefs and their prophets laid the contours for the conduct and discourse of anti-colonial resistance, while grappling with the question of how to deal with the "onrush of [European] modernity".[7] To understand Steve Biko's response to that same modernity, one has to grapple with the political and intellectual history of the Eastern Cape – and the terms this history made available for him to engage with that modernity more than a century later. It is not enough to reduce Biko's thinking, as many scholars have done, to the influence of Frantz Fanon.

Chapter 3 continues in this historical vein by locating Steve in the radical political culture of Ginsberg Location[8] in the 1960s, under the shadow of his older brother Khaya Biko. In the early 1960s Ginsberg was a stronghold of the Pan Africanist Congress (PAC), and Khaya was the organisation's leading member in the township. Formed in 1959 and banned in 1960, the PAC's influence lasted much longer than its existence

---

6   Levine, *A Living Man from Africa*, 12.
7   Eric Hobsbawm (1990). *Nations and Nationalism Since 1780* (Cambridge: Cambridge University Press), 109.
8   When I was growing up the township was simply known as a location, and it was only later that the word was replaced by township. For the remainder of the book I will be using the term "township".

as a political organisation. Thus, Khaya was expelled from Lovedale College and subsequently jailed for PAC activities as late as 1963. It is important, however, not to stretch the relationship between the PAC and the BCM too far. The BCM consisted of people from both the ANC and the PAC. Barney Pityana has always belonged to the ANC: "I personally never felt outside of the ANC that I had been part of since I was 15 or so at school."[9] Unlike the PAC – and particularly the more jingoistic elements who regarded even Coloureds as alien – the BCM built a strong black solidarity among Africans, Indians and Coloureds. The BCM also had more of a Third World than an Africanist outlook, incorporating in its ideology both the influences of African leaders such as Julius Nyerere but also Frantz Fanon, Paulo Freire and the black nationalist movement in the United States. The fact that Ginsberg was itself a mixed community throughout Steve's young life also played a role in his perception of Coloureds as part of the oppressed – their lived experience was there for all to see in Ginsberg.

Chapter 4 deals with Steve's institutional encounter with racism when he was expelled from Lovedale College because of his brother's political activism. He also objected to the authoritarianism he found at St Francis College at Mariannhill in KwaZulu-Natal. It is through these institutions of education and religion – what Ntongela Masilela calls the "political and cultural facilitators of entrance into European modernity"[10] – that many leaders come into their own. They were

---

9   Pityana interview with Rupert Taylor and Nhlanhla Ndebele, 8 February 2000, Parktown, Johannesburg.
10 Ntongela Masilela, interview with Sandile Ngidi, unpublished manuscript, 2000, 63.

spurred into action by their experience of what the sociologist Emile Durkheim called "anomie". In colonial and apartheid South Africa this would be the mismatch between the promise of educational attainment and religious conversion on the one hand, and the reality of racial exclusion and discrimination on the other. Steve tasted the injustice of apartheid when he was expelled from Lovedale College because of his brother Khaya's political activities. But Khaya was not too displeased that his brother was drawn into politics. As he put it: "Then the giant was awakened."

Steve began to assume a more conscious and assertive political role at St Francis College. That is when he started asking critical questions about the relevance of Christianity – the lynchpin of European modernity in Africa – to the lives of oppressed people. The questions were in the form of letters and conversations with his mother, a devout Christian, and discussions with a young radical cleric in our township, David Russell. It was Steve's mother, Alice (whom I shall refer to as MamCethe, the clan name by which she was fondly called in the township), who protected Russell against a congregation that did not want him on account of his race. I still have vivid memories of Russell preaching in fluent Xhosa in our church. As a young boy I could not, for the life of me, understand how this Xhosa-speaking white man found himself in our midst.

Stubbs remembers an interview with Steve's mother in the *Daily Dispatch* about her son's growing political activism. Concerned and fearing for his life she sent him a Bible in the hope that he would find answers in it: at home during the vacation she tackled him about her concern, but he replied,

"What did Jesus come into the world to do?" He told her if Jesus had come to liberate mankind, he too had a duty to seek liberation for his people.[11]

Steve continued to experience the contradictions between the liberal promise of equality and the actual reality of racial discrimination when he arrived at Rhodes University as a delegate at a congress of the multi-racial National Union of South African Students (NUSAS) in 1967. At that congress black students were required to sleep apart from the rest in the township, and Steve enjoined his white colleagues to join them in the township or to cancel the congress. When the congress voted his motion down, Steve led the historic walk-out of black students that ultimately led to the first meeting to formulate the idea of a blacks-only student organisation. **Chapter 5** is a discussion of not only the contradictory political relationship but also explores the nature of his relationship with his white friends, which caused tensions within the movement. Also, Steve was quite non-racial when it came to his relationships with white women, including an open relationship with a fellow student at the University of Natal, Paula Ensor.[12]

Chapter 6 is about the formation and the ideological evolution of the South African Students Organisation (SASO). Initially, SASO adopted nothing more than what Barney Pityana describes as a "pragmatic" black consciousness, which was no more than a gathering space for black students around the country on a social basis. I describe Steve's leadership of the movement at this stage as cautious and tactical. The elements of

---

11 Aelred Stubbs. "The story of Nyameko Barney Pityana" in *South African Outlook*, vol. 110, no. 1300, October 1979.
12 Paula Ensor is now Dean of Humanities at the University of Cape Town.

a fully-fledged philosophy began to emerge around 1970 after he had served his term as president of SASO, and had taken up the editorship of the SASO newsletter. Of critical importance here is the key role played by the University Christian Movement (UCM) as a midwife of the new movement. Even though some members of BCM were against any collaboration with UCM, Steve maintained a strategic – some might say parasitic – relationship with UCM. However, given their radical political culture, UCM leaders such as Colin Collins and Basil Moore were quite aware of the historic role they were playing in their support for SASO. In any event, Steve and Colin Collins were constantly exchanging letters about how UCM could best support SASO.

I also explore the debates and divisions around the formation of the Black People's Convention (BPC) (**Chapter 7**). Steve was firmly opposed to the formation of the BPC as a political organisation. The driving force behind the new organisation became Harry Nengwekhulu and other SASO leaders who, in 1971, were able to persuade a sceptical community meeting in Orlando, Soweto, to support the formation of a political structure. After the first generation of the movement's leadership was banned in March 1973 – and that included Steve being banished to Ginsberg – a second generation of leaders emerged with an even more militant outlook under the leadership of Saths Cooper (who was also banned) and Muntu Myeza. Against Steve's advice, this group organised the Viva Frelimo rallies in September 1974. They were ultimately arrested and Steve testified as the defence witness in the long-running SASO/BPC Trial. The trial was to be the first public political trial since the Rivonia Trial in 1964, and gave Steve a national platform to articulate to the world the philosophy of Black Consciousness.

Chapter 8 is a discussion of Steve's work in Ginsberg through the Black Community Programmes, and its evaluation through the eyes of some of the community members who worked with him. The chapter also includes a discussion of some of his personal difficulties stemming from his messy love life. While married to Ntsiki Biko (née Mashalaba) he was also having an open relationship with Mamphela Ramphele, whom he had met at the University of Natal and who would later come down to King William's Town to run Zanempilo Health Clinic. Some senior leaders of the political movement, including Robert Sobukwe, expressed their unhappiness about his multiple relationships and the impact these could have on the movement. On this one aspect of his life Steve found himself defensive and faltering. And as Christopher Hitchens writes in a critical essay on Mark Twain's biography, it is important in biography that "the private person be allowed to appear in all his idiosyncrasy".[13] This is indeed an ever-present danger for a biographer like me, who is a self-admitted admirer and follower of his subject. But for Steve to be human he must be presented to the reader warts and all – the women, the drinking, the bad temper, the stubbornness and the arrogance at times. As he put it in a letter to his friend Aelred Stubbs: "a lot of friends of mine believe I am arrogant and they are partly right."[14] To paraphrase his friend Bokwe Mafuna, Steve was a prophet, not a saint.

---

13 Christopher Hitchens (2011). *Arguably* (London: Atlantic Books), 40-41.
14 Stubbs, "Martyr of Hope: A Personal Memoir", 199.

Chapter 9 is a discussion of Steve's elusive quest for unity among the liberation movements – a quest that takes him on his abortive and fateful trip to Cape Town. From the moment Steve was banished to King William's Town, he lost control of the movement he had started, and oftentimes expressed his sense of guilt that many of the people he had brought into the movement had been arrested or killed. At one point he admitted to Stubbs that even though he regarded himself as "reasonably strong", the going was quite tough because of the restriction orders placed on him. The chapter takes us through his trip to Cape Town and back, his arrest at a roadblock and his brutal murder at the age of 31 by the South African police.

I once had a conversation about Steve with the founding father of African literature, Chinua Achebe. He said Biko reminded him of the Nigerian poet Christopher Okigbo. Both men, Achebe observed, seem to have been "possessed" in their rush to achieve their respective missions – as if they knew they would have an early death. Steve prophetically described the impact his death might have, were it to come: "You are either alive and proud or you are dead, and when you are dead, you can't care anyway. And your method of death can itself be a politicising thing."[15]

Yet another element of a good biography, Hitchens writes, is that it must leave you wishing you had known the individual. As recounted in **Chapter 1**, I still have vivid memories of Steve Biko in "my mind's eye", but I also wish I was old enough to have been able to converse with him. Each time I read his writings it feels like the first time. The last two chapters of this

---

15   Steve Biko (2004). *I Write What I Like* (Johannesburg: Picador Africa), 173.

book (**Chapter 10 and the Epilogue**) are my own subjective reflections on a man that Nigel Gibson has described as "South Africa's greatest liberation theorist".[16] Newspaper editor Donald Woods called him "the greatest man I ever had the privilege to know".[17] In those chapters I reflect on what we lost with Steve Biko and the Black Consciousness Movement, and what we might do to regain some of that movement's finest qualities and make them part of our usable past. Steve Biko's greatest historical achievement remains that of restoring the humanity of a defeated and despised people so that they might resume what Nelson Mandela has called "the long walk to freedom".

As I wrote this book over the years, I kept kicking myself for not spending more time with Steve's mother. There was a time when both of our families moved from the "Brownlee" section of Ginsberg to the "Leightonville" section that was reserved for Coloureds, until they were moved under the Group Areas Act to the neighbouring areas of Breidbach and Schornville in the 1970s. This opened space for African families to move up, so to speak, in the hierarchy of accommodation from three-roomed houses to five-roomed houses. The Biko home is still in the street behind ours. As a teenager, I would pass Mrs Biko sitting on the verandah of her new home almost every day. Sometimes she would call me over to ask how I was doing, but in all honesty, I always felt she was holding me up from some more exciting youthful engagement – such as hanging out with girls in a local shebeen. And so, in repen-

---

16 Nigel Gibson (2011). *Fanonian Practices in South Africa* (Pietermaritzburg: UKZN Press), 70.
17 Donald Woods (1978). *Biko* (New York: Penguin Books), 85.

tance, I dedicate this book to the memory of Alice "MamCethe" Biko.

1

In My Mind's Eye

"The struggle of man against power is the struggle of
memory against forgetting."
MILAN KUNDERA

I was only eleven at the time. And yet, as best as I can remember, I had already grown beyond my years. Of course I ought to be careful when reconstructing what I experienced at such an early age. Memory can play tricks on the mind. But, somehow, many of those who were around in the 1970s remember where they were when news broke of Steve Biko's death.

It was 12 September 1977. I remember my mother remarking on the oddity of the rain in the midst of the sunshine. AmaXhosa call that type of rain *ilinci*, and it is a bad omen. I also remember that it was a weekday because my mother – who was also my primary school teacher – and I had just returned from school. She had been preparing something for me to eat before I returned for after-school classes when someone knocked at the door. As she so often did, my mother asked me to answer the door. I called out: "Forbes Nyathi is here to see you," and returned to the serious business of my lunch. Forbes is Steve's first cousin, as his mother Eugenia was Steve's father Mzingaye's younger sister. I took a second glance at Forbes, normally a cheerful fellow, and noticed the sombre look on his face. They both disappeared into my mother's room, and all I could make out were whispers. When my mother came out of the room, she looked distressed. Something terrible had happened, she said: "*uBantu uswelekile*" – "Bantu is no longer with us." Everyone in our community called Steve by his first name – Bantu, a name which signifies being at one with the people.

Before I could ask more, she rushed me back to school.

Back at our school, chaos reigned. Steve's niece Nompumezo was crying inconsolably in our Standard Five (Grade 7) classroom. The older boys summoned us out of class and instructed us to go back to the township. We would not be returning to school for weeks on end. This was of great concern because that meant there was a chance I would miss the exams for the last year of primary school. I had already expressed my desire to go to one of the more prestigious boarding schools for junior high school the following year. Given what was going on around me, this seemed like a self-indulgent thought. Community members streamed from all corners of the township to gather in the public square in front of our house. The question – and there seemed to be no satisfactory answer – was what had happened to Bantu?

The minister of justice, Jimmy Kruger, had issued a statement that Steve Biko had died from a hunger strike:

> He was arrested in connection with activities related to the riots in Port Elizabeth, and *inter alia* for drafting and distributing pamphlets, which incited arson and violence ... Mr Biko refused his meals and threatened a hunger strike. But he was regularly supplied with meals and water which he refused to partake of.[18]

---

18   Jimmy Kruger's statement in Millard Arnold (ed.) (1979). *The Testimony of Steve Biko* (London: Maurice Temple Smith Publishers), 283.

The community was outraged. This explanation for deaths in detention had been offered too many times for anyone to take it seriously. I remember the anger of the crowd – especially the youngsters. I particularly remember the agitation of the twin brothers with biblical names, Joseph and Daniel, who lived at the back of our house. The youths were urging the assembled group to take revenge on the whites in town. Cooler heads prevailed and that line of action was abandoned. The anger turned inward. The discussion suddenly turned into speculation about who might have been the police informer. The next thing, a large group of youths went on a rampage. I ran home.

For the next few days a dark cloud of smoke hung over our township – literally and figuratively – as government installations and homes of suspected police informers went up in flames.

The youth targeted teachers because they were seen as part of the system of Bantu Education. My brother, who was a school principal at the nearby township of Zwelitsha, had his house destroyed by a mob of students and he moved into our home in Ginsberg. I was afraid for our home as well but nothing happened to us. My mother sent me to the shops to check out a group of youngsters who had threatened my brother about coming to find him at our house. The boys saw through my mission and warned me not to tell on them.

In the ensuing mayhem over the next few days I found myself literally staring at a policeman with a rifle. He was in camouflage behind a shrub. I turned and ran back as fast as I could. That kind of near encounter with death never left my memory. Under apartheid too many people were killed by being shot in the back, fleeing from the police – from Sharpeville to June 1976. I was lucky to come out of that experience alive, to somehow tell the story not only of Steve's death but also of his life.

Over the next two weeks our little township became the focus of the world. Hundreds of people from all over the country and from all over the globe descended on Ginsberg to hold a vigil at the Biko home in Leightonville. Every night I escaped my mother's watchful eye to listen to the fiery speeches and the freedom songs. By this time I knew the songs by heart, for I had grown beyond my years. My brother, who was a friend of Steve's, would later tell me that Steve would compose some of these songs by simply taking popular Bible hymns and replacing them with revolutionary lyrics. For example, the popular struggle song *Amabhulu azizinja*[19] – "Whites are dogs" – is derived from a famous Presbyterian hymn written by the great 19th-century priest and intellectual Reverend Tiyo Soga on his return from study in Scotland in 1857. Upon arrival at the Port of Algoa Bay (Port Elizabeth) aboard the ship *Lady of the Lake*, Soga knelt down, kissed African soil and sang this hymn in prayer. Legend also has it that he was inspired to compose the song on his first view of Table Mountain as the ship came around the Cape. Barney Pityana has described the emotional and historical significance of *Lizalis' idinga lakho* for black people as follows:

> It is a hymn that has taken on the authority of a national anthem. It is sung in churches throughout the length and breadth

---

19 This, of course, was a metaphorical reference to the way white people were colluding with apartheid.

of this land; it can be heard in political rallies; in times of sadness and in times of joy, *Lizalis' idinga lakho* is evocative of our deepest feelings, expresses our prayers in words too beautiful to fathom. It is a plaintive song of remembrance, of pain, of defiance and of dedication. [20]

Whether Steve adapted *Lizalis' idinga lakho* into *Amabhulu azizinja* is not clear. For example, others argue that the song was composed or adapted by Vuyisile Mini – one of the first people to be hanged for ANC underground activities in Port Elizabeth. It is also believed that ANC leader Govan Mbeki co-authored some of these songs. Barney Pityana recalls:

> I remember so well growing up in New Brighton with the ANC having something called *umjikelezo* singing these songs rather like religious revival meetings. The songs grew out of that.

We will probably never know for sure. History, as they say, does not proceed in a straight line. The historian Jeff Peires explains the quest for certitude as springing more from "the understandable wish to bring order into history than it does from history itself".[21] As Immanuel Kant put it: "Out of timber so crooked as that from which man is made nothing entirely straight can be carved."[22]

---

20 Barney Pityana, Tiyo Soga Memorial Lecture, University of Fort Hare, East London Campus, 7 December 2010.
21 Peires, *The House of Phalo*, 18.
22 Immanuel Kant (1784). *Kant's Gesammelte Schriften* (Berlin, 1910, vol. 8), 23.

Whatever their authorship, these revolutionary songs became our heritage. The people at Steve's home sang them as if they were singing from the same hymnal sheet, with a fervour similar to that described by Pityana.

The youth from Johannesburg's Soweto township seemed particularly fearless as they did their famous call-and-response throughout the period of the vigil. Someone would shout at the police: *Niyabesaba na?* – "Are you scared of them?" – and the crowd would respond: *Hayi, asibesabi, siyabafuna* – "No, bring 'em on". From a distance I had been fascinated by the militancy of the Soweto youth since the outbreak of the 1976 student uprisings the year before. I followed the news about Soweto student leader Tsietsi Mashinini whose famed disguises and escapes from the police were the stuff of legend throughout the country. Now Soweto had come to Ginsberg.

Steve Biko's funeral was set for 25 September 1977 at the Victoria Stadium in King William's Town – many of the most visible symbols of this most colonial of towns are named after 19th-century British monarchs or governors. The whole region is peppered with colonial names, many dating back to the arrival of German settlers in 1857 – East London, Berlin, Hanover, Hamburg, Frankfort, etc. Giving the Steve Biko Memorial Lecture in Cape Town in 2003, the famed African writer Ngugi wa Thiong'o spoke about the inappropriateness of these names in an African country. It was as if African memory was made over and dressed in the garb of European terminology. Of course, the towns had their original names too, such as Qonce or Bhisho for King William's Town. My granduncle, Benjamin kaTyamzashe (popularly known as B ka-T), composed a song for the town titled *Bhisho ikhaya lam* – Bhisho is my home. This name was later usurped by the homeland leader Lennox Sebe to build a boondoggle of a capital for the Ciskei Bantustan. Ultimately, the colonial names became the official ones.

And so there I was – an eleven-year-old, joining the throngs of adults on their way to Victoria Stadium. There are many things about that day that I don't remember. One thing that has stayed with me is that I was wearing a shirt that Bandile, my cousin from Cape Town had given to me, and that I did not have any shoes on. Saying I was without shoes is not yet another example of the narrative of ascent – the rags-to-riches posture that is the favourite posture of many successful black professionals, so as to make their rise more heroic. In the words of Henry Louis Gates Jr., successful blacks are "wedded to narratives of ascent . . . and we have made the compounded preposition 'up from' our own – up from slavery, up from Piedmont, up from the Bronx, always up".[23] I did not put on any shoes because I liked walking barefoot.

It was unusual for the funeral of a black person, let alone a revolutionary leader, to be held in town. But there was no venue big enough in our township. The community had sent a delegation, led by my granduncle B ka-T Tyamzashe, to negotiate with the municipality for the use of the Victoria Stadium. When the municipality gave the go-ahead, the white people in the neighbourhood packed their stuff and left town for the weekend.

According to newspaper reports there were more than 20 000

---

23 Henry Louis Gates Jr. (1996). "Parable of the Talents" in Henry Louis Gates Jr. and Cornel West (eds), *The Future of the Race* (New York: Vintage Books), 3.

people in the stadium that day. The numbers would have been bigger if thousands had not been turned back at various police roadblocks throughout the country. I would later learn that this was the first mass political funeral in the country – to be followed in the 1980s by such big political funerals as those of Griffiths and Victoria Mxenge in the nearby village of Rhayi, and that of the Cradock Four – Matthew Goniwe, Fort Calata, Sparrow Mkhonto and Sicelo Mhlawuli – in 1985. While the latter funerals were multi-racial events, there were only a handful of white faces at Steve's funeral. Angry militants sneered and jeered at the whites, hoping the crowd would join in their attacks. The crowd did not take the bait. These people included some of Steve's best friends, like the Reverend David Russell and *Daily Dispatch* editor Donald Woods. Throughout my childhood these people came to our township to visit the Biko family, and as children we were fascinated by the idea of whites coming to the township. This was particularly so with the Woods family, whose little children played ball with us while their parents sat in the house with the adults.

The Right Reverend Desmond Tutu delivered the sermon and former Robben Islander Fikile Bam, later judge president of the Land Claims Court, made a not-so-veiled threat that "we are not helpless". Other speakers on the dais included representatives of the South West Africa People's Organisation (SWAPO), the South West Africa National Union (SWANU) and foreign diplomats. The prominent medical doctor and community activist Nthato Motlana also gave a rousing speech.

Steve's coffin was taken to the cemetery – which has since been renamed the Steve Biko Garden of Remembrance – on an ox-drawn cart. This was a deliberate break with the tradition of fancy limousines. The coffin had a fist in the form of a black power salute on it, and was engraved with the words *One Azania, One Nation*. Everyone walked to the graveyard, led by dashiki-wearing (a dashiki is a bright, loose, coloured shirt) militants such as the president of the Black People's Convention, Hlaku Rachidi.

I had always suspected that Steve Biko was an important figure in the world. I kept a secret makeshift album made up mostly of pictures from newspaper cuttings, many of which featured his numerous courthouse appearances. I went along with him to some of the community projects he was running, including the famous Zanempilo Health Clinic he ran with Mamphela Ramphele. Black doctors were rare in those days, and black female doctors even rarer. As children we were not allowed into the clinic but we peeped through keyholes and windows nonetheless. Sometimes we would go down to the township entrance to wait for Steve to drive back from his offices which, to our puzzlement, were also in town. The Black Community Programmes, for which he was working, was renting backroom offices at the Anglican Church on Leopoldt Street in the "white" town. At other times we would spend the afternoon sitting in front of the church on Leopoldt Street watching the comings and goings of the men and women in black and gold dashikis. Among them were Peter Jones, Malusi Mpumlwana, Thoko Mpumlwana (nee Mbanjwa), Mzwandile Mbilini, Mamphela Ramphele, Thenjiwe Mthintso, Kenny Rachidi, Mapetla Mohapi, Nohle Mohapi, Thami Zani, Mxolisi Mvovo and his wife Nobandile (Steve's younger sister). There was a sense of fearlessness and urgency among them, and they had a deep connection with the community. Steve, in particular, was always surrounded by a group of Ginsberg youngsters who called themselves the Cubans and who in turn called him Castro. This was in apparent reference to both his political and physical stature. He was a big man in all senses of the word.

No one seemed more fearless to me than Mzwandile Mbilini, who lived in the shebeen directly opposite my home. The shebeen was run by his cousin, Skhweyi Mbilini, who was a childhood friend of Steve's. There was drama whenever the security police came to arrest Mzwandile. He was always dressed in military fatigues and would defiantly raise his clenched fist in the air before they drove him away. Zolani Mtshotshisa, who was a youth activist in the Black Consciousness Movement (BCM) in the 1970s before crossing over to the ANC – as many BCM youth would later do after going into exile in 1976 – quotes how Mzwandile would describe those heady days in our township: "I had Jones on my left and Biko on my right, and we had the country on our shoulders."

The last time I remember seeing Steve was from the vantage point of my home's verandah. As usual, he was going to meet up with his friends at the Mbilini shebeen opposite our home, dressed in his brown suede jacket. Maybe he had other jackets but that is the only one he ever seemed to wear. He was not a man known for his sartorial elegance, quite the opposite. In fact, among the many nicknames he picked up as a child, two stand out – *Goofy* and *Xwaku-Xwaku* – the latter a reference to his unkempt manner.

I do not recall ever seeing Stephen Bantu Biko again, hence this search.

2
Steve Biko in the Intellectual History of the Eastern Cape: The African Elite and European Modernity

> "Take your place in the world as coloured,
> not as white men, as Kafirs, not as Englishmen."
> TIYO SOGA, 1870

Most works on the life and work of Steve Biko locate his thought within the politics of the 1960s, particularly the rise of black consciousness in the United States and decolonisation movements in Africa. Steve himself acknowledges the role of the Black Consciousness Movement (BCM) in the United States:

> At this time we were also influenced by the development of a Black Consciousness Movement in the United States. There were differences, of course, because the political context simply was not the same. The conflicts in South Africa were – and are – much sharper... I do want to acknowledge the indebtedness of the Black Consciousness Movement in South Africa to the development of black thought in the USA in the 1960s.[24]

In this book I take a different tack from the dominant tendency to reduce black consciousness to the events of the 1960s. I endeavour to place Steve Biko in a longer time span of black

---

[24] Steve Biko (1977). Interview with Bernard Zylstra. "The Struggle for South Africa", An Interview With Steve Biko, 1978.

33

political and cultural thought in South Africa, in the aftermath of the late 18th-century African encounter with European modernity. This modernity in South Africa "was constituted through violence: colonial conquest, dispossession, slavery, forced labour, the restriction of citizenship to whites, and the application of violent bureaucratic routines to the marshalling, distribution and domination of the black population."[25] It was also imported through mission schools and churches. I argue that one has to delve into the traditions of African thought in the Eastern Cape and in his own community in Ginsberg township to understand why figures such as Frantz Fanon would make sense to Steve at a later stage of his life. In short, he did not come to politics as a blank slate, and neither did he slavishly follow a particular political text. Noel Mostert has this to say about Steve's historical antecedents:

> Biko, himself missionary educated, represented the last African generation to be the beneficiaries of that tradition. He personified through his lack of anti-white sentiment, his gentleness and articulate rationality, so many of the characteristic attributes of the missionary-educated African elite which had assumed African leadership after the last of the frontier wars exactly a century before; yet he embodied as well a rupture with that tradition.[26]

Daniel Magaziner makes a similar observation that the Black Consciousness student leaders were "descendants of previous

---

25 Michael Burawoy and Karl von Holdt (2012). *Conversations with Bourdieu: The Johannesburg Moment* (Johannesburg: Wits University Press), 122.
26 Noel Mostert (1992). *Frontiers: The Epic of South Africa's Creation and the Tragedy of the Xhosa People* (London: Cape Publishers), 1278.

generations of African thinkers whose ideas figure prominently in works that examine the history of African theatre and poetry, journalism and academia".[27] Cornel West captured the same theme:

> Quality leadership is neither the product of one great individual nor the result of odd historical accidents. Rather it comes from deeply bred traditions and communities that shape and mould talented and gifted persons.[28]

In this chapter I trace the traditions of African thought that preceded Steve back to the differences between two great Xhosa chiefs, Ngqika and Ndlambe, and their respective prophet-intellectuals, Ntsikana and Nxele, in the 19th century. I argue that Steve Biko's philosophical outlook should be located in this broader intellectual history. Instead of a rupture with traditions set by earlier African leaders, I speak of continuities and discontinuities, not only within African leadership traditions but also in the encounter with European modernity as well as the shifting alliances with the Khoi and the San people. Africans were never entirely free from other cultures, nor even from the ones against which they fought. Frantz Fanon captures the inextricably intertwined identities of the coloniser and the colonised in *The Wretched of the Earth*. First he points to the existential confusion wrought by colonialism on the educated elite:

---

27 Daniel Magaziner (2010). *The Law and the Prophets: Black Consciousness in South Africa, 1968-1977* (Athens, Ohio: Ohio University Press), 6.
28 Cornel West (1993). *Race Matters* (New York: Vintage Books), 56.

> Yes the first duty of the native poet is to see clearly the people he has chosen as the subject of his work of art. He cannot go forward resolutely unless he first realises the extent of his estrangement from them. We have taken everything from the other side; and the other side gives us nothing unless by a thousand detours we swing finally round in their direction, unless by ten thousand wiles and a hundred thousand tricks they manage to draw us toward them, to seduce us and to imprison us. Taking means in nearly every case being taken: *thus it is not enough to try to free oneself by repeating proclamations and denials.* [own emphasis]

And the educated elite cannot resist the seduction by simply returning to a romantic and pure past in the name of the people:

> It is not enough to try to get back to the people in that past out of which they have already emerged; rather we must join them in that fluctuating movement which they are just giving a shape to, and which, as soon as it has started, will be the signal for everything to be called into question. Let there be no mistake about it; it is to this zone of occult instability where the people dwell that we must come; and it is there that our souls are crystallised and that our perceptions and our lives are transfused with light.[29]

In characteristically dramatic language, the writer Lewis Nkosi describes black nationalist movements as "bastard children of Western modernity".[30] Nkosi argues that in their efforts to

---

29 Frantz Fanon (1963). *The Wretched of the Earth* (New York: Grove Press), 226-227.
30 Lewis Nkosi (2006 [1981]). "Negritude: New and Old Perspectives" in Lindy Stiebel and Liz Gunner (eds) (2006) *Still Beating the Drum: Critical Perspectives on Lewis Nkosi* (Johannesburg: Wits University Press).

liberate themselves from the "civilised decorum" of Western culture, black writers "were obliged to make use of the weapons which that culture had itself furnished" – mostly education and religion.

Bheki Peterson notes that the educated elite often joined protest and rebellious movements because of their own frustration with the contradictions between the promises of European modernity and their exclusion from the fruits of that very same modernity. Their participation in struggle was an attempt to show up and correct this contradiction. The more conservative among these educated elites relied on moral persuasion to get the European colonisers to extend political rights to Africans. Here is the legendary African intellectual DDT Jabavu on the prospects for change through moral persuasion – and see the importance he attaches to the two central features of European modernity – education and religion:

> It is our belief that with the spread of better understanding in Church and college circles the future of South Africa is one we can contemplate with a fair degree of optimism in the hope that Christian influences will dispel illusions, transcend the mistaken political expedients of pseudo-segregationists and usher in a South Africa of racial peace and goodwill.[31]

---

31 DDT Jabavu (1928). *The Segregation Fallacy and Other Papers* (Alice: Lovedale Press). Cited in Gail Gerhart (1978). *Black Power in South Africa: The Evolution of an Ideology* (Berkeley: University of California Press), 35. Jabavu was the first black professor at the University of Fort Hare and later became president of the South African Institute of Race Relations and the All African Convention. Like his father John Tengo – discussed below – DDT became a towering force in black political and intellectual life.

Peterson further notes that even the more progressive elite such as John Dube and Pixley kaSeme tended to be accommodating and deferential towards colonial authorities. And yet, "it was precisely in occupying the intermediary ground, a diffuse, marginal space, that the *kholwa* were compelled to forge profoundly new forms of African identity in response to modernity".[32] This is not to say that the hybridisation of modernity – and the making of new African identities – was a uniquely elite affair. Far from it. As David Attwell notes, "modernity is experienced 'objectively' as much by the migrant labourer as by the writer-artist . . . in oral popular genres and in the African independent churches, for example. It is true, nevertheless, that elites are, indeed, deeply involved in such work of interpretation and re-inscription."[33] While the elites may lead this process, this is not a one-way street. One of Fanon's major contributions was a recognition of the tensions that would emerge between the African elite and the working people at the moment of freedom as they each sought to define their identities and find their place in the post-colonial world. This is "the struggle over post-coloniality" that we see in South Africa today as the wealthy elite lead lives that are at a far remove from the masses of people – politically, economically and culturally.

The fact that the elite historically came from European institutions – educational and religious – explains why the leaders of the various liberation movements were all educated in the mission schools: Nelson Mandela and Robert Sobukwe at Healdtown, Chris Hani and Steve Biko at Lovedale. Ian Macqueen

---

32 Bhekizizwe Peterson (2000). *Monarchs, Missionaries and Intellectuals* (Johannesburg: Wits University Press).

33 David Attwell (2005). *Rewriting Modernity* (Scottsville: University of KwaZulu-Natal Press), 23.

observes that "as men schooled in the liberal crucible of Lovedale and, for Pityana, at Fort Hare College, they [BC leaders] were well-placed to judge the gulf between liberal ideals and actions",[34] just like their 19th and early 20th century predecessors. And it is no surprise that the BC movement was born within the bosom of European modernity – the white universities in South Africa.

I argue that Steve Biko did more than any other political leader to form a political movement whose primary aim and achievement was to challenge the intellectual foundations of European modernity while engaging with that modernity itself through the weapons it had itself furnished. Attwell argues that the Black Consciousness Movement fashioned a response to European modernity that would be on the terms of black people themselves, by drawing on the diaspora: "for the invasive effects of racial capitalism were such that intellectuals such as Steve Biko and his followers were, to a degree, culturally disenfranchised at home."[35]

As shall become apparent in Chapter 5, the reframing of Christianity through Black Theology was one of the signal achievements of the Black Consciousness movement.

Macqueen takes the liberty of saying that Biko was describing his personal experience when he wrote that "no wonder the African child learns to hate his heritage in his days at school. So negative is the image presented to him that he tends to find solace only in close identification with white society."[36]

---

34 Ian Martin Macqueen (2011). "Re-imagining South Africa: Black Consciousness, Radical Christianity and the New Left, 1967-1977", PhD thesis, University of Sussex, 24.
35 Attwell, *Rewriting Modernity*, 20.
36 Biko cited in Macqueen, *Re-imagining South Africa*.

However, I shall stop short of making Biko "a subjective projection of the mind of the biographer".[37] It is indeed the temptation of many psychobiographers to seek to explain leadership in terms of some crisis that the individual must have undergone, either within the family or in the community. In my research, I never once found evidence that somehow Steve had a troubled youth, therefore explaining his leadership. As I shall argue in Chapter 5, Steve's writings about religion may be as much of a window into his identity as it may be an attempt to reinterpret Christianity in the South African context.

The African response to European modernity has historically been multiple and multi-vocal, characterised by all manner of shifting alliances. Of relevance here is the social fissure between the Red People, those Noni Jabavu called the Ochre People[38] – the *amaqaba*; and those who accepted the civilising ways of European modernity – the *amakholwa*. Even on this point it is important to avoid watertight opposites. There were often alliances between the *amaqaba* and *amakholwa*. Jabavu writes: "I belong to two worlds with two loyalties; South Africa where I was born, and England where I was educated. When I received a cable sent by my father, I flew back to South Africa to be among my Bantu people, leaving my English husband in London." She later lived in East Africa, and describes her book as "a personal account of an individual African's experiences between East and South Africa in their contact with Westernization".[39]

---

37 Hitchens, *Arguably*, 41.
38 Noni Jabavu (1963). *The Ochre People: Scenes from a South African Life* (London: Murray). Noni Jabavu was one of DDT Jabavu's daughters.
39 Noni Jabavu (1960). *Drawn in Colour: African Contrasts* (London: Murray).

Sometimes the conservative elite joined forces with traditionalists for political reasons, as happened when John Dube – when challenged by a younger ANC leadership in 1917 – decided to join forces with the Zulu royalty. Indeed, Solomon ka Dinizulu had a close if ambiguous relationship with both Dube and Seme. One of the outcomes of the relationship between the educated elite and the Zulu royalty was the formation of the Inkatha Movement in 1924. The more radical elite joined up with the peasants against the colonial system, as happened in the case of the Bambatha Rebellion against the imposition of the poll tax.

Earlier in history, elders who did not entirely accept Western "civilisation" did not necessarily prevent their children from adopting Christianity or obtaining an education. Even as he remained sceptical, Tiyo Soga's father, Jotelo Soga, allowed his son to be taken in by the missionaries to be taught at Lovedale College. The same is true of amaNtinde chief Kote Tshatshu, who allowed his son, Dyani, to be trained by missionaries at Bethelsdorp under the tutelage of James Read and Johannes van der Kemp (known to the Xhosa as Nyengane).[40] Donovan Williams is thus mistaken in saying that Tiyo Soga was "the first black missionary among Africans".[41] Dyani was taken in by Read and Van der Kemp when he was still a ten-year-old boy in 1804. He briefly returned to his father but in 1810 went back to the mission to become a full-time missionary.

---

40   In his book *A Living Man From Africa*, Roger Levine calls the chief Jan Tzatzoe. Here I use the Xhosa version of his name, Dyani Tshatshu, except where it is in a direct quotation from Levine.
41   Donovan Williams (1983). *The Journal and Selected Writings of the Reverend Tiyo Soga* (Cape Town: AA Balkema).

According to Levine, "by serving the mission, Tzatzoe operates from within the ambit of colonial society, and preaches in part as its representative. He makes the Word available. When he claims its power he does so on behalf of the mission, and not for himself, as individuals like Makana appear to do."[42]

Dyani Tshatshu retained relationships with the Xhosa chiefs, who were angry at him for collaborating with the white church. He was at once a collaborator and an ally. Thus, unlike the earlier Soga who had refused to read to Maqoma the colonial letters the chief had acquired, Tshatshu maintained good relations with the chiefs. He even participated in the great Xhosa uprising of 1834-1835 – known as the Sixth Frontier War. He is reported to have said in response to colonial provocation, which included the shooting of Maqoma's brother Xoxo: "Every Xhosa who saw Xo-Xo's wound went back to his hut, took his assegai and shield; and said it is better that we die than to be treated thus . . . life is no use if they shoot our chiefs."[43]

His earlier deference to Europeans notwithstanding, the later Tiyo Soga, mission-educated himself, admonished those who created a gulf between the Christians and the "heathens": "You Xhosas, Thembus and Fingos who have accepted the word of heaven should not be accused of lack of respect to those who deserve respect as chiefs or lack of honouring those who deserve honour." Soga disapproved of the use of foreign words in Xhosa, and he warned against "the Xhosarising of foreign words – especially in relation to addressing chiefs . . . we would suggest that words like *molo* – 'good morning', *rhoyi-*

---

42   Levine, *A Living Man from Africa*, 54.
43   In Mostert, *Frontiers*, 653.

ndara – 'goeie dag', *rhuyinani* – 'goeie nag' . . . should be eliminated from our language."[44]

My concern here is to trace in this history of the Eastern Cape encounter with European modernity the lineaments of Steve's political and intellectual thought – the continuities and discontinuities with the leadership tradition that developed over time between the educated elite and the people, without falling into the romantic search for a pure African past that Fanon warns against. Mostert observes how both Ntsikana and Nxele embraced Christianity but sought, each in his different way, to reframe it to serve their people: "While both Nxele and Ntsikana looked westward to colonial society for their initial inspiration, each in his different way began serving the emergent Xhosa nationalism."[45] Before I go further into Steve Biko's intellectual heritage, I want to draw a connection between the struggles of the Eastern Cape frontier waged by Xhosa chiefs and earlier struggles that were waged by the Khoi and San people in the Northern Cape frontier in the 17th and 18th centuries.

Steve Biko's political articulation of Black Consciousness is reminiscent of the solidarities forged by the Xhosa and the Khoisan in the 17th and 18th century Northern Cape frontier and the Xhosa on the 19th century Eastern Cape frontier – in short, between Africans and the diverse communities that go under the term "Coloured". Black Consciousness sought to overcome all of these separate identities and construct a hybrid political identity that included Africans, Indians and

---

44 Williams, *The Journal and Selected Writings of the Reverend Tiyo Soga*, 172-173.
45 Mostert, *Frontiers*, 463.

Coloureds. The creation of this common identity was yet another important achievement of the movement. We shall see in Chapter 7 how Steve was opposed to the formation of the Black People's Convention because there had not been enough consultation with the Coloured and Indian communities. Steve Biko's writings and new philosophy of action in the 1970s distinguish him; according to Magaziner he was "this era's most famous political thinker".[46]

And so, even though this chapter is primarily about Biko's inheritance from the Xhosa warriors, both coloniser and the colonised were building on past precedents of oppression and resistance. It was in the 18th century that the "commando system" of cattle raiding was created by the Dutch, and later developed with force and ferocity by the British on the Eastern Cape frontier in the 19th century. In other words, the Northern Cape frontier was the training ground for the perfection of a brutal system of domination. Equally, it was in the San resistance to colonial attacks that we see the beginnings of Maqoma's "guerrilla warfare" – which would later be adopted by decolonisation movements in the 20th century, drawing of course from the experiences of other countries as well. The earlier history foregrounds the formation of Xhosa-Khoisan alliances and identities. As Levine observes, "the amaNtinde have had a significant degree of integration with Khoisan groups".[47] The missionary station of Bethelsdorp was "a thriving centre of Khoisan life", and there were many visitors from Xhosaland because of "the preponderance of Khoi-

---

46 Magaziner, *The Law and the Prophets*, 23.
47 Levine, *A Living Man from Africa*, 13.

san kinship ties among the Xhosa".[48] Indeed, the amaGqunukhwebe, which to all intents and purposes is a Xhosa clan, has its origin in intermarriage between the Khoisan and the Xhosa. Martin Legassick describes the Kat River settlement as "an area of intermingling of all the peoples of the Eastern Cape (save whites), including Maqoma".[49] In his biography of Tiyo Soga, Donovan Williams describes the same settlement as follows:

> Between the Amatole and the Great Fish River lay an area which, by the early nineteenth century, was the last cushion for absorbing the increasing European thrust from the Cape colony. Therefore it was worth fighting for. It was also rich in cultural diversity: amaXhosa and Mfengu mingled with European missionaries, traders and travellers, administrators and military. To the northwest of the Amatole lay the Kat River valley. After Maqoma had been expelled from it in 1829 it was filled with Hottentot (Khoi) and Coloured farmers, a sprinkling of European missionaries, and after 1851, white farmers.

Dutch Rule and the Khoisan Resistance: 1657-1806

When the Dutch East India Company settled at the Cape, they immediately sought to establish a farming system that would provide them with food and meat. The Company thus settled the Cape with free burghers (independent farmers) who would provide passing ships with food supplies, which was itself a

---

48 Levine, *A Living Man from Africa*, 24-25.
49 Martin Legassick (2010). *The Struggle for the Eastern Cape 1800-1854* (Johannesburg: KMN Review Publishers), 59.

recipe for disaster given the existence of Khoi-Khoi communities with cattle in the area. In fact the Dutch governor Simon Van der Stel had feared that the free burghers could not be trusted not to encroach on the Khoi-Khoi by force, and in the process jeopardise the steady supply of food and meat to the settlement. He also feared that "in place of a class of sedentary agriculturalists, there would be created a class of roving herders, continually in search of better nourishment for their animals".[50]

Van der Stel's son Willem Adriaan succeeded him in 1699, and encouraged the free burghers to practise pastoralism, and the colony spread to places such as Stellenbosch, Franschhoek, Paarl and Tygerberg. As the older Van der Stel had feared, that was the beginning of interminable wars between the free burghers and the Khoi-Khoi for the first half of the 18th century – culminating in the ferocious 1739 Khoi-Dutch war. According to Nigel Penn there was a respite in the fighting between 1700 and 1740, as the free burghers moved further and further into the interior, reaching the escarpment. The vast escarpment with its little rainfall and a sparse population meant that the colonists – or *trekboere* as they were now called – did not meet much resistance as they forayed and foraged into the interior. They were in no mood to stay as they could not sustain pastoral farming in such an inhospitable terrain. They had their eyes on the better-watered lands of the Eastern Cape. But first they had to reckon with one more obstacle – the unanticipated existence of the San people in the Sneeuberg region of the Karoo. The *trekboere* had simply assumed – as

---

50 Nigel Penn (2005). *The Forgotten Frontier* (Athens: Ohio University Press), 28.

colonialists tend to assume to this day – that there were no people in the area. But, according to Penn, "the entry of the *trekboere* into the region was to inaugurate the most violent period in the colony's history".[51]

Unlike the Khoi-Khoi, the San could not be brought under the control of the free burghers because they were of no economic value to the Dutch pastoralists – they could not be forced to labour as pastoralists. When they had cattle, it was with the intention of eating instead of herding them. Central to colonial pastoral farming was what was arguably its most important institution – the commando system, whereby a group of armed men would violently put under their control those whose land and cattle they raided. The San were not easily conquerable by the commando system because they could not be put to use. And so the free burghers approached them with a shoot-to-kill policy. The San also seemed to come from a mystical world that was completely foreign to one of the fundamental aspects of Christian societies – the idea of a settled, sedentary life. The differences between the Khoi-Khoi and the San did not, however, prevent the emergence of a strong Khoisan resistance, leading to pleas by various commandos for government assistance as the loss of livestock was becoming intolerable – the San ate the livestock, making its recovery by the pastoralists a moot point. In 1774 the colonial government decided to put all of the commandos under one general command – the General Commando. The San became the target of the most genocidal campaigns precisely because they could not be caught with the cattle or be captured and

---

51 Penn, *The Forgotten Frontier*, 113.

put in service of the pastoralists. What frustrated the burghers most was that they could not easily win against the San:

> The San were not passive, unsuspecting victims of colonial aggression. The General Commando was, after all, an attempt to crush a most threatening and no doubt concerted campaign of resistance. Nor was this resistance overcome by the General Commando. Although the great numbers of casualties suffered by the San and the negligible losses suffered by the colonists would seem to suggest that the commando had been an overwhelming colonial success, this was not in fact the case. The struggle was far from decided and for many years the colonists were unable to find a military solution to the most effective guerrilla war that was being waged against them.[52]

Penn further notes that:

> ... on the eve of the British occupation, there was little to indicate that conditions in the Roggeveld were conducive to peace negotiations between the *trekboere* and the San. Neither side appeared to be defeated, though it is possible that both had come to realise that there was no military solution to their conflict.[53]

It is to the entry of the British into the Cape and their encounter with the Xhosa people that I now turn. Here we see the antecedents of what Steve Biko would later achieve when he forged an identity of Blackness that included Africans,

---

52 Penn, *The Forgotten Frontier*, 123.
53 Penn, *The Forgotten Frontier*, 227.

Coloureds and Indians. To be sure, there were wars between the Xhosa and the Khoi and San people. War between pastoralists and hunter-gatherers is inevitable because the latter want to eat what the former want to preserve. Equally, though, there were also efforts by warriors from both sides to bridge the gap and stand together against the *trekboere*. This unity was to be of crucial importance in the ensuing resistance to the British who, unlike the Dutch pastoralists, now sought to entrench a more elaborate administrative system over the colony. Their aim was to anglicise what was still a Dutch-dominated colony by bringing their language and culture to bear on the entire landscape. According to Mostert,

> the British were indeed to do all these things, to impose their language, their currency, their legal system and their political concepts and to bring the single greatest alteration in the course of South African affairs since the Dutch East India Company's sanction of permanent settlers in 1657.[54]

British Colonial Rule and the Xhosa Resistance: 1779-1909

Events in Europe at the beginning of the 19th century changed the pattern of colonial rule in the Cape. Napoleon Bonaparte dominated Europe and occupied Holland, which meant that the Cape was an indirect colony of the French, except for one factor: England retained "mastery of the seas"[55] and was able to inflict severe damage on the French navy. According to Georges Lefebvre, France had 1 500 vessels in 1801 but this number had

---

54 Mostert, *Frontiers*, 1992, 480.
55 Georges Lefebvre (2011). *Napoleon* (New York: Routledge), 306.

been reduced to a mere 179 in 1812. In 1806 Britain had 36 000 French prisoners and the number increased to 120 000 in 1815 – "a large part of them captured by the British sea forces".[56] Britain's naval supremacy guaranteed her control of maritime trade, and at this point colonial conquests were secondary to British interests: "England, mistress of the seas, was now in other parts of the world the only nation capable of imposing the authority of the white man. It was a task to which she was not so much disposed . . . the example of American colonisation did not encourage further colonisations."[57] It would seem, then, that Britain's wrestling of the Cape from the Dutch in 1806 was motivated first and foremost by commercial interests. "In January 1806 Popham, Baird and Beresford landed at the Cape and forced Janssens to surrender",[58] an event apparently witnessed by the Xhosa chief and missionary Dyani Tshatshu together with Read and Van der Kemp when they were all in Cape Town.[59] What mattered most to the British was control of the sea trade, including the Cape, which from 1806 they controlled. Their entry broke the stalemate between coloniser and colonised.

From then onwards the colonial enterprise consisted of a double assault on the humanity and dignity of African people – military conquest in the 100-year wars of resistance, otherwise known as the frontier wars; and cultural indoctrination primarily through religion and education.

This is not to underplay the role played by some missionar-

---

56   Lefebvre, *Napoleon*, 307.
57   Lefebvre, *Napoleon*, 47.
58   Lefebvre, *Napoleon*, 308.
59   Levine, *A Living Man from Africa*, 12.

ies in giving sustenance to the Xhosa warriors. (For instance, James Laing, who lived in Burnshill, looked after Maqoma's children while the latter went out to fight the colonists.) On the whole the contrasting responses to colonialism at the end of the 18th century and the beginning of the 19th century by Xhosa chiefs Ndlambe and Ngqika laid down the contours for African politics for the coming generations, all the way to the era of the Black Consciousness Movement in the 1970s. To trace this resistance to the Xhosa is not to deny the role of other groupings in South Africa – for they would also play just as crucial a role as the Xhosa. We may simply attribute the role of the Khoisan and the Xhosa to a historical and geographical coincidence – that is where these groups were when the colonialists landed. We also see the emergence of contrasting ideological responses by two prophet-intellectuals, Ntsikana and Nxele, advocating submission – and resistance.

The encounter with Europeans coincided with what the historian Jeff Peires has described as "the most significant feature of Xhosa internal politics in the second half of the eighteenth century".[60] This was the split in the Xhosa kingdom at the turn of the 19th century. Because Xhosa chiefs had polygamous marriages, the tradition was that the heir to the throne came from the Great House, and it was often the eldest son. At times the son from the more junior Right Hand House usurped power, often because the rightful heir was regarded as too weak to lead the nation.

For example, around 1600 Chief Tshawe from the junior house of his father Nkosiyamntu usurped power from the

---

60 Jeff Peires (1981). *The House of Phalo: A History of the Xhosa People in the Days of Their Independence* (Johannesburg: Ravan Press), 53.

rightful heir, Cirha. Cirha enlisted his brother Jwara to resist Tshawe but the latter enlisted the even more powerful and numerous amaMpondomise and amaRhudulu. To this day the Tshawe are regarded as the legitimate chiefs of the Xhosa. Almost a hundred years later, Ntinde and Gwali, who were from the Right Hand House of Tshiwo, sought to usurp power from the rightful heir Phalo, who was too young to take over at the time. The usurpers were fended off by Mdange, who was the regent holding the chieftaincy until Phalo came of age. Phalo in turn had two sons, Gcaleka from the Great House and Rharhabe from the Right Hand House. Instead of attempting to usurp the throne, Rharhabe separated from Gcaleka's kingdom because of the latter's decision to become a traditional healer. Rharhabe thought this was unbecoming of a Xhosa king and he asked for his father's permission to leave. According to SEK Mqhayi, Rharhabe had no match in terms of wealth, generosity and courage and "these were convincing reasons for him to attract many people to himself and he welcomed them all. The Ntinde, Hleke, Mbalu and Dange formed independent chiefdoms, but at his kingdom they recognised his authority and held him as their paramount chief."[61] His father Phalo agreed with him and they crossed the Kei River into what is now known as the Ciskei.

It was the amaRharhabe, and those chiefdoms which had preceded them across the Kei River, who would now take centre stage in the century-long sequence of anti-colonial wars, first against the Dutch *trekboere* and then against the British.

---

61 SEK Mqhayi (2009). *Abantu Besizwe: Historical and Biographical Writings, 1902-1944* (Johannesburg: Wits University Press), 286.

Divisions arose, however, when Rharhabe's eldest son, Mlawu, died before his father. The rightful heir was Mlawu's Great Son, Ngqika (c. 1770-1829). However, Ngqika was too young to rule and Mlawu's brother Ndlambe acted as regent. In 1795 the young Ngqika pushed his uncle aside and seized the throne. Ndlambe regrouped to avenge his humiliation by his nephew, aided by the house of Gcaleka in the Transkei. But Ngqika's formidable army defeated the Gcalekas as well, following which Ngqika declared himself the paramount chief of all the Xhosa. This usurpation bred resentment in all Xhosaland for not even Ngqika's grandfather, Rharhabe, had claimed such authority over the Gcaleka – choosing instead to leave and cross the Kei. Mqhayi describes Ngqika's calumny as follows:

> ... the reader must understand that Xhosa kingship passes down in a direct line and minor princes assume their appropriate rank – no one usurps another's rightful place. For this reason no one was much impressed with Ngqika's prowess in battle.[62]

But Ndlambe did not just roll over and allow Ngqika to assume authority. He rallied his allies, Tshatshu of the amaNtinde, Kobe of the amaGqunukhwebe and Bhotomane of the imiDange. They were incensed that Ngqika had declared himself paramount chief over them – and in alliance with the British colonial governor, Lord Charles Somerset, with whom he was

---

62 Mqhayi is here enunciating the principle and not the reality of usurpation. As stated above, the practice of usurpation was not unheard of among amaXhosa.

now openly collaborating against his own people, giving away much of their land for a pittance or alcohol. His uncle Ndlambe lamented Ngqika's betrayal thus: *Lo mfo wam selegqibile ukusithengisa kumzi wasemzini* – "This chap of mine has already sold us out to a foreign nation."[63] And so it was that in 1818 Ndlambe and his allies launched an all-out attack on Ngqika in what became known as the Battle of Amalinde – in reference to "the saucer-like cavities" that characterised the valley of Debe at the foot of the Amathole Mountains.[64] In retreat, Ngqika was forced to call upon Governor Somerset to come to his aid, something the latter had always cherished. The victorious Ndlambe chiefs were ferociously put down by a commando led by Lieutenant-General Brereton, an event which led to Nxele's calamitous revenge assault on Grahamstown.

Aligned to Ngqika and Ndlambe were two influential prophet-intellectuals – Ntsikana and Nxele (aka Makana) respectively. Ntsikana was one of the first African leaders to embrace the new Christian religion. He claimed to have had a vision in which the rays of the sun shone on his favourite ox's horn. A whirlwind sprang up when he attended a traditional ceremony, whereupon he went to the river to cleanse himself of all that was impure, taken to mean the "heathen" traditions of his people. He authored one of the most popular hymns in isiXhosa, *UloThixo Omkhulu*, which urged his people to submit to the will of God. Ngqika himself was only stopped by his counsellors from formally converting to Christianity. We should be careful, however, not to assume that Ntsikana had no religious or spiritual anchor before the mis-

---

63 Mqhayi, *Abantu Besizwe*, 312-313.
64 Mostert, *Frontiers*, 465.

sionaries came. Mqhayi was sceptical that Ntsikana was converted by Christianity:

> What do people say today? They say Ntsikana was influenced by the first missionaries, that they converted him. Who are those missionaries? Because Williams is the first missionary, apart from Van der Kemp, who did not stay long at any one place in our country. I say who are those missionaries, because the first missionary Ntsikana met is the one who dropped to his knees before Ntsikana, confessing guilt. My fellow countrymen, this opinion should not be spread, because it does not fit the facts, even though the missionaries have already published in books the opinion that Ntsikana was their first convert. I would not say this unless the missionaries had the power and authority to make the sun rise through Hulushe, unless they could control and direct the winds, so that they could stir them to rage, on the day Ntsikana grew anxious and could not dance, so that he gave up, washed off the ochre and went home. And so it seems to me our fathers the missionaries are making too much of this, they are robbing God of his power, the power to convert someone without them, without their intervention. That is a grave error, because it is written "Render unto God the things that are God's".[65]

AC Jordan was not entirely convinced by the mysticism surrounding Ntsikana in Xhosa folklore. For example, there is the story that Ntsikana prophesied the arrival of white people with a coin on one hand and a Bible on the other. Yet this had

---

65 Mqhayi, *Abantu Besizwe*, 212.

nothing to do with Ntsikana's prophetic powers. As one of Van der Kemp's earliest converts in Bethelsdorp, Ntsikana drew on his direct experience with the missionaries and on the Bible. Jordan also argues that in Ntsikana's world divination was not uncommon, and could not be reduced to the influence of white missionaries. More importantly, Jordan offers a secular interpretation of Ntsikana's significance, and it is within this intellectual trajectory that I seek to place Steve Biko. In his own way, Steve was, as Mostert observed, a beneficiary of a long tradition started by Ntsikana but also a critic of that culture. Here is how Jordan describes Ntsikana's enduring legacy:

> The importance of Ntsikana lies not in the smitings by the shafts of sunrise, or in the rising winds and readings from karosses. The fact that his *Hymn of Praise* is the first literary composition ever to be assigned to individual formulation – thus constituting a bridge between the traditional and the post-traditional period – is of great historical significance. Even more important than this is the fact that, through his influence, a few young disciples were introduced to the arts of reading and writing, and that, inspired by his exemplary life and teaching, these men became the harbingers of the dawn of literacy among the indigenous peoples of Southern Africa. [66]

The differences between Ntsikana and Nxele were more political than spiritual. When Ntsikana attempted to proselytise

---

66 AC Jordan (1973). *Towards an African Literature: The Emergence of Literary Form in South Africa* (Los Angeles: University of California Press), 50-51.

Steve Biko in the Intellectual History of the Eastern Cape

Ndlambe, the latter cautioned that "each ear will hear a different thing because I am still listening to Nxele".

Nxele, Ntsikana's chief rival, preached in a more innovative idiom. After an unsatisfactory dalliance with Christianity, and through increasing dissatisfaction with white cattle-raiding, Nxele rejected the concept of a white God in the heavens and preached that Mdalidiphu under the ground was the true God of the Xhosa. He subsequently led the Xhosa army in the Battle of Grahamstown (1819) where the Xhosa suffered severe casualties – estimates of casualties range from 1 000 to 2 000. Incarcerated on Robben Island, he participated in a prisoner break-out but the boat in which he was travelling capsized and he was drowned in the cold Atlantic Ocean. He had promised his people that he would come back, and in apparent fulfilment of that promise he died trying to escape from the island by swimming across the Atlantic. Today the Xhosa people speak of *ukuza kukaNxele* – the return of Nxele – to mock a failed promise. Noel Mostert is of the view that "victory for Nxele at Grahamstown would have seen the collapse of the frontier as the colonists fled westwards towards the Cape, as they usually did on such critical occasions".[67]

According to Peires, notwithstanding the differences between Ntsikana and Nxele, both individuals were grappling with adapting to the "irruption of the European":

> Nxele's nationalist theology emerged as a result of white hostility to his version of Christianity and to his patron Ndlambe, whereas Ntsikana's pacifism was due to the political circumstances of his sponsor, Ngqika ... Their attraction depended

---

67 Mostert, *Frontiers*, 480.

> not on their charisma or their supernatural abilities, but on their power to reinterpret a world which had suddenly become incomprehensible. They are giants because they transcend the specifics to symbolise the opposite poles of Xhosa response to Christianity and the West: Nxele representing struggle, Ntsikana submission. [68]

Peires argues that after the Xhosa were subdued, particularly around the Fourth Frontier War of 1811–1812, the political leadership passed from the chiefs to the prophet-intellectuals. People hoped that they might answer the questions: "Who were these white people? What did they want? What should be done about them?"[69] These existential questions went to the heart of Black Consciousness in the face of white racism in the 1970s. In the early 1800s the answers to these questions were not so clear – they ranged from submission to various forms of resistance. After Nxele (aka Makana), subsequent Xhosa chiefs found themselves confronted with the same questions – not only in response to the colonial government but also to the missionaries. And here we can see the parallels with the questions that the Black Consciousness Movement was faced with in the 1960s – not just how to deal with the colonial government but also with those who sympathised with the cause of black people, whom the founder of the Pan Africanist Congress (PAC), Robert Sobukwe, called *abelungu abasithandayo* – "whites who love us".

---

68 Peires, *The House of Phalo*, 83-84.
69 Peires, *The House of Phalo*, 75.

Relationships with Missionaries – Friends or Enemies?

In his book *The Struggle for the Eastern Cape*, Martin Legassick describes missionaries as "the main mediators of colonial politics and culture among the Khoisan and the Xhosa". Early missionaries such as Van der Kemp were opposed to the racist and murderous policies of the colonial government. One of the early exponents of liberatory theology, Van der Kemp believed that God would intervene on behalf of the oppressed. He immersed himself in the life of the Khoisan – ate their food, wore their clothes and married a slave girl. He established his mission in Bethelsdorp as "an imperium in imperio – a place with its own moral code" – an example of non-racial co-existence among the different races. Although he had been sent to civilise the "savages", Van der Kemp protested the evil among the Boers and the British who enslaved them. He warned the colonists – a warning that would fall on deaf ears for the better part of the next two centuries – that "there is no way of governing this country other than by the government doing justice to the natives. In no other way can the Boers escape the hand of Providence than by acknowledging their guilt."[70]

Even after Van der Kemp's death in 1811, his contemporary James Read – called Ngcongolo[71] by the Xhosa – continued to insist on humane treatment of "the natives", and opposed the expulsion of the Xhosa from the Zuurveld. As pointed

---

70 Martin Legassick (2010). *The Struggle for the Eastern Cape 1800-1854: Subjugation and the Roots of South African Democracy* (Johannesburg: KMM Review Publishers), 8.
71 A *ngcongolo* is a reed, which suggests Read may have been a tall man.

out earlier, Governor Somerset had succeeded with his divide-and-rule policies by buying off the Xhosa chief, Ngqika. He corralled the missionaries who followed Van der Kemp and Read to be on the colonial government's side. Missionaries were expected to be the government's "eyes and ears" among the Xhosa, enabling the government to enforce its policy of punishment by reprisal. This entailed the burning of crops and the raiding of cattle in retribution for one transgression or another. An increasingly racist policy of extermination was now in place in Britain and was being enforced with the utmost ruthlessness by colonial governors and some of the missionaries, who evangelised in support of Britain's growing imperialism.

And here one begins to see the emergence of a patronising attitude among the missionaries towards the "natives". John Philip, superintendent of the London Missionary Society, for example, rejected slavery but only because he saw a potential consumer market among the Khoisan and the Xhosa. What was needed was to "elevate" them to a level of cultural development more aligned with missionary and European norms. We see the same condescending but ultimately contemptuous approach as that adopted towards the Khoi and the San in the preceding century. Philip's mission was to:

> ... raise uncivilised and wandering hordes, which formerly subsisted by chase and by plunder, to the condition of settled labourers and cultivators of the soil, to lead them to increase the sum of productive labour and to become consumers of the commodities of other countries, to convert such as were a

terror to the inhabitants of an extended frontier into defenders of that frontier against the inroads of remoter barbarians. [72]

By the 1820s this "humane" approach was increasingly supplanted by a portrayal of the Xhosa as lazy, libidinous and thieves. Philip, who had written that "the Caffres are not the savages one reads about in books"[73], was replaced by the openly racist Henry Calderwood. And here we see the church laying the seeds of the prohibition of inter-racial relationships:

> The radical evangelism of Van der Kemp and Read, which allowed and even encouraged interaction with the proselytised to the point of marriage, was being replaced by a conservative, culturally chauvinistic and racially charged ideology that demanded, above all, that its agents adhere to accepted norms of British respectability that would not allow for marriage with Khoisan or African women, and certainly not condone adultery. [74]

The chiefs were already critical of the missionaries for taking decisions on their behalf by amending treaties with the British government. While the Xhosa gave a modicum of respect to missionaries such as James Read and John Philip, they treated racists such as Robert Moffat and Henry Calderwood with disdain. Read succinctly remarked to Philip that "as for Calderwood, they hate him".[75] As Legassick puts it:

---

72 Legassick, *The Struggle for the Eastern Cape*, 25-26.
73 Legassick, *The Struggle for the Eastern Cape*, 38.
74 Levine, *A Living Man From Africa*, 74.
75 Legassick, *The Struggle for the Eastern Cape*, 73.

> . . . humanitarian liberalism had given way to utilitarian liberalism for which results were more important than the state of people's souls, in which efficiency and discipline were necessary for progress and coercion could be employed to impose them.[76]

In an early precursor of the Black Consciousness critique of the commitment of white liberals to the struggles of black people, Xhosa chiefs increasingly questioned missionaries' intentions. Neither James Read nor John Philip could resist the stampede of their more conservative brethren and they threw in their lot with the whites in the 1846 war against the Xhosa. Increasingly, the Xhosa chiefs regarded the missionaries as legitimate targets of war. One can see the antecedents of the Black Consciousness critique of white liberalism in the language they used.

The question Steve Biko posed: "Can our white trustees put themselves in our place? Our answer was twofold: 'No! They cannot'," had been posed by his ancestors more than a century earlier. Just as Steve Biko said: "As long as the white liberals are our spokesmen, there will be no black spokesmen . . . the white trustees would always be mixed in purpose."[77] Chief Maqoma said this about the duplicity of the missionaries:

> You are a teacher. You say it is your object in coming among us to teach us the word of God. But why do you always give over teaching that word, and all leave your stations and go to

---

76 Legassick, *The Struggle for the Eastern Cape*, 66.
77 Interview with Bernard Zylstra, 1977.

military posts when there is war? You call yourselves men of peace; what then have you got to do at any of the forts, there are only fighting men there? I am doubtful whether any of you be men of peace. Read, I think he is, but look at Calderwood; what have you to say about him? Now he is a magistrate, one of those who make war.

Maqoma's younger brother, Sandile, described the collusion of the missionaries as follows:

> I have always spared the teachers, but now I will kill them too. What do they do? Only teach men that they are not to fight even though their chiefs be in danger. The white men! The white men put the Son of God to death although he had no sin: I am like the Son of God, without sin, and the white men seek to put me also to death.[78]

The Modern Intellectuals from Tiyo Soga to Steve Biko

It is often assumed that the colonial conquest of the Xhosa was a clean sweep. In fact, it was the colonial government's failure to completely subdue the Xhosa that led to a rethink of policy and the colonial government's decision to introduce a qualified franchise. All adult males who earned 25 pounds could vote. Legassick argues that the introduction of the franchise was an effort to restabilise the colony in the wake of the 1846 Frontier War, to incorporate as many whites as possible into the political system in Britain and in the colony, and to recruit many of the Khoisan who had thrown in their lot with the Xhosa. All of this was too late to stop the emerging soli-

---

78 Legassick, *The Struggle for the Eastern Cape*, 90.

darity among the Xhosa and the Khoisan, transcending more localised tribal and ethnic identities rooted in the previous century. For example, Maqoma's brother and rightful chief of the Rharhabe, Chief Sandile (1820–1879), worked hard to forge a unified identity among the Xhosa and the Khoisan. He promised to re-establish the Khoisan dynasty if they should switch their allegiance from the British to the Xhosa:

> I see that notwithstanding all the assistance you have given the government to fight against us in every war, you are still very poor ... you have been ... starved and oppressed ... If you join me ... you shall be completed with cattle and all that a man should have.[79]

It was only in 1865, when the so-called "British Kaffraria" was united with the Cape Colony, that significant numbers of Xhosa men began to qualify for the franchise. By this time a handful of Xhosa intellectuals had emerged, the most prominent of whom was Tiyo Soga, described by his biographer Donovan Williams as "the father of black consciousness".[80]

Tiyo Soga: The Father of Black Consciousness?

In what would become one of the most consequential decisions in Xhosa history, the prophet-intellectual Ntsikana approached Ngqika's counsellor Jotelo Soga and asked if he could bring Soga's son Tiyo into his church. Jotelo could see the benefits of

---

79 Legassick, *The Struggle for the Eastern Cape*, 101.
80 Williams, *The Journal and Selected Writings of the Reverend Tiyo Soga*, 5.

the new religion and education for his son. In his book *Zemk' Iinkomo Magwalandini*, WB Rubusana argues for a direct link between Ntsikana and the Soga family. He writes that the last line in Ntsikana's hymn *UloThixo Omkhulu* is a reference to Ntsikana's invitation to the Soga family to join in his crusade. In the recorded text the line reads: *lo mzi wakhona na siwubizile*, which does not make sense in that context. Rubusana argues that it was a misprint and should have read *Lo mzi kaKhonwana siwubizile* – "we have invited Christ to the house of Khonwana, ancestor to the Soga family". Rubusana writes in isiXhosa:

> *Kukho indawo esinqwenela ukuyilungisa kulo eli culo lika-Ntsikana kuba ayivakali into eliyithethayo. Le ndawo kumgca wokugqibela ithi, "Lo mzi wakhona na siwubizile" iyimposiso. La mazwi ebefanele ukuthi, "Lo mzi kaKhonwana siwubizile." Lo Khonwana wayethetha yena nguyise boJotelo noJiyelwa nabanye; yinto yasemaJwarheni, kaMtika, yomlibo wakwa-Soga. Lo mzi wayewumemela enguqukweni kuba ubulumelwane oludala lwamaCirha olwalububukhwe bakhe, kuba umkakhe wasekunene, unina kaMakhombe wayengumJwarhakazi.*[81]

The rough translation of this would be:

> There is a place we wish to correct in this rendition of Ntsikana's hymn because it does not make sense. The part in the last line that says, *Lo mzi wakhona na siwubizile* is false [and

---

81 Rubusana, Benson Walter and SC Satyo (2002 [1906]). *Zemk'Iinkomo Magwalandini* (Cape Town: New Africa Books), 4.

indeed not translatable into English]. It should actually read as follows: "We have also called the house of Khonwana." The Khonwana he was referring to was the father of Jotelo (Tiyo Soga's father) and Jiyelwa and others; he is a man of the Jwarha clan, a Mtika, from the line of Soga. Ntsikana was inviting this house to the gospel because they were from the amaCirha, and his in-laws because his wife from the Great House, Makhombe's mother, was also from the Jwarha clan.

Tiyo Soga would become the most influential Xhosa intellectual of the 19th century.[82] He was taken in by Presbyterian priest William Chalmers who educated him at Lovedale College, the mission school established by the British John Bennie in 1841 to "civilise" the natives. The college was closed during the Frontier War of 1844. Fearing for his protégé's life, Chalmers took Soga along to Scotland. They returned to South Africa in 1846 and Soga worked as a teacher and a missionary at Uniondale in Keiskammahoek.[83] Soga refused to be drawn into the Xhosa resistance. For example, he declined Xhosa warrior Maqoma's request to translate the contents of letters that the chief had confiscated from the British. He told the chief that "he would not mix himself up in a context which carried death to his fellow creatures".[84]

When another war broke out in 1851, Soga and Chalmers left for Scotland again to return only in 1856. While in Scotland, Soga enrolled for a theology degree, was ordained as a

---

82 Levine (2010), *A Living Man From Africa*.
83 This Uniondale is not to be confused with the one in the Karoo.
84 Quoted in Mcebisi Ndletyana (2008). *African Intellectuals in 19th and Early 20th Century South Africa* (Cape Town: HSRC Press), 20.

minister and fell in love with a Scottish woman, Janet Burnside. In keeping with Christian teachings Soga dissociated himself from African cultural traditions and rituals. He did not undergo circumcision, which was the rite of passage from boyhood to manhood in Xhosa custom. In his writings and teachings Soga extolled European culture and values, and yet he implored black people to self-reliance:

> As men of colour, live for the elevation of your degraded, despised, downtrodden. My advice to all coloured people would be: assist one another; patronise talent in one another; prefer one another's business, shops etc.[85]

Soga's political outlook took a radical turn when he read a newspaper article written by his childhood friend John Chalmers in the newspaper *Isigidimi SamaXhosa*. Chalmers wrote that black people were indolent and inevitably drawn to extinction. Soga wrote a response which is worth reproducing at length – it has been described as a precursor to the development of black consciousness and Pan Africanism:

> Africa was of God given to the race of Ham. I find the Negro from the days of the Assyrian downwards, keeping his "individuality" and his "distinctiveness", amid the wreck of empires, and the revolution of ages. I find him keeping his place among the nations, and keeping his home and country. I find him opposed by nation after nation and driven from his home. I find him enslaved – exposed to the vices

---

[85] See Donovan Williams (1978). *Umfundisi: A Biography of Tiyo Soga, 1829-1871* (Alice: Lovedale Press).

and the brandy of the white man. I find him in this condition for many a day – in the West Indian Islands, in northern and South America, and in the South American colonies of Spain and Portugal. I find him exposed to all these disasters, and yet living, multiplying and "never extinct". Yea, I find him now as the prevalence of Christian and philanthropic opinions on the rights of man obtains among civilised nations, returning unmanacled to the land of his forefathers, taking back with him the civilisation and Christianity of those nations (see the Negro Republic of Liberia). I find the Negro in the present struggle in America looking forward – though with still chains on his hands and chains on his feet – yet looking forward to the dawn of a better day for himself and all his sable brethren in Africa.[86]

In addition to preaching self-help and inspiring African churches through his hymns, Soga counselled his children, on the eve of their departure to study in Scotland, to regard themselves as black, despite having a white mother:

> I want you, for your future comfort, to be very careful on this point. You will ever cherish the memory of your mother as that of an upright, conscientious, thrifty, Christian Scotchwoman. You will ever be thankful for your connection by this tie to the white race. But if you wish to gain credit for yourselves – if you do not wish to feel the taunt of men, which you sometimes may be made to feel – take your place in the world as coloured, not as white men, as Kafirs, not as Eng-

---

[86] Tiyo Soga's reply to Chalmers under the pseudonym Defensor, *King William's Town Gazette and Kaffrarian Banner*, 11 May 1865.

lishmen. You will be more thought of for this by all good and wise people, than for the other. [87]

A proud man, he once lamented that "this 'morning sir' of the Xhosa people whenever they see a white face is very annoying"[88] – Biko would make a similar point about how black people would grin and smile even as they were insulted by white people:

> I had a man working in one of our projects in the Eastern Cape on electricity; he was installing electricity, a white man with a black assistant. He had to be above the ceiling and the black man was under the ceiling and they were working together pushing up wires and sending the rods in which the wires are and so on, and all the time there was insult, insult, insult from the white man: push this, you fool – that sort of talk, and of course this touched me; I know the white man very well, he speaks very well to me, so at tea time we invite them for tea; I ask him: why do you speak like this to this man? And he says to me in front of the guy: this is the only language he understands, he is a lazy bugger. And the black man smiled. I asked him if it was true and he says: no, I'm used to him.
>
> Then I was sick. I thought for a moment, I don't understand black society. After two hours I came back to the (black) guy, I said to him: do you really mean it? The man changed, he became very bitter, he was telling me how he wants to leave

---

87 John Chalmers (1877). *Tiyo Soga: A Page of South African Mission Work* (Edinburgh: Andrew Elliott), 430.
88 Williams, *The Journal and Selected Writings of Tiyo Soga*, 175.

any moment, but what can he do? He does not have any skills, he has got no assurance of another job, his job to him is some form of security, he has got no reserves, if he does not work today he cannot live tomorrow, he has got to work, he has got to take it. And if he has to take it, he dare not show any form of what is called 'cheek' to his boss. Now this I think epitomises the two-faced attitude of the black man to this whole question of existence in this country.[89]

David Attwell would later observe that "Soga was indeed 'a man of two worlds', but he was also a transitional figure within Xhosa history, marking a choice that subsequent generations would have to remake for themselves".[90] Soga's biographer Donovan Williams described Soga as placed in the cross-tide:

> ... caught in the cross-tide of cultures, as a navigator his responsibilities were enormous. Yet he had no precedents and struggled alone trying to plot a course through the restless seas which were to try the skill and patience of others for the next hundred years.[91]

Soga's radical turn notwithstanding, the tension persisted between the politics of submission passed down from Ngqika and Ntsikana, and the radical defiance passed down from Ndlambe and Nxele, such that by the end of the 19th century there had evolved what Ntongela Masilela describes as conservative and

---

89 Biko, *I Write What I Like*, 113.
90 David Attwell (2005). *Rewriting Modernity: Studies in Black South African Literary History* (Scotsville: University of KwaZulu-Natal Press), 46.
91 Williams, *Umfundisi*, 125.

radical modernisers. Among the former group would be the early Tiyo Soga, John Tengo Jabavu and his son Don Davidson Tengo Jabavu, the editor of the influential *Bantu World*, RV Selope Thema, and the man who would become the first president of the South African Native National Congress (later named the African National Congress), John Dube. The conservatives had been exposed to the self-help principles of the conservative African-American leader Booker T Washington when they were studying in the United States. Dube was studying at Oberlin College when Washington started the Tuskegee Institute. The radicals came under the influence of WEB du Bois and, to a lesser extent, Marcus Garvey. Masilela points out that Selope Thema was vehemently opposed to any radical nationalist influence in South Africa, particularly the Garveyist movement:

> Selope Thema could not accept in many ways that the philosophy of his master, Booker T Washington, had evolved and taken the mantle of Garveyism. To conservative modernisers such as Dube and Selope Thema, the black radicalism of Garveyism was viewed as a threat to their conservative and middle class construction of African nationalism.[92]

The battle between the conservative and radical modernisers played itself out in many ways. The leading and arguably the most influential African leader of his time in the Cape was John Tengo Jabavu. He was one of Soga's successors as a leading opinion maker in black society. He was the proprietor of

---

92 Masilela, interview with Sandile Ngidi, 2000.

the black newspaper *Imvo Zabantsundu*, and was also one of the people behind the establishment of the University of Fort Hare as the first institution of higher learning for black people in South Africa. *Imvo Zabantsundu* became the single most important mouthpiece for African rights. He used the newspaper to launch protests and call for a conference against the Parliamentary Voters Registration Act, which sought to nullify tribal tenure as a basis for the property qualification. According to André Odendaal, the conference authorised Jabavu to call for the creation of a national organisation to represent Africans on a political basis.[93] However, Jabavu refused to do this mainly because it would take away from his personal leadership but also because he felt this would alienate whites "and stimulate racial distinctions instead of promoting practical non-racialism".[94] The philosophical foundations of a cautious non-racialism were indeed laid in that period, despite Jabavu not responding to the call of national leadership.

Jabavu's Achilles heel was that he was beholden to his white financiers. He made two fatal mistakes, politically speaking, that cost him support among Africans. The first was his support for the Afrikaner Bond which threatened to bring Cecil John Rhodes's government down in the 1898 elections. Going into those elections the Afrikaner Bond, under the leadership of JH Hofmeyr, wooed African supporters by promising them the vote, and Jabavu threw in his lot with them against his erstwhile liberal supporters, including Rhodes. The second mistake Jabavu made was to come out in support of the Land

---

93   André Odendaal (1984). *Vukani Bantu!: The Beginnings of Black Protest Politics in South Africa to 1912* (Cape Town: David Philip).
94   Odendaal, *Vukani Bantu!*, 15.

Act of 1913. This earned him the ire of one of the leading radical modernisers of the time, Sol Plaatje. Plaatje was a well-known author and edited *Koranta ea Becoana* – The Bechuana Gazette. He had been elected secretary of the South African Native National Congress (later the ANC) in 1912. Plaatje challenged Jabavu to a public debate, offering to travel all the way from Mafeking in the north to Jabavu's home in King William's Town:

> Now I challenge *Imvo* or Mr Tengo Jabavu to call a series of three public meetings, anywhere in the district of King William's Town. Let us both address the meetings from the same platform, or separately, but on the same day and at the same place. For every vote carried at any of these meetings, in favour of his views on the Act, I undertake to hand over 15 pounds to the Grey Hospital (King William's Town) and 15 pounds to the Victoria Hospital (Lovedale), on condition that for every vote I carry at any of the meetings, he hand over 15 pounds to the Victoria Hospital (Mafeking) and 15 pounds to the Carnarvon. That is 30 pounds for charity.[95]

As if to demonstrate that he would not stoop to respond to Plaatje, Jabavu asked someone else to reply on his behalf with a pithy but characteristically arrogant response:

> I am instructed by the editor of *Imvo* to acknowledge the receipt of your letter, and to inform you that as he has not been reading and following your writings etc., he cannot

---

95 Sol Plaatje (2007). *Native Life in South Africa* (Johannesburg: Picador Africa), 165-166.

understand what you mean by it. In short, to let you know that he takes no interest in the matter.

Plaatje regarded Jabavu as nothing less than a sell-out:

> God forbid that we should ever find that our mind had become the property of someone other than ourselves; but should such a misfortune ever overtake us, we should at least strive to serve our new proprietor diligently, and whenever our people are unanimously opposed to a policy, we should consider it a part of our duty to tell him so; but that is not Mr Jabavu's way of serving a master. Throughout the course of a general election, we have known him to feed his masters (the SA Party), upon flap doodle, fabricating the mess out of imaginary native votes of confidence for his master's delectation, and leaving them to discover the real ingredients of the dish, at the bottom of the poll, when the result has been declared.[96]

Jabavu's other nemesis was the highly respected teacher and priest Walter Benson Mpilo Rubusana, who, in 1909, became the first representative of Africans in the Cape Parliament. In 1914 he lost in a three-way race to a white candidate – mainly because Jabavu chose to enter the race and split the black vote. Rubusana and a number of more radical modernisers such as Allan Kirkland Soga – one of Tiyo Soga's sons – had broken away from Jabavu to form *Izwi Labantu* – The Voice of the People – in protest against Jabavu's politics. However, as Frantz Fanon warns, we should be careful not to overlook the con-

---

96 Plaatje, *Native Life in South Africa*, 162-163.

traditions that come with fighting modernity – for *Izwi La-bantu* was financed by none other than Cecil John Rhodes, who was bitter at Jabavu for breaking ranks and siding with the Afrikaner Bond in 1898. Not only did Rhodes finance *Izwi* but he also entrusted its finances to CP Crewe, a member of the Cape Legislative Assembly. That did not stop *Izwi* from calling for a national convention to support the Progressive Party while also becoming the springboard for the formation of the South African National Convention (SANC) under the leadership of Rubusana – 14 years before the formation of the South African Native National Congress (SANNC). By this time Rubusana had "eclipsed Jabavu as the leading Cape African politician".[97] The SANC sent a delegation to protest the passage of the South Africa Act of 1910, consisting of Thomas Mapikela, Daniel Dwanya and WB Rubusana – who was picked over AK Soga, to the latter's enduring bitterness, swearing to the end that he would oppose any form of unilateralism.

Perhaps the one individual who would come to symbolise a more radical African nationalism was SEK Mqhayi – the founding genius of Xhosa literary culture. Mqhayi was a man of many talents. As a journalist he served as editor of *Umteteli waBantu* and *Imvo Zabantsundu*; as a novelist he wrote *uDon Jadu* and the classic *Ityala Lamawele*; as a non-fiction writer he wrote the biographies of several prominent African leaders including Rubusana; but it was for his poetry that he was best known, earning himself the title of *Imbongi Yesizwe Jikelele* – The Poet of the Nation.

Mqhayi was unusual in that even though he graduated from Lovedale College and qualified as a teacher, he spent a great

---

97 Odendaal, *Vukani Bantu!*, 15.

deal of time at his father's kraal in Centane, where he learned the rituals of his people. This gave him an enormous amount of self-confidence and pride in himself and in the history of his people. For instance, he refused to write in English. Presaging Biko's call for African people to study their history before they can begin to define a new course for themselves and their new nation, Mqhayi enjoined the Xhosa to study the history of their people. The great writer AC Jordan had the highest praise for Mqhayi, calling him "the soul of his people": "Mqhayi takes the highest place in Xhosa literature."[98]

In his autobiography Nelson Mandela remembers a display of cultural nationalism by Mqhayi at his college in Healdtown:

> There was a stage at one end of the hall and on it a door that led to Dr Wellington's [the headmaster's] house. The door itself was nothing special, for no one ever walked through it except Dr Wellington himself. Suddenly, the door opened and out walked not Dr Wellington, but a black man dressed in a leopard skin kaross and matching hat, who was carrying a spear in either hand.

To Mandela's surprise, Mqhayi proceeded with a blistering critique of white racism despite the presence of Dr Wellington himself. Mqhayi said:

> ... we cannot allow these foreigners who do not care for our culture to take over our nation. I predict that one day, the forces of African society will achieve a momentous victory

---

[98] AC Jordan (1973). *Towards an African Literature: The Emergence of Literary Form in South Africa* (Los Angeles: University of California Press), 116.

over the interloper. For too long we have succumbed to the false gods of the white man. But we will emerge and cast off their foreign notions.

Mandela concludes:

> I could hardly believe my ears. His boldness in speaking of such delicate matters in the presence of Dr Wellington and other whites seemed utterly astonishing to us. Yet at the same time it aroused and motivated us, and began to alter my perception of men like Dr Wellington, whom I had automatically considered my benefactor.[99]

Although Mqhayi falls squarely among radical modernisers such as the later Tiyo Soga, WB Rubusana and Sol Plaatje, it is important to keep in mind that all these individuals were complicated. They were part of the very modernity they were contesting, and thus their lives were often characterised by contradictions. AC Jordan reminds us, for example, that Mqhayi had a "double loyalty":

> As a Xhosa he was loyal to the Xhosa chiefs and their ancestors, and as a British subject he had to be loyal to the British king. A poem written during the Anglo-Boer War in the *Izwi Labantu* of 13 March 1900 shows how very sincerely Mqhayi had accepted British guardianship. Each stanza has a refrain, *SingamaBritani* – We are Britons.[100]

---

99 Nelson Mandela (1994). *Long Walk to Freedom* (Little, Brown), 35-36.
100 Jordan, *Towards an African Literature*, 113.

It was only in the 1940s that a younger generation of radical modernisers emerged through the formation of the ANC Youth League under the leadership of Anton Lembede, AP Mda, Robert Sobukwe, Nelson Mandela, Walter Sisulu and Oliver Tambo. To this day the Unity Movement claims it was the first to preach non-collaboration with government institutions, which became an important plank in the Black Consciousness Movement. An even more radical group of modernisers arrived on the scene with the breakaway of the Pan Africanist Congress (PAC) from the ANC in 1959. As we shall see in the following chapter, this breakaway would have a direct bearing on Steve Biko's life in Ginsberg Location. In his brilliant summary of Steve's testimony, Millard Arnold notes that "there was no indication in his childhood or early background that Biko possessed the political genius that would lead him to develop an ideology and a mode of action that would irreversibly change the course of history in South Africa".[101] Yes and no. As a young child he was not particularly interested in political life – which he left to his older brother Khaya – until he left Ginsberg for Lovedale College. As Khaya put it: "Then the giant was awakened."

---

101 Millard Arnold (ed.) (1979). *The Testimony of Steve Biko* (London: Maurice Temple Smith), xv.

3
Formative Years in Ginsberg Location, King William's Town

"Ah, Biko, *uya kuba yinkokheli mfana wam!* –
you will grow up to be a leader, my boy!"
HEADMASTER XOLELA MBONI, 1957

King William's Town is arguably the most important town in the entrenchment of colonial rule in South Africa. Cape Town laid the foundation for the northern Cape frontier in the 17th century and King William's Town provided the base for the establishment of the Eastern Cape frontier. The town was established on John Brownlee's twice-abandoned mission station. During the Sixth Frontier War the Xhosa had destroyed John Brownlee's mission station, after Dyani Tshatshu had tried in vain to get Brownlee and his family to leave. Their lives were spared. The 1834 uprising by the Xhosa was met with a strong show of force by the British. The British governor, Benjamin D'Urban, and his trigger-happy commanding officer, Harry Smith, travelled all the way from Cape Town to launch the most brutal assault on the Xhosa in 1836: "British soldiers burn Xhosa fields, grain stores and homesteads. They shoot artillery rounds into dense vegetation where women and children take refuge with their cattle."[102] This was a 19th-century reprise of what had befallen the San in the 18th century, and what had happened at the Battle of Grahamstown.

---

102 Levine, *A Living Man from Africa*, 102.

D'Urban and Smith went about creating and fortifying King William's Town as the military headquarters of the newly established Province of Queen Adelaide, which D'Urban annexed thinking that the Boers leaving the Cape Colony might try to grab it. The Annexation of the Province of Queen Adelaide was reversed by the colonial secretary and Brownlee was allowed to return in 1836. He was chased out again during the War of the Axe in 1846. The British re-annexed the area as British Kaffraria. The town's first native location was built in 1846 through a colonial government grant of 14 acres to Brownlee's London Missionary Society, which was extended by an additional 8 acres. The new town fell under neither the missionary society nor the chiefs but under the colonial government. From then on King William's town became "the new hub for a military system that was intended to descend like an imprisoning grid upon all the Xhosa, underneath which they would be made over".[103] A native location was established on the old mission, but extending beyond it, under Dyani Tshatshu. According to Peires, "for the Xhosa, British Kaffraria was a monster which swallowed them up".[104] But it was also the beginning of new forms of struggle.

One of the turning points in the defeat of the Xhosa was the cattle killings of 1857, when the young girl Nongqause called on the Xhosa to burn all their fields and kill all their cattle in anticipation of future bounty. The reasons for the tragic event have been explored elsewhere.[105] Suffice to say

---

103 Mostert, *Frontiers*, 772.
104 Peires, *The House of Phalo*, 191.
105 See Jeff Peires (1989). *The Dead Will Arise: Nongqawuse and the Great Xhosa Cattle-Killing Movement of 1856-7* (Cape Town: Jonathan Ball). Others who have taken a different view from Peires include Mqhayi, *Abantu Besizwe*; Zakes Mda; and Timothy Stapleton.

that the cattle killing left the Xhosa people decimated. When the tragedy took place, King William's Town had the only hospital in the vicinity. The Hospital was established in 1857 by George Cathcart and further developed by George Grey. It was initially called the Native Hospital; its name changed to Grey Hospital only in 1887. Yet again we see that the line between tradition and modernity should not be drawn too tightly: Chief Maqoma's son Ned worked here as an assistant and an interpreter for the medical staff, earning "2 pounds a month plus rations and a few articles of furniture".[106] In the 1970s, Steve's mother Alice Biko also worked at this hospital, as a cook.

In 1857 thousands of starving people flocked to the hospital from all over the colony. According to GS Hofmeyr, a considerable number of the people who died of starvation following Nongqause's prophecy were buried around King William's Town. The survivors stayed in the vicinity and some found work in the growing industrial centre. Photographs from the late 19th century show a settlement consisting of a handful of traditional rondavels. It quickly grew with the development of the town.

This was a general trend throughout the country as Africans were forced off the land and started working in emerging industrial and mining towns. With the rise in Africans in towns, the Cape Provincial Government formalised African settlements into what were called "locations". The Cape Provincial Government passed the Native Reserves Act of 1902 to regulate locations as labour reservoirs.

In addition to Brownlee there was another settlement made

---

106 GS Hofmeyr (1986). "Grey Hospital, King William's Town: Its Formative Years", *South African Medical Journal*, vol. 70, 615-617.

up of wattle-and-daub huts called Tsolo on the other side of the Buffalo River. Tsolo would become part of the new location of Ginsberg that was beginning to take shape after local industrialist Franz Ginsberg started building brick huts and pitches alongside the existing wattle-and-daub huts. According to Ginsberg historian Luyanda Msumza, Ginsberg was practising a form of enlightened capitalism by building these houses. He was concerned by the drudgery of the long daily commute and how it affected his workers' productivity. Describing the industrialist's push to develop the township, Msumza says "the idea of a location close to his factory must have appealed to him and he threw every ounce of his energy into it. He worked so hard on this such that when the settlement was finally established it was named after him."[107]

The township's expansion was in reality part of the municipality's overall plan to relocate black people from the white section of town and from Brownlee, which was regarded as too close for comfort and a health hazard. Ginsberg argued that the improvements had to be of such a nature that the "natives" would have no desire to return to town. As Ginsberg said in response to a query by another councillor, Dr Charles Brownlee: "We are going to make it so comfortable for the Natives in the location and so cheap that I am quite sure in a very short time every native will be glad to go to the location."[108]

At Ginsberg's insistence and initiative, in 1901 the King William's Town council built 50 brick huts in five rows of 10 houses, adjacent to the existing wattle-and-daub huts in Tsolo village. These houses were rented out to the early inhabitants

---

107 Luyanda Msumza, unpublished manuscript.
108 Msumza, unpublished manuscript.

at 10 shillings per hut. The uptake was very slow because people were not used to paying for accommodation. Despite Ginsberg's initial optimism, only 18 out of the 50 huts had been let by December 1901. There was as yet no systematic enforcement of racial segregation, and many people chose to remain in town rather than move to the new houses. The houses only started filling up as an increasing number of migrants from as far as the Transkei started arriving, looking for work, and particularly when those known as the amaBhaca arrived. For the most part these people worked for the municipality as toilet cleaners, which meant that they occupied the lowest rung in the social status system, even in such a working-class community. By 1904 the municipality had built 30 more huts, taking the number of newly built houses to 80, and by 1908 there were 116 houses.

Throughout the 1920s there was a housing freeze, with the next major housing construction taking place in the 1930s and '40s. The boom had to do with the fact that the old Brownlee Mission was razed to the ground in 1939 and the residents relocated to Ginsberg. The new arrivals nostalgically named their section Brownlee. It is important to understand the history of Brownlee Mission to understand the cultural dynamic the new residents would bring to the growing settlement of Ginsberg.

This dynamic was the continuation in Ginsberg of the social division between those who embraced modernity and those who stuck to traditional ways. Roger Levine describes the piety of life at the original Brownlee mission, and the strict regimen that the residents had to follow. Almost all their time was occupied with the Scriptures. A typical day would consist of the reading of the Scriptures in the morning and a catechism in the evening, with extra services on Sundays. John Brownlee insisted on a strict separation between the converts and the world of their chiefs. The missionaries warned that those who rebelled faced eventual death at the hands of the colonial army. A circular issued on 10 February 1885 stated that "no one shall be allowed to reside on the Mission Station who does not seek the benefit of the Mission Institutions viz. church and school. All residents are therefore required to attend church and send their children to school." The rules also stipulated that "no resident shall make or sell kaffir beer or any intoxicating liquor".

Those families that refused to live by the new Christian doctrines were ostracised and sent to live in a separate settlement called Mnqayi. (*Mnqayi* is a stick rural boys used for fighting.) In Mnqayi the boys could continue brewing traditional beer and observing their cultural rituals. The social division between the mission residents of Brownlee and their Mnqayi neighbours was so stark that when the mission station was demolished in 1939, Mnqayi residents were relocated to the existing working-class section of Ginsberg. Many preferred it that way, not wanting to be forced to live with "the stiff upper lip" elite and their constricted and, some might say, pretentious lifestyles in the Brownlee section. The addition of this new section increased the number of houses significantly; by December 1950 there were 371 houses in Ginsberg. An additional 105 houses were built between 1950 and 1960. According to a letter from Chief Commissioner FH De J Brownlee, there were 486 houses in Ginsberg as of March 1961. In that same letter the commissioner conceded that the houses in

Ginsberg were "seriously overcrowded".[109] In another memorandum, the chief health inspector wrote to Commissioner Brownlee that the average population density per house in Ginsberg was nine people, leading to an increase in tuberculosis by 245% since 1953. The local municipality sought to alleviate this situation by building an additional 300 houses for the African population in a new area known as Juliwe – with the name, meaning "dumped", an allusion to the fact that people were simply abandoned there.

By the end of the 1960s Ginsberg would grow to about 700-800 houses. When he was asked to describe Ginsberg at the SASO/BPC Trial (more about that later), Steve described it as "a small township of about a thousand houses, very poor".[110] If the old sections of Tsolo and Ginsberg were most adversely affected by overcrowding, the Brownlee section became the location of choice for the emerging middle class – the teachers, nurses, clerks, priests.

The municipality appointed the Brownlee elite as guardians over the rest of the community through the Ginsberg Native Advisory Board, a colonial government creation set up to advise on community needs. The advisory boards were toothless bodies used to enforce influx control, repatriating people who were illegally in the township to their proper homes in the rural areas. The dominant figures in the community were called *izibonda* – headmen. The more prominent among them were Wycliffe Zaula, Gordon Gcilishe, Peter Ngesi, Baldwin Gqaliwe and Richard Gushman. They even had the streets in

---
109 (N9/15/3/54), Eastern Cape Archives, Port Elizabeth.
110 Biko, *I Write What I Like*, 126.

"Brownlee" named after themselves – old Tsolo did not have street names, let alone proper streets.

The generation of *izibonda* was followed by a more urbane and better educated group in the 1950s. One of the most influential among them was my granduncle on the Mangcu side of our family – George Mayile Mangcu. He was born and raised in Brownlee and obtained a scholarship to attend the prestigious Methodist mission school for Africans, Healdtown College, near the town of Fort Beaufort, about 50 kilometres from the University of Fort Hare in Alice. Upon graduating from Healdtown, Mangcu taught in the growing and buzzing town of Port Elizabeth. He returned to King William's Town in 1939 to join his family in their new home in Ginsberg. Because there was no primary school in the township, Mangcu taught young pupils out of the local community hall, until he persuaded the local education authorities to start a primary school. The school was established in 1941 and named after the then white school inspector, Charles Morgan. Mangcu was the first principal. He was later appointed the first black inspector of schools in the area, before moving to work as a school inspector in Cape Town in 1965.

During his stay in Ginsberg, Mangcu established a jazz ensemble, the African Melodies, as well as the famous iXhanti Choral Society. A man for all seasons, he also coached the local boxing and cricket clubs. He preached a conservative brand of self-reliance and started a community garden with exactly that goal in mind. (On that site now stands the Steve Biko Memorial Centre.) Mangcu also set up a community organisation called Masizakhe in collaboration with local leaders, such as his next-door neighbour and prominent teacher Mr Gushman, as well as local women leaders such as Mrs Ngesi and local nurse Winnifred Nolutshungu. Although it received its funding from liberal-minded white lawyers the organisation was based on the idea of self-help. Community members worked in a communal garden to produce food, particularly for the poorer residents of the old section of Tsolo. Curiously, the produce was sold in Mangcu's own shop, which caused many to say that he was working for his own gain. One of the residents of Tsolo, Bra Kimbo, reminded me that Mangcu kept the community piano in his own house even though it was meant to benefit the entire community. As a result Mangcu's son, Mthetho, could play the piano well while the other children were reduced to makeshift guitars. (Mthetho also dated Steve's younger sister Nobandile.)

Despite the unhappiness with Mangcu, he remained an authority figure with the exalted status of teacher and school inspector. Masizakhe also provided bursaries to local pupils enabling them to attend Forbes Grant Secondary School – buying books and uniforms for those who could not afford them. To add to the controversy, my oldest brother, Mzwandile, received help from this organisation though he did not qualify as coming from a poor family. Masizakhe also helped students who wanted further education. Thus Masizakhe paid for Steve to attend Lovedale College in 1963.

Yet another influential figure in Ginsberg was the legendary Harry Mjamba, the second principal of the newly established local secondary school. If Mangcu was the conservative moderniser, then Mjamba was Ginsberg's radical moderniser. He had graduated from the University of Fort Hare, where African leaders such as Seretse Khama, Nelson Mandela, Oliver

Tambo, Robert Sobukwe and Robert Mugabe had studied. The late cabinet minister Steve Tshwete once informed me that he was recruited into the ANC by Mangcu and Mjamba while he was a student at Forbes Grant Secondary School in the 1950s. I suspect Tshwete was being polite for I cannot imagine the conservative Mangcu taking on such a role. Tshwete's conscientisation was more likely to have been Mjamba's work.

Ginsberg also had women leaders such as Peter Ngesi's wife, Mrs Ngesi, who had trained as a social worker. She founded the Ginsberg Village Women's Unity Club to foster cooperative projects among local women. That tradition continued under the auspices of the Young Women's Christian Association (YWCA). By the 1970s the Y had become a permanent feature in the township's life although its members were mostly teachers and nurses from Brownlee. Some of these meetings were hosted at my home – to my great delight because the leftover cookies were there for the taking, raising my popularity among the other kids to an all-time high.

This is the social milieu Steve's parents, Mzingaye and MamCethe (also known as Alice), found when they arrived in King William's Town in 1948. Mzingaye had resigned from the police force and worked for a short while at Fort Cox Agricultural College near Keiskammahoek. He subsequently obtained a job as a clerk in the Native Affairs office in King William's Town while pursuing a degree with UNISA. The family initially moved into Temperance Boarding House before renting a house from Sam Makhubalo, a Ginsberg businessman who worked at Fort Cox on weekdays and lived in another new section of Ginsberg, New Rest. Makhubalo agreed to let the Bikos use the house until they found a place on the

Formative Years in Ginsberg Location, King William's Town

famous Zaula Street in the Brownlee section. Steve, only two at the time, was taken to live with relatives in Cathcart, about 60–70 kilometres from King William's Town. He rejoined his family once they moved into their own house on Zaula Street.

Upon joining the Brownlee set, Mzingaye signed up as a pianist at the local church. He also enrolled with the local rugby club, Lily White, for which he played lock forward. According to Lily White founder member Toyo Mkhencele, Mzingaye never really stood out as a player. He was instead drafted to be the club's executive secretary. Unfortunately, tragedy struck the family when Mzingaye suddenly fell ill. His abdomen became distended with water, which made it difficult for him to take any food, and he died suddenly in 1950, leaving MamCethe to fend for their four little children: Bukelwa, Khaya, Bantu (Steve) and Nobandile. Mzingaye's youngest sister also lived with them, and so did MamCethe's grandchildren, nephews and nieces: Solly, Nomagqwetha, Pumla, Thembile (Sekelezi), Mandlakazi, Lungisa, Thabo, Sipho and others. Steve was only four when his father died.

The young Steve was greatly affected by his mother's daily struggles to keep the family going. He could not bear to see her work as a cook at the local Grey Hospital where she had to single-handedly mind the burning coal furnace. He eventually persuaded her to leave that job and did all he could to support her. She in turn became a strong pillar of support for her son, even later when she feared for his life. In his personal memoir Steve's friend and spiritual mentor Aelred Stubbs, a missionary who was posted in South Africa by England's Community of the Resurrection, describes the relationship between Steve and his mother:

> Closer at home his mother provided from the first an indomitable base of support. Unlike the parents of one or two of Stephen's contemporaries, Mrs Biko never had a chance to be a political activist even if she had had the inclination. She had been too poor and had had to work unsparingly to bring up four children after the early loss of her husband. But she showed that she knew how to cope with the 'system', as the Security Branch is everywhere called in the black world. She stood no nonsense from them: enquiries as to the whereabouts of her son were met with a vacant stare and blank denials. Even if she felt fear, she never showed it. Nor, on the other hand, was she rude to them. She simply treated them with a cold polite correctness ... his mother's courage was all the more heroic in that it was not her natural disposition. Her son made it clear from the first that he was in no way going to be subjugated by his restriction order. Out of love for him she complied. Her strong Christian faith helped her; whatever his spoken criticism of the church might be Stephen never denied being an Anglican, and this was due chiefly to loyalty to his mother, and to admiration of the quality of her faith.[111]

But, as James MacGregor Burns argues in his magisterial *Leadership*, children's experiences with their peers tend to have a greater impact on their subsequent leadership development than their interaction with their parents:

> As children participate more widely in home, school and play groups, confront diverse personalities, exchange confidences,

---

111 Stubbs, "Martyr of Hope" in Biko, *I Write What I Like*, 185.

and take part in group divisions, they are drawn more and more into new roles. Ultimately young people move into wider educational, occupational, legal and political milieus . . . Qualities of leadership emerge out of these imitative, selective and role-taking or empathetic processes.[112]

This is exactly the line that Steve's life would take – learning to lead among his peers in Ginsberg.

Survival of the Fittest: Youth

Ginsberg had a particularly fearsome reputation among the townships of the Eastern Cape. This was due in no small part to the living conditions in the community, especially the overcrowding and the lack of educational opportunities for the youth. Some of the Brownlee youth were better positioned because of the social status of their parents. They looked to a local body builder and rugby coach Sigqibo Ndwalaza for protection against the *tsotsis* – township street thugs or gang members – from Tsolo. Ndwalaza came from one of the nearby rural communities of Debe-Nek where he was a famous stick fighter. Embarrassed by using sticks in an urban setting, he started a body-building gym at his home.

One of his protégés was Doctor Pringle Jack, a youth leader named in gratitude after the doctor who delivered him at birth – apparently his mother had a difficult delivery. The Jack family lived just a few paces from the Biko home on Zaula Street. "I was as fit as a fiddle in those days," Doctor Pringle Jack says wistfully. He led the Brownlee boys in their battles

---

112 James MacGregor Burns (1978). *Leadership* (New York: Harper Row Publishers), 77-78.

against the notorious Tsolo *tsotsis* who bullied other youth, whether caddies at the golf course or at the shebeens on weekends. In order to get to town, the youth from Brownlee had to walk through Tsolo, where they would be held up or beaten up by the bullies, whose weapon of choice was the knife. However, Doctor Pringle Jack was just as adept at using the knife as he was at fist-fighting. He made money by holding up passengers in stowaway train rides between King William's Town and East London. And he wore the best clothing in town – two-tone shoes, Dobbs of London. As the reigning township boss and "swanker" he dated the beautiful Nomsa Peteni, who belonged to a prominent family in nearby Zwelitsha township. Doctor Pringle Jack is also remembered for leading Ginsberg youths into battle with youths from Zwelitsha township in a battle over Nomsa. Zwelitsha boss Mpungutyane detested the fact that a boy from Ginsberg could go out with someone from his own territory. And so it was that one night Pringle Jack and Mpungutyane stood toe to toe in an epic battle during a music concert at the Zwelitsha Community Hall. The concertgoers ignored the band and became riveted by these two raging bulls. As it became clear that Doctor Pringle Jack was about to prevail, Mpungutyane's lieutenants stabbed him and he had to retreat with his group back to Ginsberg. While his lieutenants were no "softies" either, Pringle Jack described the Biko boys – Steve and his older brother Khaya – as "mama's babies" who had to pay him protection money on the streets:

> The Biko and Gqaliwe boys were mama's babies. They never ventured beyond their yards. When they did we would take

their money and go buy traditional beer in Tsolo; and then we would go to the all-night church service and make a nuisance of ourselves until the early morning, and then set off for the golf course as caddies as soon as the sun came out the following day.

Sport and Politics

The social rivalry between the Brownlee and Tsolo boys was most intense during rugby matches between their respective teams, Star of Hope and Head of Lion. Star of Hope was seen as the team of the elites while Head of Lion was seen as the team of the working people. Star of Hope was started by the "mama's babies". Every day after school they gathered to play rugby in front of the Biko home on Zaula Street. The youngsters naturally gravitated to the Biko home after school because it was the only home on the street where there was no adult supervision; Steve's mother was at work until late.

Under Khaya Biko's leadership these youngsters formed a rugby club, first called Sea Lions, which later formed the core for Sigqibo Ndwalaza and Michael Mbeki's famous rugby team, Star of Hope. Star of Hope and Head of Lion dominated local, regional and national rugby for many years. Many of the players would later become architects of the new South Africa. As mentioned earlier, democratic South Africa's first minister of sport, Steve Tshwete, studied at Forbes Grant, where he was captain of the school rugby team. He was head prefect while working underground for the ANC. Tshwete later joined Welsh High School in East London, where his political activism grew more intense. Tshwete subsequently hired my older brother, Mthobi Tyamzashe, as the country's first director-general of sport. Mthobi's parents died when he was very young and he lived with my family throughout his school and university years. He served as the secretary for Star of Hope. Mthobi never forgets that it was Steve Biko who later organised a bursary for him to attend Fort Hare in the 1970s.

Other prominent sports figures who were ever-present in my youth included Smuts Ngonyama, who played for Star of Hope. Ngonyama and I would later lock horns when he became head of the presidency during Thabo Mbeki's rule but when I was a young boy I used to carry his kitbag to the rugby field. The former deputy minister of defence in Mbeki's cabinet, Mluleki George, was a prominent member of the rival team, Head of Lion, and so too was the first mayor of Buffalo City, Sindisile Maclean. Beyond the field of sport, two ANC underground activists slain by apartheid assassins in the 1980s – Griffiths Mxenge and Victoria Mxenge – also studied at Forbes Grant Secondary School under Harry Mjamba. In the days of segregated sport the community produced six players for the black national team: PV Maneli, Tommy Esterhuyse, Jack Dolomba, Zanemvula Lefume, Mveleli Nyakathi and Liston Ntshongwana. The little township of no more than a thousand houses also produced two national boxing champions – Nkosomzi Moss and Tyumphrie Krune.

Khaya Biko, two years older than Steve, emerged as the intellectual leader among his peers. He was articulate and suave, having honed his English through his friendship with the McNamee children – Michael, Peter, Margaret and Anne – the children of the white local superintendent for whom his mother had worked before she became a cook at Grey Hospital. Through his friendship with the McNamee children Khaya

Formative Years in Ginsberg Location, King William's Town

also developed a life-long passion for newspapers. He became the news reporter for the student newspaper at Forbes Grant, thereby expanding his growing sphere of influence among his peers.

Khaya also came under the influence of Harry Mjamba at Forbes Grant. However, unlike his fellow schoolmates, Tshwete and Mxenge, Khaya was attracted to the more radical politics of the Pan Africanist Congress (PAC). The PAC had broken away from the ANC in 1959 on the grounds that the latter was under the undue influence of white liberals and communists. PAC leaders were unhappy with the Freedom Charter's declaration that "South Africa belongs to all who live in it, black and white". As far as they were concerned, the country belonged to African people. They argued that the land had been forcibly taken from them by whites. With that simple message the PAC caught on like wildfire throughout the country. By some estimates it had registered more than 100 000 members in the six months of its existence – it was banned along with the ANC in 1960. Ginsberg was one of its strongest bases because of its youth. In his book *Sharpeville*, Tom Lodge argues that in trying to understand the success of movements such as the PAC we have to:

> ... do more than look at leaders, organisations, strategies, and ideologies ... the most effective challenges were those that brought together the high culture of nationalist elites with the concerns and preoccupations of everyday life, animating people around tangible and sometimes parochial grievances.[113]

---

113 Tom Lodge (2011). *Sharpeville: An Apartheid Massacre and Its Consequences* (Oxford: Oxford University Press), vi.

Lodge further suggests that key to understanding such movements is "intimate local knowledge" for "without the insights from such knowledge it would be impossible to explain the relationships between political leaders and the people they led". Effective political movements, Lodge argues, were those that were able to combine the aspirations of the nationalist elite with the daily grievances of ordinary people, particularly marginalised groups such as unemployed youths and school leavers with few opportunities. Lodge further argues that the PAC's language about land appealed to rural migrants living in barracks in townships such as Langa in Cape Town:

> The PAC's rhetorical militancy, its war-like language, the reference in its oratory to conquest, dispossession and restitution, and its identity as an indigenous African movement were going to make it increasingly attractive to those migrant workers who were still influenced by rural culture.[114]

Lodge further argues that because of its rural social base, the military wing of the PAC departed from "the liberal democratic foundations of the African elite", most of whom were missionary-trained university graduates. I shall later show how the intimate relations between Black Consciousness activists and local communities made it such an effective movement, particularly in Ginsberg. Suffice to say that in the early 1960s Ginsberg was fertile ground for the PAC precisely because of the conditions that prevailed, and the relationship between people such as Khaya Biko and the local youth. The PAC sent

---

114 Lodge, *Sharpeville*, 194.

a nonconformist. He hated the idea of joining the boys' choir – where he was required to sing soprano. He would wake at 4am and climb to the roof of the communally shared toilet behind his home and sing at the top of his voice. If anyone protested, he would ask them to talk to the school. And yet this "clown" was best friends with Zaula Street's beautiful Maniwe Nombamba, and was dating equally beautiful Mandisa Mayeye, who lived in the New Rest section of the township.

According to Sonwabo Yengo, one of Steve's closest friends in Ginsberg, the principal at Charles Morgan Primary, Mr Mboni, had a tendency to typecast students. For example, Fikile Mlinda – who would later become one of Steve's close comrades in Ginsberg – was always late for school. His family made their living by brewing traditional beer and Fikile had to go to town to buy the ingredients before school. He was thus invariably late. Mboni would bellow out: "Ah, Mlinda my boy, you will always be late in life." To another student, Boy Mgubelo, who was a caddy, Mboni would say: "Ah, Mgubelo, *uya kuhlala uyingxungxu okokoko* – you will not amount to anything, boy." And then Yengo remembers that one day they were working in the school garden and Mboni bellowed out to Steve: "Ah, Biko, *uya kuba yinkokheli mfana wam!* – you will grow up to be a leader, Biko, my boy!" Yengo does not recall what occasioned Mboni to say this but insists that looking back he can now see Steve's leadership qualities among his peers. Everyone tended to gather around him and his brother Khaya.

While Khaya's efforts went into political proselytising, Steve put his energies into helping other kids at school. Major Sihunu, who later became a successful businessman, credited Steve with helping him through the highly sought-after Standard Six certificate in 1959. Major was born into a large but poor family who lived right behind the Biko home. He was determined to break out of his family's poverty by going into business. But he also knew that he would never get his foot inside a bank to ask for a loan without a Standard Six certificate. So he approached Steve to help him with his grades: "Standard Six was the gateway to everything. Without Standard Six you were nothing. You could not enter bars, get decent jobs or date respectable women." Major approached the much younger boy and asked: "Tell me, boy, how do you do it? Can you help me?"

Steve simply said: "Sure, come to my house at four o'clock tomorrow morning."

Major found Steve already on his way out at the appointed hour: "Oh, I thought you were not coming, it's already after four."

"So where are we going?" asked Major.

"Don't ask," replied Steve, "let's just go."

The two boys waded through the thicket of forest where Charles Morgan Primary was located, about two kilometres outside the township. They stopped at a dam on the way to the school where Steve said they should rinse their faces so they could stay awake. Major recounts: "Steve, of course, passed the year with flying colours and I obtained a second-class pass – a big improvement for me. Remember, I was failing my subjects before that. That opened the gateway to the world for me."

Major Sihunu says that when they got to Forbes Grant Secondary School in 1960, "the men were separated from the boys".

The "Steve and Larry Show"

At Forbes Grant, Steve developed a special friendship with Larry Bekwa from the small rural town of Peddie, about 50 kilometres southwest of King William's Town. Steve and Larry's friendship was of the kind called *babelala ngengubo enye* – a Xhosa saying for inseparable friends. Larry came to Forbes Grant Secondary School with a history of political activism. He had been to Lovedale College in Alice on the prestigious Andrew Smith Bursary. Larry is not shy to say that "I was a bright spark at Lovedale". However, he was expelled after a strike in protest against the declaration of South Africa as a republic in 1961. The real ringleaders were older students such as Charles Nqakula, also there on an Andrew Smith Bursary. (Nqakula later served as a cabinet minister in Thabo Mbeki and Jacob Zuma's governments.)

Larry's father was a well-connected man and quickly secured his son a place at Forbes Grant after his expulsion from Lovedale. As a condition for his son's acceptance he promised the principal – Mr Sidney Qaba had replaced Mjamba at that point – that his two daughters, Thozama and Ntombomzi, who were already at the school, would keep an eye on their wayward little brother. The girls lived as boarders with the Jojozi family directly opposite the Biko home on Zaula Street. Larry was supposed to live with them but he hardly spent any time there. Steve often insisted that he should sleep over at his home.

While Steve empathised with Larry for his expulsion from Lovedale, he also reminded him that "at Forbes we don't play, we study". And, indeed, the two of them took over the intellectual leadership of the school. Larry was proficient in Latin and Steve excelled in Mathematics and English. Sometimes teachers would complain that Steve and Larry gave the same answers to exam questions and Steve would joke and say: "Great minds think alike!"

Steve and Larry entered their final year for what was then known as the Junior Certificate in 1962. They were teenagers – Steve was 16 – who were also attracted to girls and vice versa. And so the principal was sceptical when they approached him to ask if they could have night studies. Ultimately they prevailed on the principal to let them start the class. The intellectual leader of the group, Steve would sit on top of the table, his legs swinging back and forth, and just start talking. He would encourage others to participate in the discussion. He introduced to his fellow students a novel way of studying that he called "brainstorming". No one really knew where he got the idea from, and he was not telling. When the final-year results came no one was surprised that Steve was at the top of his class (with four As and one B), with his friends Larry Bekwa and Mzwandile Ngcelwane close behind.

As the top student at Forbes Grant, Steve was selected to give the valedictorian address, whereafter the boys were expected to join the girls at a formal dance. With his wicked sense of humour Steve prevailed on the boys to arrive late at the ceremony, wearing raincoats. Their classmate Baba Gcweni recalls:

> We arrived on time looking very nice and ready for the dance. But the boys were not there. And we loved them because they were all so brilliant. All of a sudden the boys appeared – wearing raincoats! And these raincoats were smelly! We just refused to dance with these guys. We were so disappointed.

Steve also had a tendency to dress skimpily during icy weather, and would wear an overcoat during scorching heat. When asked he would say he was preparing for the next World War. Apparently Steve had told his mother, MamCethe, not to worry about getting him anything for the farewell because "everything has been organised". One wonders whether this was his own way of saving his mother from finding the extra money, using his sense of humour as a way of getting around the need for new clothes.

An oft-told story is that of a prank Steve pulled on one of his classmates, Mantyoyi. The story is that Steve and his friends were very fond of the Beatles, especially their song "A Hard Day's Night". One night Steve was on top of the desks at school singing "A Hard Day's Night" when Mantyoyi complained that they were making too much noise. The following day Mantyoyi approached the school principal to ask to be allowed to study by himself in the laboratory. The boys were annoyed by Mantyoyi's actions and considered beating him up, until Steve came up with an idea. One night the ever-studious Mantyoyi was seriously preparing for exams when Steve and some other boys sneaked into the laboratory and started flicking the lights and flashing their buttocks at him. One of the students was Retsi Pule, later a famous musician. (I grew up singing the funny lyrics of one of his songs: *Sidudla, ngane yam, ndiyakuthanda. Kutheni izolo ubungekho?* – a popular song about a man who misses "his fat lady".) Retsi was particularly light-skinned, and seeing Retsi's buttocks at night convinced Mantyoyi that the witches of Ginsberg had finally come for him. He jumped out of the window and dashed home. He stayed away from school for days and went to a witch doctor for protection from Ginsberg's evil spirits. He came back with cuts on his face from the witch doctor's knife. The school took the matter very seriously and Steve was suspended from school for a joke that had gone wrong. His mother MamCethe had to come to school to apologise and Steve was only allowed to come and write exams. That notwithstanding, he came out top of his class.

Steve had also taken it upon himself to ensure that everyone in his class applied to go to post-secondary college to finish matric (i.e. high school of Grade 10 to 12). Steve was awarded a bursary by Masizakhe to study at Lovedale. The fact that the people of Ginsberg had sent him to college stayed with him throughout his life, and would inspire him to do the same when he was banished to Ginsberg, in setting up the Ginsberg Bursary Fund in 1975. (See Chapter 8.)

I now turn to Steve's formative political experiences at Lovedale College and St Francis College at Mariannhill.

4
Leaving Home: Lovedale, St Francis College

> "I had unsuccessfully tried to get Steve interested in politics. The police were able to do in one day what had eluded me for years."
> KHAYA BIKO

In 1963 Steve Biko and Mzwandile Ngcelwane were admitted to Lovedale College but soon discovered that Larry Bekwa had failed to apply. Steve persuaded Larry to come with them to Lovedale, but he was reluctant because of his earlier expulsion from the college. Steve insisted that the school would have forgotten or forgiven him, and he convinced Larry to come along anyway. They were put together with the brightest of the bright in the Form IV A class at Lovedale. Khaya had been at Lovedale for a year already and had a sterling reputation as one of the leading students at the school. One of his classmates, prominent businessman Wiseman Nkuhlu, remembers that Khaya had been "particularly good in English."

Then one day at the beginning of the school year, Larry's former Maths teacher, Mr Paterson, recognised Larry's face. "Do I see a Bekwa in my class or are my eyes failing me?" Paterson mocked.

"No, your eyes are not failing you, sir. I am Larry Bekwa," replied Larry.

"What puts you here, Bekwa?" asked Paterson.

"I have come to learn, sir," Larry answered.

"No, no, no, no, you have come to spoil these children, Bekwa." Paterson then left the room and came marching back down the hallway with the school principal in tow.

"Get out of Lovedale now!" bellowed the principal. Steve tried to intervene but was ordered back into the classroom.

"He's my brother, he's my brother!" he protested as the police took Larry to the train station.[116]

In April 1963 Lovedale was hit by a student boycott of classes soon after Larry's expulsion – but not because of it. Khaya Biko was identified as one of the "ringleaders". The police had uncovered his political activities in the PAC in Ginsberg and he was removed from the school by plain-clothes security policemen. Khaya recalls the events of that morning:

> It was the Tuesday just before Easter, and I was attending Mrs White's English class when someone came to call me. I saw a white Corolla CD 143 with Steve inside. I thought maybe there was a death in the family. I soon discovered there were actually two cars – and that these were cops. We were separated, and Steve went in the other car to fetch our clothes from the dormitory. I was handcuffed all the way from Alice to King William's Town at the back of the sedan – for 60 long kilometres. All the time the cops were boasting about how they had broken the guys from Ginsberg into confessions. Indeed, when I got to the King William's Town police station I found the whole Star of Hope team there. I really did not know who to trust, but I knew I could always trust Pringle Jack.

---

116 Some students have a positive recollection of Mr Paterson, whom they called Oom Pat, as one of the more enlightened teachers at Lovedale.

Khaya was charged for being a member of an unlawful organisation POQO, the armed wing of the Pan Africanist Congress in the 1960s – later it was called the Azanian People's Liberation Army (APLA). He was convicted and sentenced to two years' imprisonment, with 15 months suspended. He spent several months at Fort Glamorgan jail just outside East London, while Steve was stranded in Ginsberg, also expelled from Lovedale. Fearing that he too would be arrested, Steve – who was only 16 at the time – ran away from Ginsberg and joined Larry at the latter's home in Peddie for the remainder of the year. Larry recalled that "the police would come in their vans to my house looking for us. We would sleep in the trees and among the cornfields behind my father's house."

It would have been impossible for Steve to avoid the highly charged political atmosphere at Lovedale. Barney Pityana, with whom Steve would later establish the Black Consciousness Movement, remembers the first time the two of them met at Lovedale. After finishing primary school as one of the top students in Port Elizabeth, Barney received the Andrew Smith Bursary to attend Lovedale. He remembers that Lovedale under principal John Benyon was run like a typical English public school with very rigid rules, lots of hard work and plenty of sport, and was also very religious. Barney was also in the so-called academic track – Form I A, Form II A and Form III A. A class ahead of them was Sam Nolutshungu, who was then a star of Lovedale, and a favourite of the school principal:

> We got there at the time of the strikes. Thabo Mbeki had just been expelled, and there were rumblings about that. Chris Hani had finished and was now at Fort Hare but would sneak

in to give political classes. Zola Skweyiya was doing Form V at the time, and would give us classes in political education, and so did Andrew Masondo.

Pityana also remembers Steve as a bright student: "Then in 1963 a guy arrived to join us in Form IV A. At that time we had little academic respect for township high school students. But this guy was giving us a run for our money. And that was Steve."

Upon release from prison Khaya Biko was barred from attending any public school in South Africa. "Troublesome" students were blacklisted as a matter of course. Khaya had no choice but to leave school. He started working as a clerk with a King William's Town law firm, Squire, Smith and Laurie, and wrote to schools around the country, trying to have his younger brother admitted. On the strength of his excellent Forbes Grant grades – and despite having missed a full year of school – Steve was admitted in 1964 into one of the most competitive schools in the country, St Francis College in Mariannhill, Natal – essentially to start with Form IV again (in today's parlance that would be Grade 11). As in Lovedale, Form IV A at St Francis was a collection of the brightest students from all over South Africa – Larry's ever-resourceful father had secured him a place at Healdtown College, where he completed high school.

According to Khaya, the Lovedale experience was the most politicising moment in Steve's life:

> Steve was expelled for absolutely no reason at all. But in retrospect I welcome the South African government's gesture of

exposing a really good politician. I had unsuccessfully tried to get Steve interested in politics. The police were able to do in one day what had eluded me for years. This time the great giant was awakened.

Early Activism at St Francis College

St Francis College was established in 1883 by Abbot Francis Pfanner to produce "Christian leaders of the African race". Some of its illustrious alumni include the likes of BW Vilakazi (an early African intellectual), Ben Ngubane (former cabinet minister), Sibusiso Sibisi (head of the Council for Scientific and Industrial Research), Ivy Matsepe-Casaburri (former cabinet minister) and the late Jeffrey Baqwa (Black Consciousness activist and close friend of Steve's). Steve encountered stiff academic competition from fellow students such as Sizo Mazibuko, Olaf Baloyi, Boardman Mbhele and Dorrington Mathanda, but he still held his own among the top five in his class. He was without peer in English and History and soon became the vice-chairman of the school's Literary and Debating Society.

The debates, or what his classmate Boardman Mbhele described as "the battle of words", were focused on broad political questions such as: "Is the Third World War possible?"; "Is the press a servant or a tyrant?"; and "Men and women should have equal rights". The motto of the debating team was: "Virtue lies not in the prize but in the struggle." Steve's debating skills would stand him in good stead later in his leadership of the BCM, particularly in his famous testimony at the SASO/BPC Trial.

Steve's growing political consciousness did not dull his sense of humour. He often joked about a debate his school won on "the importance of milk and milk products in family feeding". He penned a glowing report for the school magazine:

> We were invited to Lamontville for the distribution of prizes, where our school had been asked to render a musical piece. We were confident of gaining at least one prize. On the 15th May, the big convertible (school lorry) took us to Lamontville. We arrived in good time. The musical performance was appreciated. Sizo Mazibuko snatched the first prize in the region. The great applause was interrupted by the Master of Ceremonies announcing Steve Biko had secured the second prize for the district. In all directions people were grinning and clapping hands.[117]

For the first time in his life, St Francis provided Steve with the space for serious political reflection. The school had a liberal political culture which allowed it to admit even politically "troublesome" students. One of those "troublesome" students, Eric Jose, had been imprisoned for three years on Robben Island before being admitted to the college. He later became headprefect and led most of the political discussions at the school. These discussions often took place in the evening in the dining hall where Jose would talk as if he was addressing a mass meeting.

In 1964 Jose led a strike against the bad quality of the food at the school. He argued that while mission schools afforded black students a certain degree of freedom, this should not be used to hide unjust practices within the schools themselves.

---

117 St Francis College School Magazine, 1965.

The food strike lit the political fervour at St Francis. It is at these evening meetings that students began to notice the quality of Steve's political contributions. After dinner the students would meet under the trees, and this is where Steve continued in a mostly understated way to make his inputs. He emerged as one of the leading political thinkers at the school when Rhodesia's Ian Smith announced the Unilateral Declaration of Independence (UDI). Students converged around him as he explained the implications for black people in South Africa.

Steve's schoolmate at St Francis, and later one of his closest comrades in the BCM, Jeffrey Baqwa, described Steve's growing profile as a political thinker:

> We needed clarity on UDI in Rhodesia, and that's where Steve shone ... and when Churchill died Steve was there to describe the political implications. He was able to make all these connections and link them to what was going on in South Africa.

Baqwa also recalled how Steve invited him to come out to King William's Town and had a sheep slaughtered for him before he went into exile: "The next thing I heard they had killed him."

Steve had one more hurdle before he could even think about assuming a leadership position. The tradition of *ukwaluka*, or initiation, is the most important part of a Xhosa male's "rite of passage" into adulthood. The initiation takes the form of circumcision accompanied by a series of other "character-moulding" rituals conducted in a forest away from the community. The initiation marks the passage from being a boy to a man with social responsibilities. No amount of educational or financial qualification exempts a Xhosa man from this institutionalised cultural practice. The practice has come under fire in recent years because of the number of deaths that have accompanied it.

Because his mother could hardly afford the costs that go with the ritual, in December 1964 Steve went to his initiation at the home of his relative OB Biko in Zwelitsha, together with Sipho Biko and Sipho Kila, and returned to St Francis as a man in 1965.

At the close of 1965 Steve reflected on the impact St Francis College had on his own consciousness:

> Mariannhill has been a source of great inspiration to us. This history of the college shows that she has produced teachers by the thousands, doctors and lawyers galore, priests and many other distinguished figures. Therefore may we not expect to swell this list one day also?[118]

He presciently singled out the Debating Society "which has trained many of us in public speaking, and play-acting which has revealed and developed potential histrionic talents in some of us. No less important is character-moulding and training self-knowledge."

---

118 St Francis College School Magazine, 1965.

5
The Trouble(s) with NUSAS

"[Steve Biko] . . . defined a problem hitherto unrecognised."
From SASO statement signed by Don Espey,
Goolam Abram and others

As testimony to his intellectual abilities, Steve was admitted to the prestigious Durban Medical School at the University of Natal Non-European section (UNNE) in 1966. His arrival in Durban precedes, and some might say prefigures, what Tony Morphet called "the Durban moment" – the years 1970-1974 – when, according to Morphet, a new sense of the possibilities of "brushing against the grain" of South African history arose. Flowing from the intellectual ferment of radical student politics and labour struggles of the time,[119] this "moment" made real the possibility of going against the grain of an increasingly militaristic and racist police state. In 1960 the government had outlawed the ANC and the PAC, leaving them with no option but to pursue an underground armed struggle. The leading theoretician of apartheid, Hendrik Verwoerd, had been elected prime minister in 1958 and he enlisted known Nazi sympathiser BJ Vorster as minister of justice, if ever there was a misnomer. Together they erected what sociologist Dan O'Meara has described as "walls of granite" around white privilege:

---

119 Tony Morphet, Richard Turner Lecture, Durban 1990.

> Under the new Minister of Justice, BJ Vorster, South Africa was rapidly turned into a grubby (and increasingly corrupt) police state ... lengthy prison terms and a number of death sentences were handed out to organisers of political resistance. By 1964 the underground networks of the ANC and the PAC had been wiped out, the various rural revolts brutally suppressed, and the member unions of the South African Congress of Trade Unions bled white.[120]

Going against this grain were liberal political institutions and individuals such as Helen Suzman, the sole voice of the opposition in the all-white parliament. Liberal universities assumed the role of extra-parliamentary opposition because of their relative autonomy from government interference. The establishment of the Durban Medical School in 1951 relieved a situation in which black students had nowhere to study medicine. Throughout the 1920s and '30s, neither Wits nor the University of Cape Town (UCT) medical schools were prepared to accept black students. The practice at places like UCT was to dissuade black students from applying. After World War II there were only a handful of black students at UCT – Fikile Bam, Archie Mafeje, Thulani Gcabashe and Welsh Makanda. The medical school would not have any African students until 1985. Refusing admission to African students exposed the Wits and UCT medical schools' liberal credentials, an awkwardness ended only by the establishment of the medical school at the University of Natal in 1951. Wits had competed hard to house

---

[120] Dan O'Meara (1996). *Forty Lost Years: The Apartheid State and the Politics of the National Party 1948-1994* (Johannesburg: Ravan Press) 109-110.

a medical school for blacks, located within its campus but with its own segregated classes. Bruce Murray notes that the number of blacks at the Wits Medical School between 1950 and 1959 stayed static at 73 to 74 students – and these were mostly Indian and Coloured students. The first major intake of African students would be at the new medical school in Durban.[121] The Durban Medical School was opened on a separate campus known as the University of Natal Non-European section (UNNE). Popularly known as Wentworth because of the area in which it was located, the university attracted the brightest black – including African – matriculants from right across the country.

On his arrival Steve joined a peculiarly sophisticated and cosmopolitan group of students. The group consisted of a cross-section of young leaders from across the country – Ben Ngubane and Charles Sibisi from upper-crust African families in Natal, Goolam "Geez" Abram from Lenasia, Aubrey Mokoape and Chippy Palweni from Soweto and the dashing Vuyelwa Mashalaba from the Transkei. Each of these individuals brought something unique to the group. Charles Sibisi, who had access to academic journals and newspapers at his home, often led the discussions on foreign affairs. Vuyelwa Mashalaba, who came from a prominent family in the Transkei, was beautiful, classy and sophisticated. She listened to classical music, put on the finest wear, and could hold her own in the male-dominated political discussions. According to Mamphela Ramphele, who joined the group on her arrival in 1968, Mashalaba was "the only woman who participated in those debates, while the rest

---

121 Bruce Murray (1979). *Wits: The 'Open' Years, A History of the University of the Witwatersrand, 1939-1959* (Johannesburg: Wits University Press).

of us watched silently, though with interest".[122] Ramphele recalls that Mashalaba was sent to launch a South African Students Organisation (SASO) branch at the University of Fort Hare: "Her public smoking at the meeting left the students horrified! How could they be associated with an organisation that had such women in leadership positions? It took some skilful smoothing of ruffled feathers by Pityana to get the launch back on track."[123]

Mashalaba became a role model for younger female medical students such as Mamphela Ramphele. Ramphele arrived in 1968 as a transfer student from the University of the North. Many members of this nucleus would come to play prominent roles. Ngubane became a cabinet minister in the first democratic government of Nelson Mandela and South Africa's ambassador to Japan; Ramphele became the first black and female vice-chancellor of the University of Cape Town and, later, a managing director at the World Bank; Mokoape, who served eight years on Robben Island, later became a prominent businessman; and Charles Sibisi became a surgeon in London.

The University of Natal also accepted black students who had been expelled from black universities after protesting against the Extension of University Education Act of 1959 – only the National Party could come up with such a misnomer. This new law formally divided university admissions by race and ethnicity. Under its provisions Xhosas would study

---

[122] Mamphela Ramphele (1991), "The Dynamics of Gender Within Black Consciousness Organisations" in Barney Pityana, Mamphela Ramphele, Malusi Mpumlwana and Lindy Wilson, *Bounds of Possibility: The Legacy of Steve Biko and Black Consciousness*, 215.
[123] Ramphele, "The Dynamics of Gender", 219.

at Xhosa universities such as Fort Hare, Zulus at the University of Zululand, Sothos at the University of the North (Turfloop) etc. Expelled students from these universities brought their radicalism to the University of Natal, adding dynamism to black student politics at the university. Among this group were the likes of Justice Moloto, a fiery student leader at Fort Hare who later married Vuyelwa Mashalaba. Moloto became a judge in the Land Claims Court. Another student, Louis Skweyiya, would become a distinguished lawyer and a judge of the Constitutional Court in the democratic South Africa.

The black students at Natal had their own Student Representative Council, which was affiliated to the multi-racial but predominantly white student organisation, the National Union of South African Students (NUSAS). Black students were divided when it came to the relationship with NUSAS. The African Students Association (ASA), aligned to the banned African National Congress (ANC), was in favour of collaboration with NUSAS. This was hardly surprising given the ANC's history of collaboration with white groups such as the Congress of Democrats and the South African Communist Party (SACP), going back to the 1950s. The African Students Union of South Africa (ASUSA), aligned to the Pan Africanist Congress (PAC), rejected any association with white groupings.

It is testimony to his political and intellectual talent that Steve was elected to the Student Representative Council (SRC) at Wentworth. All SRCs at the white liberal universities were affiliated to NUSAS. The policy of affiliation to NUSAS was a bone of contention not only among black students but among whites as well. This was because even conservative students were by dint of their SRC membership at any university also members of NUSAS. Because of his leadership position in the SRC and NUSAS, Steve got caught up in the debates over the role of white liberals in the struggle. Leading the charge against his participation in NUSAS was Aubrey Nchaupe Mokoape.

The Pan Africanist Influence . . . Again

By the time he arrived at the University of Natal, Aubrey Mokoape was "long in the tooth"; he had been a member of the PAC since the age of 15. He belonged to the PAC branch in Mofolo, Soweto, whose membership included the organisation's founder, Robert Sobukwe. He was a volunteer in the PAC's anti-pass campaign in 1960 and, along with the adults, he presented himself at a police station for arrest on the principle of "no bail, no fine, no defence". Some of the protesters were sentenced to imprisonment for periods of up to three years, which in the case of Robert Sobukwe became nine years. The moment his three-year term in the Pretoria prison was up, Sobukwe was detained without trial on Robben Island under the so-called Sobukwe Clause for a further six years. The clause enabled parliament to renew his detention every year as he came up for release. The government put him in a house separated from the other prisoners for six solitary years. His family was allowed to visit him once a year for a week or two. For the remainder of the year he was all by himself with only the sound of the ocean and the guard dogs. According to his wife, Victoria, he had started forgetting how to speak by the end of his sentence. His son, Dinilesizwe, often talked about the pain of leaving their father behind after those short visits. Despite the hardship Sobukwe registered for postgraduate economics degree with the University of London.

He was eventually released but banished to a place he hardly knew – Galeshewe in Kimberley. There he took up studies in law through private correspondence and qualified as an attorney. He also immersed himself in the life of the community and became a preacher in the local church – until the government realised that he was using prayer to make political statements. So afraid was the apartheid government of Robert Sobukwe that they banned him from praying in public. BJ Vorster once described him as the most dangerous black man alive.

During the SASO/BPC Trial Steve recalled visiting Sobukwe in Kimberley with his friend and comrade Stanley Ntwasa. Steve referred to people like Nelson Mandela, Govan Mbeki, Ahmed Kathrada and Robert Sobukwe: "The common factor is that they are people who have been pushing forward the struggle for the Black man in a selfless sense." And then he continued with respect to Sobukwe: "I have met Mr Sobukwe, for instance . . . it was in 1972." And then the prosecutor asked him: "In what connection?" and Steve replied rather cheekily: "Because I wanted to meet him . . . I was on a tour of the country for Black community purposes which took me to collect some information from Mr Stanley Ntwasa in connection with some cases that he had had that year, and because we were in Kimberley, of course we took the opportunity of seeing Mr Sobukwe."[124] The urban legend is that Steve once walked into a room where Sobukwe was present and exclaimed: "*Tyhini, noThixo ulapha!*" – Phew, even God is here! Whether this is legend or fact is not clear but it does demonstrate the

---

124 Arnold, *The Testimony of Steve Biko*, 147.

respect with which the Black Consciousness students regarded Sobukwe. Sobukwe, however, was not always impressed with the social behaviour of the student leadership, particularly their drinking and womanising – a topic to which I shall return.

The 1960 anti-pass campaign had involved many young activists and their parents collectively approached the PAC leadership to help get the younger ones released. Upon his release Aubrey Mokoape went back to Orlando High and finished high school. Unfazed by his prison experience, he then left the country to join the PAC's military wing, POQO, in neighbouring Lesotho. Passage into countries further north on the continent proved difficult. He soon returned to work as an underground operative inside South Africa while holding a job at OK Bazaars grocery store in downtown Johannesburg.

Under the controversial leadership of Potlako Leballo, POQO started preparing for its "final assault" on the apartheid regime. Leballo had left the country on a one-way exit permit with a letter from Sobukwe that designated him acting president of the PAC. When it was banned, the PAC had established a fairly elaborate system of underground cells throughout the country – all waiting for commands from Maseru for the "final assault". At the beginning of 1963 Leballo summoned leaders of these cells to Maseru where they would be given instructions about the impending uprising. He eventually decided that the uprising – which was set for 7 April 1963 – should be executed on written orders from Maseru. But the police had infiltrated the PAC. One of the couriers was intercepted. On her were the addresses of all those instructed to lead the insurrection. "Within a month, 3 246 POQO suspects had been arrested" and "1 162 of them were eventually jailed", according to Tom Lodge.[125] Mokoape recalls the interception of a letter carried by one Mrs Molapo:

> ... the Boers mounted the biggest arrest campaign. That is how people like Dikgang Moseneke got arrested. There were mass trials all over the country. The courts were kangaroo courts, willy-nilly sentencing our people to death or sending them away for long terms in prison. That broke the PAC's back and permanently arrested its development. After that there was really no political activity. Everyone was terrified. There was total silence even at dinner tables. Mutual suspicion ruled the day.

Mokoape was lucky to be in prison for a criminal misdemeanour at the time of the swoop – he had been caught stealing goods at the grocery store where he worked. While he was in prison his parents applied for him to study medicine at the University of Natal. He had been an extremely bright student and was accepted on the strength of his matric grades.

Mokoape found the liberal campus environment strange. As an underground operative, he remained aloof from student politics in order to cover his trail: "I told them that this whole thing of passing conference resolutions from the comforts of the university campus was a joke."

Steve would argue with him, saying that NUSAS had resources they could utilise. Mokoape was impressed by Steve:

---

125 Lodge, *Sharpeville*, 202-203.

> In those days a "freshman" was there to be seen, not heard. But I remember this gangly, awkward youth who would not shut up. Not only was I more experienced in these matters but I also came from Jo'Burg, wearing Florsheims and I was a big *mjita* on campus. But he was not fazed. I got attracted to him by that quality. He did not feel disempowered by people who had more privileges than he did. And because of my background I could not be really intimate with anyone. But I detected in him someone more committed and more sincere. That made it easier to seek out his company. He was probably the first person to whom I intimated my background. We just grew on each other. When I wanted serious debate I would seek him out. And when I wanted to be a *mjita* I would seek out other people.

In his later testimony at the SASO/BPC Trial Steve recalled his disagreements with Mokoape and other radical nationalist students who wanted to have nothing to do with NUSAS:

> Their attitude was one of a very deep level of distrust of the attachments of Whites to the concept of non-racialism. They felt that this would always be propounded as an idea only, but that in effect Whites in general are satisfied with the status quo as it exists now, and are not going to assist completely in moving away from this situation to one of non-racialism. My view was that I do not believe this. I believe that there are equally committed Whites who want the situation changed – who would like to share with us everything that the country can produce.[126]

---

126 Arnold, *The Testimony of Steve Biko*, 6.

The Conference at Rhodes University

In this testimony, Steve referred to the arguments of his antagonists, which were essentially about the duplicity of NUSAS. They alleged that NUSAS would hold parties in places where they knew blacks would not be allowed, or they would cite a NUSAS president who was overheard speaking in support of racial segregation. The truth of what Aubrey Mokoape had been saying dawned on Steve at a NUSAS conference at Rhodes University in Grahamstown in July 1967.

Steve attended this conference on behalf of the Wentworth campus. The representatives from Wentworth travelled to Grahamstown by train, giving them time to caucus. They resolved that should they be asked to stay in racially segregated accommodation, they would withdraw their participation in protest:

> It so happened that when we got to Rhodes University in the first instance the conference organiser could not quite say where we were going to stay. We were all put out in the hall in different places, and we eventually noticed that all the White students first went, then some of the Indian students, then eventually he came to us to say he had found a church where we could stay. At that moment I felt we had ample reason to stick by our decision in the train.[127]

Steve consulted with the other black students on what action they should take. The NUSAS executive was quick to condemn the university's decision, causing a split in the black delega-

---

127 Arnold, *The Testimony of Steve Biko*, 7.

tion. The black delegates were also informed that they could not eat at or participate in racially mixed social functions. Steve began canvassing white students to go with the black students to the church. Robert Schrire, who was vice-chairman of NUSAS and head of the UCT delegation, remembers someone reporting to him that there was a "troublemaker" intent on breaking NUSAS: "I became particularly indignant that it was a black person who was trying to destroy NUSAS, the most important multi-racial institution in the country." Schrire asked for a meeting but Steve refused to go to his dormitory. A fuming Schrire walked over to a dormitory where Steve was temporarily staying. He found him with a group of other black students. Schrire remembers Steve asking him how he saw the struggle progressing, given the position taken by the white students. Schrire replied that the only road to liberation was through the persuasion of whites. The black students had to be careful not to alienate the white students, even more so as NUSAS was trying to extend its membership to the Afrikaans-speaking campuses. Schrire remembers: "Steve was a very attractive individual with a great sense of humour. He was polite, but basically treated me with good-humoured contempt."

The NUSAS congress started the following day with the various NUSAS regions giving their reports. Steve rose to make a point of order. He started speaking in isiXhosa and everybody started laughing. But Schrire realised what he was trying to do. As it became clear that he was not about to stop, the white students started protesting that they could not follow him. But that was exactly the point, Steve argued, to make white students understand how it felt not to be heard.

NUSAS president Margie Marshall, who later became chief

justice of the State of Massachusetts, argued that NUSAS could not be held accountable. The decision against racial mixing and shared accommodation was the university's decision, not a NUSAS decision.[128] Robin Margo, president of the Wits SRC, proposed a motion condemning the university council's position and asking for a 24-hour hunger strike in protest. The motion passed, but then Steve proposed a more radical amendment: that NUSAS had not handled the organisation of the congress properly. Steve contended that NUSAS headquarters knew in advance that accommodation would be a problem, yet they did not make alternative arrangements to either postpone the congress or change the venue. He therefore proposed that the congress be suspended.

The discussion lasted from around midnight to 5am but Steve's motion was ultimately rejected.

Steve left and returned to Durban a broken and disappointed man. He told his friends at Alan Taylor Residence what had happened. He had publicly defended NUSAS, and he saw the incident at Rhodes University as a slap in the face: "I realised that for a long time I had been holding on to this whole dogma of non-racialism almost like a religion, and feeling that it is sacrilegious to question it, and therefore not accommodating the attacks I was getting from other students." [129]

Mokoape gleefully confesses that he felt vindicated by the turn of events in Grahamstown: "What happened there hurt him deeply. He saw this blatant hypocrisy I had been telling him about unfolding in front of his own eyes."

---

128 John Kane-Berman says Margie Marshall was quite hurt by the walk-out at Rhodes.
129 Arnold, *The Testimony of Steve Biko*, 8.

For Mokoape, NUSAS's inability to accept Steve's proposal reflected an inherent limitation that came from its demographic make-up. It was essentially a student body led by privileged white students from elite universities such as Wits, UCT and Natal. Its opposition to apartheid was tempered by the desire to maintain a strong presence among conservative white students.

Sam Nolutshungu would later explain the birth of Black Consciousness in the following terms: ". . . the movement presents itself as secession from a world that rejects or frustrates or cannot comprehend its concerns and needs, but the secession precedes the shattering of that world and the creation of another."[130]

The NUSAS Congress at Wits: More Accommodation Trouble

The issue of accommodation preoccupied the organisation as it prepared for its next annual congress, to be held at Wits University in 1968. Letters went back and forth about where the black students would be accommodated. A solution was found only after a series of consultations between the president of the Wits SRC, John Kane-Berman, and the vice-chancellor, Ian MacCrone.

Kane-Berman came from a radical background in Johannesburg. His father, Louis Kane-Berman, had been a leader of the War Veterans' Torch Commando, which consisted of World War II veterans who, after returning from fighting Nazism on the war front, found its replica in the National Party. Es-

---

130 Sam Nolutshungu (1982). *Changing South Africa: Political Considerations* (Manchester, Manchester University Press), 152.

tablished in 1941 out of the work of the Springbok Legion – some of whose members included Joe Slovo, Rusty Bernstein, Jack Hodgson and Fred Carneson – the Commando became for a while the most powerful opposition to the National Party government. The government passed a law to ban anyone in public service or the military from joining the organisation and as a result it did not survive beyond the first five years of its existence. But one might say the seed of militancy – at least among some whites – had been planted.

Eschewing the more radical path chosen by the likes of Slovo (who joined the ANC's Umkhonto we Sizwe), Louis Kane-Berman became an activist in the Liberal Party. His son, John, graduated from St John's College, a preserve of Johannesburg's liberal elite, and entered Wits in 1965. He assumed the leadership of the Students' Representative Council in 1967. Kane-Berman was at the Rhodes University conference as an alternate delegate from Wits. He had seen how upset Steve was by the whole debacle and he was determined that a black breakaway from NUSAS would not happen under his watch: "I could see that this could be a nail in the coffin for NUSAS. I knew Steve would not come to the Wits congress if this issue was not resolved."

Kane-Berman lobbied the university vice-chancellor Ian MacCrone to turn a blind eye to racial mixing at the 1968 congress. In 1952 the Wits University Council had adopted a resolution that allowed for "academic non-segregation and social segregation". What this meant was that while the university was willing to admit black students, this did not extend to social mixing with whites on the campus. The policy specifically stated that "the Non-European student has access to every educational facility which the university provides, but he is not admitted to the sports facilities provided for Europeans nor to European dances or other social functions". Wits did not intend to be an island of racial equality in an otherwise unequal society.

This was the custom at Wits when Kane-Berman approached MacCrone. MacCrone in turn asked Kane-Berman to get him a legal opinion that would provide the university with a loophole in the legislation. Kane-Berman obtained that legal opinion from Cecil Margo, who later became a prominent judge. Margo opined that for the purposes of the law, the university was a private space and for that reason was entitled to host mixed gatherings. In that respect Margo exposed the collusion of the university in the enforcement of segregation on the campus. Kane-Berman also shuttled back and forth to see Steve at the University of Natal, if only to assure him of his efforts to have an integrated congress.

The negotiations between John Kane-Berman and Ian MacCrone bore fruit. The Wits University administration and SRC had managed to resolve for NUSAS what seemed to be an intractable dilemma. Consequently, Steve and other SASO students, such as Strini Moodley, attended the 1968 conference, where Moodley put on his play *Black on White*.

In reality, race remained the elephant in the room. For example, some students suggested that future congresses not be held at white universities, while others viewed this as an impractical proposition. The latter position prevailed. Also, when an Afrikaner student addressed the conference in Afrikaans, Steve instructed Geez Abram to speak in Urdu and he would speak in isiXhosa. At the conclusion of the conference the white students all stood up to sing the apartheid-era national anthem, *Die Stem*. Steve and his colleagues remained seated. After the white students had finished with *Die Stem*, they stood up to sing the black anthem *Nkosi sikelel' iAfrika*. There was a stunned silence in the hall.

At the conference, Steve proposed the election of Duncan Innes as president of NUSAS before leaving the conference. He would characterise that particular congress as follows:

> The 1968 NUSAS Congress was uneventful. The overriding impression was that we were there in name only. The swing to the right in the organisation did not meet with the usual counter from the blacks. It was clear none of the blacks felt a part of the organisation. Hence the Executive that was elected was all white.[131]

Before the congress, John Daniel was acting president of NUSAS because the president-elect, John Sprack, had been deported by the government in 1967. Speaking at a NUSAS meeting in early 1968,[132] Daniel noted that "from the government, hostility is tremendous and undiminishing". He commended NUSAS for holding the fort despite those pressures:

> I think it is miraculous that NUSAS has survived the involvement of two former Presidents (1960, 1961, 1962) and numerous students in sabotage, the 90-day detention of the 1964

---

131 Biko, *I Write What I Like*, 12.
132 John Daniel's address to NUSAS at an undisclosed venue in early 1968. Daniel had also volunteered to take over the leadership of NUSAS at a time of heightened government reaction to the student body, evidenced by the bannings and deportations of its leadership.

> President, banning of 1966 President, deportation of the 1968 President-elect, the banning of other executive members and advisers, constant verbal attacks from the Government and continual security police harassment.

Daniel also critically reflected on NUSAS's composition as a body of 22 000 white students and only 1 776 "non-white" students that had only one non-white member in its ten-member executive and "has never had a non-white president." He also lamented the fact that NUSAS leadership was dominated by the most conservative campuses, Wits and UCT – which "held policy back" – the conservatism would indeed be on display at the 1968 NUSAS congress at Wits.

This is the political context that Duncan Innes found when he took over the NUSAS leadership – a government onslaught and a conservative student body. Innes was a product of the preppy Bishops College where he distinguished himself playing rugby. He was at the University of Cape Town when Robert Kennedy visited the country in 1966. According to Innes, Kennedy's historic speech, Ripple of Hope, which equated the South African struggle to the civil rights struggle in the United States, galvanised an otherwise timid middleclass and upper-middle-class student body:

> The following year I was elected president of the UCT SRC. My liberal UCT colleagues and I were harassed by the security police and I had my passport removed which prevented me from taking up an overseas scholarship, the Abe Bailey Bursary. But we didn't care because we now felt part of a global movement for freedom.[133]

---

133 Duncan Innes in *Cape Weekend Argus*, in Helen Bamford, "Ripple of Hope that Kennedy Brought to SA", Sunday 1 August 2010, 22.

A Liberal UCT?

Innes's first major challenge took place at UCT in 1968. The university had appointed the prominent anthropologist Archie Mafeje as a replacement for the leading left intellectual Ray Simons. The university was almost entirely white at that time, with a handful of Coloured students and absolutely no African students. Two days after Mafeje's appointment, the Minister of national education Jan de Klerk, FW de Klerk's father, wrote to the university asking it "not to proceed with the appointment of the non-white person". The minister argued that this would flout the accepted tradition in South Africa. He argued that although there was no law prohibiting Mr Mafeje's appointment, there was a general understanding that even at open universities such as UCT the staff would always be white. The University Council was cowed by government pressure and rescinded Mr Mafeje's appointment. A mass meeting was called where the council would address students on the Mafeje affair. The leader of the Radical Students Society, Raphael Kaplinsky, stood up to give a scathing critique of the meeting. He saw it as an attempt to salve the university's conscience, and called for more radical action. The result was another meeting which resulted in a sit-in at the Bremner Administration Building. Innes says:

> ... there was simply no way that we, as liberal student leaders, were going to sit back and allow the UCT council to withdraw the appointment of a black lecturer (Archie Mafeje) simply because the apartheid government told them to.

Although he saw himself as more of an intellectual than a politician, Jeremy Cronin (later to become the deputy general secretary of the South African Communist Party and a cabinet member in Jacob Zuma's government) remembers coming under the influence of Rick Turner, who came into his own as a student leader during the sit-in. Cronin says he was increasingly being influenced by other leftist intellectuals such as Jack Simons and Martin Versfeld. Turner had studied philosophy at Nanterre under the French intellectual Henri Lefebvre, and wrote his doctorate on Sartre and Marxism. On his return, he became part of a circle of progressive Afrikaner intellectuals at the University of Stellenbosch, under the leadership of philosophy professor Johannes Degenaar. He later taught at the University of Natal and produced the classic *The Eye of the Needle*, a book of essays that included a chapter on the Black Consciousness Movement. Turner was later assassinated by apartheid hit men at his home in Durban in 1978.

Despite the protests, the University of Cape Town Council insisted that under the circumstances they could not appoint Mr Mafeje. They offered instead to create a University Academic Freedom Award, as well as to dedicate a plaque to academic freedom. The SRC accepted this offer. The black students saw this as further confirmation of the limits of white student politics. Innes admits that they were indeed still operating from within the liberal tradition. He had never encountered black leaders like Steve and Barney, and he was immediately bowled over by Steve. For the first time he had met a black leader whom he was ready and willing to follow.

By all accounts, Steve would easily have been elected to lead NUSAS, were it not for the events at Rhodes in 1967. Ben Ngubane, who did not walk out with the other black students, was elected vice president to John Sprack. Innes and Steve agreed that even though SASO had a right to exist as a separate organisation, it would be important to keep a strategic relationship between the two organisations.

Innes shared Steve's "weakness" for the opposite sex. So notorious was Innes's playboy image that at a NUSAS congress, the men would compete for the "Duncan Innes Trophy" – which went to the man who slept with the greatest number of women. The women activists hated this but the men, including Steve, were not the least bothered. Innes used the presidential visits as an opportunity for his sexual exploits. Innes describes the routine whenever Steve visited from Natal:

> I stayed in a big house and Steve, Ben Ngubane and Barney would come and stay for weeks. We would keep the curtain closed all the time. We used to go around in my Ford Anglia and then we would go hang out at the Hussar Steakhouse. The owner knew us and did not have problems with a multiracial grouping at his place. The racists were the Pig & Whistle Restaurant down the road. Steve liked the ladies, and we were sometimes jealous because he hit on "our" white women. He was quite non-racial when it came to that, and our resentments of him dating our women tested our own commitment to non-racialism.

NUSAS's general secretary Sheila Lapinsky remembers going up to Steve once and angrily telling him off: "You're a sexist!" Steve's retort was: "Don't worry about my sexism. What about your white racist friends in NUSAS?"

Thus, even though Steve was pushing the race debate, he never in his politics addressed issues of gender, a point made eloquently by Mamphela Ramphele in her critique of the Black Consciousness Movement, but disputed by other women as we shall see in Chapters 7 and 8.

At the NUSAS congress at Wits University in 1968, Horst Kleinschmidt, who was a student at Wits, was sitting directly opposite Steve. He immediately identified with the points that Steve and the black students were making. His background as the child of a poor Afrikaner family created a social distance between him and the English-speaking, often well-off, liberal leadership of NUSAS. He was born to a conservative German family in Swakopmund, Namibia, and came to South Africa to join the Afrikaans section of Paarl Boys' High School. NUSAS leaders had gone to the best of the country's private schools, where they were taught social etiquette and the rules of debate. This made the Afrikaans-speaking students feel inadequate and awkward at public gatherings.

Because of this social distance from the NUSAS leadership, Kleinschmidt spent much of his time with Steve and the black students at the University of Natal. He owned an old Borgward, which he drove down to the medical school to see Steve on weekends. They would go out to the shebeens in Umlazi, and Kleinschmidt formed a very strong relationship with Steve's friends Strini and Samantha Moodley.

Kleinschmidt was nonetheless still committed to NUSAS. He saw increased black membership as key to the transformation of the organisation. As NUSAS regional director in the Transvaal, he drove up and down to the University of the North ("Turfloop") to register a branch there, which ultimately happened in 1969. Kleinschmidt looks back on that achievement: "I can proudly say that I increased black representation in NUSAS to just under 50% during my time as regional director." Unfortunately for him, this was also the time of growing calls for a new black student organisation separate from NUSAS.

Steve missed the 1969 NUSAS conference at the University of Cape Town. He was travelling around the country mobilising support for the newly formed blacks-only SASO. One of the handful of black students at that conference rose to call for a black caucus outside the conference proceedings. They returned with a statement signalling their intention to walk out completely from NUSAS. The statement read as follows:

> The white can afford to indulge in conceptualising for he always has access to material sufficiency. The first priority for blacks is physical existence. The implications of this have been on the Congress floor where debates have been initiated on premises arising from white backgrounds. Even if Congress were integrated in all its forums, debate would nevertheless be affected by the background of delegates. This should not be seen as the posing of an insuperable problem but as the definition of a problem hitherto unrecognised.

The statement was signed by Don Espey, Goolam Abram, M Omar, S Pather and Ben Ngubane. Kleinschmidt confesses to feeling ambushed by the black students' action. He felt Steve should have informed him of their intended course of action. His response was, however, different from that of the rest of the NUSAS leadership. Whereas people like Robert Schrire took the black walkout as a betrayal, Kleinschmidt became part of a more radical tradition within NUSAS, starting with

Duncan Innes in 1968-69 and intensifying with Neville Curtis in 1969-70.

Not for the first time, NUSAS was urged to abandon its liberal position for a more radical approach. Martin Legassick had made a similar call during a conference in Dar es Salaam in 1965. He had written to NUSAS president Jonty Driver, calling for a repositioning of NUSAS as a student wing of the liberation movement. He argued that NUSAS should move away from the model of campus affiliation to one of individual membership. A smaller organisation of genuine radicals would make it possible for the organisation to elect a black president, unencumbered by the conservatives that came into the organisation by virtue of their campuses' affiliation to NUSAS. Legassick's radical proposal was leaked to the National Party press, which used it to scare white students away from NUSAS.

NUSAS Takes A Radical Turn

Duncan Innes's presidency of NUSAS was in the end a bridge to the more radical turn under Neville Curtis, who was elected in 1969-70.

Neville Curtis was raised on the Johannesburg gold mines where his father, Jack Curtis, had risen from mine labourer to mine manager. He was demoted because of his affiliation with the Progressive Party, which had broken away from the conservative United Party, the party of Anglo American. In 1958 Jack Curtis ran as a candidate for the Progressive Party and ended up as a lecturer in the School of Mining at Wits University. When he was 17 years old, Neville was diagnosed with a fatal bone disease. He was given no more than four years to live. Neville survived and matriculated from Jeppe Boys

High, a public school in Johannesburg, and entered Wits University in 1965.

Like Horst Kleinschmidt, Neville Curtis did not share the background of the majority of the NUSAS leadership: "I came from the wrong side of the tracks, at least among whites." His parents were devout Christians but also politically conscious. He counted his History teacher Patrick Laurence as one of the most influential people in his early life. Laurence later became a well-known journalist and columnist who covered the Black Consciousness Movement in the 1970s. Curtis also counted Marius Schoon as yet another great influence. Schoon came from a conservative Afrikaner family. His father was a teacher, an active member of the National Party and a member of the Broederbond (the secret organisation that was the brains behind the apartheid government). The rebellious Marius was arrested and sentenced to 11 years' imprisonment for sabotage, a charge that Curtis insists had been the result of a set-up by the police. Schoon later married Neville's sister, Jeanette Curtis. In 1984 Jeanette and her six-year-old daughter Katryn were killed by a parcel bomb sent by notorious spy Craig Williamson.

By the time he arrived at Wits University, Curtis had a highly evolved political consciousness accompanied by a sense of urgency. He found at Wits a network of student leaders from the privileged sections of white society – Margie Marshall, John Kane-Berman and Mark Orkin. These students had a career path which often started with a Rhodes Scholarship at Oxford University, all the way to the heights of private industry or the academy, if they so chose. Many of them had connections with influential people in the American and British establishment. Renfrew Christie described them to me as "the Anglo American liberals". They chose who could attend NUSAS congresses as delegates, and that often meant people within their networks.

Curtis's rise to the leadership was also unusual because he did not hold a position on the Students' Representative Council at Wits. Curtis channelled his energies into the student publication *Wits Student*, where he eventually became editor. *Wits Student* was in turn affiliated to the South African National Student Press Association (SANSPA), through which he could attend NUSAS congresses. One of NUSAS's great strengths was its ability to identify and groom new leadership. Their liberal outlook notwithstanding, the NUSAS leadership co-opted him onto its national executive. He was elected president in 1969. He attributed his election to the fact that no one really wanted to stand because of increasing government pressure. John Kane-Berman declined because he wanted to take up his Rhodes Scholarship but promised that he would return should something happen to Curtis.

Neville Curtis brought a far more confrontational approach to NUSAS than his predecessors. In 1968 he led a motorcade to the Union Buildings to confront John Vorster about his government's racial policies. They caught Vorster sneaking out the back door and approached him right there. That was the first time Vorster had been confronted in this way, and in revenge he visited his wrath on the NUSAS leadership in the years to come. On 27 February banning orders were served on Neville Curtis, Clive Keegan, Paul Pretorius, Sheila Lapinsky, Chris Wood, Philippe le Roux and Paula Ensor.

The issue of SASO as a blacks-only student organisation was

a sore point for Curtis. His reasons were quite different from those of the Anglo American liberals. Curtis was a true socialist who wanted to build non-racial alliances. As far as he was concerned, SASO took all the talent for such an alliance with it. Curtis was an idealist who believed that progressive black and white students could lead the socialist revolution. He reorganised NUSAS and set up new divisions to deal with social issues such as education (NUS-Ed) and wages (NUS-Wage). His executive consisted of dedicated and highly principled cadres that included Kleinschmidt, Paul Pretorius, Paula Ensor and Sheila Lapinsky. A further indication of a growing radicalism was the election of another Afrikaner radical, Paul Pretorius, as the NUSAS president for the period 1970-71.

The most crucial moment for NUSAS-SASO relations came at the 1970 NUSAS congress in Eston, Natal. Steve attended that congress as an observer and the newly elected president of SASO. Steve had over a period of time explained the SASO position to the white student leadership at the University of Natal. Paul Pretorius, president of the SRC, and Paula Ensor, on the NUSAS executive, were regular visitors to the students at the black section – at this point Steve was also dating Paula Ensor. As Duncan Innes had put it, Steve could be quite non-racial when it came to members of the opposite sex.

However, it would be patronising to Ensor and other women to reduce their participation to love relationships. Speaking at the Platform for Public Deliberation a few years ago, the feminist intellectual Phyllis Ntantala said there is a tendency to assume that women joined the struggle through their men. She was already active in the movement before she met AC Jordan, who became her husband. Govan Mbeki also met his future wife Epainette through her activism in the movement.[134] Pumla Gqola has also written about the tendency to reduce women to props in a struggle otherwise waged by men. She cites the case of Albertina Sisulu, who, despite her leadership role, was frequently described either as Walter Sisulu's wife or "the mother of the nation":

> She was occasionally described as an ANC "veteran" and "stalwart", but there was very little discussion of her leadership in the African National Congress (ANC), the United Democratic Front (UDF); or of her subversive work against Bantu Education, her multiple spells in detention, or her insistence that women were at the vanguard of various key political successes against apartheid South Africa.[135]

During the research for this book I asked Paula Ensor to reflect on Steve beyond their love relationship, and this is what she wrote:

Biko and White Student Politics
By Paula Ensor

The most dramatic impact of Biko and the BCM on white student politics was of course the formation of SASO and its call for black campuses to withdraw from NUSAS. In retrospect,

---

134 Phyllis Ntantala, speech delivered at the Platform for Public Deliberation at Wits University, August 2006.
135 Pumla Gqola (2011). "Unconquered and Insubordinate: Embracing Black Feminist Intellectual Activist Legacies" in Xolela Mangcu (ed) *Becoming Worthy Ancestors* (Johannesburg: Wits University Press), 68.

this was inevitable. When I think back to my first NUSAS conference in 1969, I remember the slick accomplishment of the white student leaders there (mainly male), especially from Wits and UCT. Among them were the scions of wealthy families, the products of the best schools, who were well read, articulate and urbane and who dominated the discussions and debates. For those with less cultural, social and economic capital at their disposal, NUSAS conferences were often a silencing and alienating experience.

For many white male student leaders, involvement in SRC and NUSAS politics was a stepping stone to an Abe Bailey Scholarship, or a Rhodes Scholarship to Oxford. That these scholarships were not open to women or blacks caused no greater concern than the fact that NUSAS conferences were held on white campuses which obliged black students to find accommodation elsewhere. NUSAS in the late 1960s was largely a debating forum where students took motions on a range of international and local issues and then returned to life as usual. Liberal ideals were energetically defended, but hunger, oppression and transformation were not placed seriously on the agenda.

Biko, and the leadership that formed around him in SASO, identified the moral vacuum within NUSAS and challenged the white student body to question itself and where it was going. White students, he said, needed to decide whether they would continue to be part of South Africa's problem, or become part of its solution. SASO's withdrawal polarised white student politics and posed the question of how change in South Africa would come, and under whose leadership. It provoked intense discussion and strengthened the hand of those like Neville Curtis who wished to restructure NUSAS in order to slough off its "debating chamber" image and provide a vehicle for white students to engage more meaningfully in social change.

The withdrawal of SASO and the transformation of NUSAS were outward manifestations of Biko's influence on white student politics. But his influence was also felt in more personal ways, especially by students based in Durban at that time, as I was. When Biko entered the student scene in the late 1960s, he entered something of a political void. The ANC and SACP, as well as the PAC, were operating in exile and there was no organised internal political presence of any significance. Among many activist youth at the time, the ANC and SACP appeared ineffectual, something that was attributed to the conservative influence of their white middle-class members. Biko's emergence coincided with the tail end of the period of severe repression following Sharpeville and chimed with the radicalism of students in France, Germany and the USA. For a small group of white students, SASO represented the re-emergence of radical politics and needed to be actively supported. While some attempted to do this through campus-based politics, others turned their attention towards the building of trade unions.

Whether oriented towards student politics or the labour movement, we found in Steve an energetic, articulate and tireless interlocutor: patient, kind, humorous and always razor sharp. He didn't try to convert, but to challenge us with the imperatives of his political programme and oblige us to take a position of our own. The debates were always serious, but we also found time to drink, dance, listen to music, and for those who qualified, play rugby. Durban in the late 1960s and early 1970s was a hub of intense political debate and activity, involving many brilliant young minds. Dominating that space with the dazzling power of his intellect and political courage was Steve Biko.

Paul Pretorius arrived at the university in 1967 with virtually no interest in politics. He was popular more for his rugby-playing skills. But the oddity of separate university life angered him, and in an act of rebellion he organised an illegal rugby match against a team of black students. They locked themselves behind gates and played the famous Paul Pretorius XV vs. Steve Biko XV match, which the white students narrowly won. Pretorius recalls that "we had a referee who was not politically correct. During the scrum Ben Ngubane had a tendency to have his feet up before the ball was in. The referee stopped the scrum and berated this highly articulate medical student Ben Ngubane in *Fanakalo* (a mix of English and simplified Zulu whites used in addressing miners). We were all so embarrassed, but Ben just laughed it off."

The match drew scathing criticism from government officials, but the students had made their point. Pretorius caused a stir at the NUSAS congress by proposing a motion that NUSAS recognised SASO as the organisation best able to represent the interests of black students. The motion read as follows:

> NUSAS, while expressing disagreement with the principle of racial exclusion in any student organisation, recognises SASO as the body best able to represent the views and needs of black students in South Africa.

The motion went on to suggest that the NUSAS executive should enter into discussions with the SASO executive with a view to establishing "maximum contact and cooperation". It further stated that non-racialism was the goal of both organisations, even if they adopted different views about how to best attain that goal.

The motion was so controversial that it promised to derail the whole congress. Wits University and the University of Cape Town, which were the most important and powerful NUSAS affiliates, threatened to walk out if the motion was not withdrawn. Ken Costa and Deon Irish from Wits and UCT respectively were the most vocal opponents of the motion, while Pretorius and Kleinschmidt stood their ground. Paula Ensor left the podium to sit on Steve's lap, ostensibly to give him support but really to give the finger to the conservative white students. She was annoyed by the fact that white students assumed it was up to them to recognise a black student body. Sensing the possibility of a NUSAS split, NUSAS president Neville Curtis sent a note to Kleinschmidt that they should withdraw the motion for a caucus discussion later that evening. Even though Pretorius and Kleinschmidt withdrew the motion, the two organisations had reached a moment of no return in their relationship. Sheila Lapinsky remembered the drama of the moment:

> At that point it became clear that the black students were peripheral to NUSAS. The white students' understanding of the black students' position was minimal. They stood up to say the most patronising things about NUSAS giving permission to SASO to exist. That's when Paula went to sit on Steve's lap. But it was clear that this was the end.

At the end of the session Steve stood up to walk out. He scribbled a note to Paul Pretorius: "Thanks Paul for your support, we are leaving now. Cheers, Steve."

Former NUSAS students have often argued that the incident was traumatic for Neville Curtis. He took time out from the congress after that session, and was not to be found until the following morning. The truth is that Curtis was engaged in a night-long caucus discussion which sought to find some compromise on the motion. The compromise was that SASO was not "best able", but "well able" to represent the interests of black students. The motion was carried but Pretorius abstained as a sign of protest. "To me it was obvious that SASO was the body best able to represent the interests of black students."

Despite that setback, in wording the resolution Pretorius would be part of a new generation of NUSAS radicalism that had started with Duncan Innes and intensified with Curtis. Even though Curtis himself was not in favour of the breakaway and was ambivalent about the recognition given to SASO, those reservations were of a different order to those of conservative students like Ken Costa, Deon Irish and Steve Jooste.

There was a difference of style between Curtis and Pretorius. Pretorius advocated a shift from Curtis's focus on individual action to put more emphasis on the representative nature of the organisation on its affiliate campuses. This reignited the earlier debate about the efficacy of individual over affiliate membership, initiated by Martin Legassick. Pretorius felt that the growing radicalism among white students in general should have put paid to fears about white student conservatism on the white campuses. He saw the growing radicalism as an opportunity to build a beachhead into the white community through NUSAS. Pretorius appealed to liberal values such as freedom of speech and freedom of association to garner greater support for NUSAS's radical shift.

Shortly thereafter, however, the Schlebusch Commission – set up by Vorster to investigate student organisations – was to deal a devastating blow to student politics. On 27 February 1973 the commission slapped bannings on the NUSAS leadership. As a result of the 1973 bannings NUSAS had made a tactical decision not to elect a new president at the end of that congress, and Pretorius stayed on as president for the period 1971-72.

Steve and Curtis maintained cordial relations. Even after that raucous NUSAS congress in Eston, Steve continued to attend NUSAS seminars. For example, he was present at one of NUSAS's leadership formation schools in Stellenbosch in 1970 along with the young NUSAS student Geoff Budlender, who later had a sterling legal career at the Legal Resources Centre and the Cape Bar. Budlender recalls Steve's response to David Curry, a Labour Party politician invited as a guest speaker. (The Labour Party was a Coloured organisation that had decided to work within the system under the leadership of Allan Hendrickse.) Curry complained about how his son was constantly talking about issues of race, asking: "Why do the white people hate us so much?" Steve stood up to tell the Labour Party politician: "Your son understands politics better than you do, Mr Curry."

After the seminar, Steve hitched a ride to the Eastern Cape with Budlender, who was returning home to Port Elizabeth. As they neared Port Elizabeth, Steve asked Budlender to drop him off at Barney Pityana's home in New Brighton. Budlender went cold. Even though he was born and raised in Port Elizabeth, he did not know where New Brighton was.

Sensing the young man's nervousness, Steve burst out laughing and said: "You don't have a clue where it is, do you?" Here he was a senior leader in NUSAS but found himself "shit scared" by the whole experience: "I dropped him off at Barney's house. I just liked him enormously. He could differ with a person politically and yet could engage with the person socially. But above all he helped me to understand myself in relation to society. I learned how to listen better because of Steve."

During my research for this book I asked Budlender to sum up his thoughts on Steve's legacy for South Africa. The article has not been published elsewhere and so I reproduce it here in full:

Reflections on Steve Biko
By Geoff Budlender

Steve Biko spoke primarily to black South Africans – but he also spoke to white South Africans. He spoke particularly loudly to white students in the National Union of SA Students. NUSAS was inevitably dominated by white student concerns and perceptions – through numbers, through the language used by the organisation, and as a result of accumulated benefits and privilege. Black students were required to fit into an organisation which operated within a predominantly white discourse. It was an example of white power in a nominally non-racial organisation which sought to challenge that power.

Biko said that black students had to challenge white power

both within student organisations, and within the society at large. The most effective way for them to do this, he said, was to stand together to assert their own power. Most black students withdrew from NUSAS. The organisation was left to face the spectre, within itself, of white power and privilege. This caused great pain. It led to a fundamental re-think by students in NUSAS. The black student challenge coincided with a deep disillusionment about the politics of protest, and particularly the ritualised forms of protest which had become the norm.

And so NUSAS started to shift. It moved from protest towards projects – from words to action. Students tried to find ways in which their skills, resources and energy could be made available to black people in a way which did not lead to white domination. The result was a generation of white activists who tried to find new ways of engaging white power – through support for nascent black worker organisations, and through their activities as journalists, lawyers, academics and community workers.

What Biko said more than 25 years ago remains relevant today, in at least two senses. First, white power and privilege remain potent. Biko's message reminds us that white people carry the benefits and the burden of that legacy. White arrogance is sometimes thinly disguised as a non-racial critique of the new (black) holders of power in government and elsewhere. Humility does not come easily to the privileged. We continue to see an arrogance which fails to recognise the generosity which black South Africans have shown their white counterparts, and which also fails to recognise that our democratic constitution did not produce social transformation –

rather, it created one of the necessary preconditions for the transformation which must still come.

Biko's critique also continues to speak to black South Africans. It speaks to the need for black people to assert the power which they hold, in a way which does not depend on and gain its strength from the negative critique of white power. It also speaks to the need for empowerment which empowers all, and not just a new elite. It speaks to a form of affirmative action which is about power, and not just numbers.

This will be the foundation of the self-confident power-sharing which Biko predicted would be the long-term outcome of black consciousness. We should not be surprised that we have not arrived there after a few short years of political liberation. We continue to struggle, often painfully, with the results of our history. Steve Biko's message continues to give us a powerful tool for doing so.

6
Steve Biko and the Making of SASO

> "We should begin to talk about
> the problems affecting us as Black students."
> Steve Biko at the Stutterheim conference

The late 1960s were the heyday of radical student politics all over the world. Student uprisings broke out in major capitals – Tokyo, Madrid, Paris, Chicago, Berlin. These movements were influenced by a number of momentous political developments worldwide, including the Chinese revolution, the civil rights movement in the United States and movements for decolonisation in both Africa and Europe. According to Risto Lehtonen, the revolts were also a reaction to the industrialisation of higher education and the authoritarian culture of university administrations at a time of growing youth rebelliousness all over the world.

The church also played a big part in the revolutionary turmoil that gripped the world in the years between 1968 and 1972.[136] The turn towards a more secular theology inspired Christian students around the world to reflect on their role in the here and now – as opposed to the futuristic orientation of established religions. These events were preceded by the Life and Mission of the Church programme of the World Student

---

[136] Risto Lehtonen (2004). "Dialogue and Ecumenical Vision", *Student World*, 2004 (1).

Christian Federation (WSCF) – which was a federation of Student Christian Associations (SCAs) around the world – and the World Council of Churches conference on "Church and Society" in 1966.

A similar turn towards a more ecumenical movement was taking place in South Africa. In the early 1960s liberal Christians were beginning to speak out against apartheid – the Catholic Archbishop Denis Hurley described it as "immoral" – in direct contrast to the Dutch Reformed Church's defence of the separation of races that was at the heart of apartheid.

Even though the SCA in South Africa was one of the WSCF's earliest affiliates, the relationship between the two bodies was bound to be tumultuous because of the radical culture of the WSCF. Matters came to a head when the SCA delegation to a WSCF conference in Strasbourg in 1961 refused to condemn apartheid. When the WSCF urged its member associations to put pressure on their governments to dissociate themselves from the apartheid government, the SCA offered itself as a bridge among the races in South Africa – a completely untenable proposition under Hendrik Verwoerd's government. According to Macqueen, "the polarisation imposed by apartheid necessitated a choosing of sides".[137] The renowned American social scientist Seymour Martin Lipset observed that the worldwide protests, notwithstanding what was happening in South Africa, were of even greater consequence because of the immoral nature of apartheid: "The politics of South African students, therefore, may turn out to have a greater impact on the future of their country than do those of French, Ger-

---

137 Ian Macqueen, "Re-imagining South Africa", 31.

man or American students." While students from the latter countries "turned quiescent" when their specific demands were met, "the moral questions which concern South African students and intellectuals, however, have no resolution other than a radical change in the major social institutions of the country".[138] It is this moral dimension of the struggle and the role occupied by the church in society – more than any internal identity struggle – that explains Steve's relationship with the University Christian Movement (UCM) and their subsequent collaboration on Black Theology (of which more later).

In 1965 the SCA ultimately buckled under the weight of its own irresolution about apartheid, and disbanded into its ethnic components – Africans, Coloureds and Indians. The first formal meeting to discuss an alternative ecumenical, non-racial, university-based Christian organisation took place at the home of the Archbishop of Cape Town, Robert Selby Taylor, in Bishopscourt in late 1966. It had the backing of five denominations: the Presbyterian, Methodist, Congregational, Anglican and Roman Catholic churches. In an article titled "Servant to the University", John Davis noted that "the new movement has a very demanding mandate to live up to, a mandate to be as free and inclusive, racially and theologically, as are the five main churches which at present support it".[139]

After he walked out of the NUSAS conference at Rhodes, Steve stopped off at Barney Pityana's home in nearby Port Elizabeth. Pityana had just returned from the launch of UCM

---

138 Hendrik van der Merwe and David Welsh (1972). *Student Perspectives on South Africa* (Cape Town: David Philip), 7.

139 John Davis, "Servant to the University", 1967, UCM Papers, Wits Historical Papers, Johannesburg.

in Rosettenville, Johannesburg. Pityana was now studying law at Fort Hare University, and was a leading member of the Anglican section of students at Fort Hare, and a leading UCM activist on the campus. Raised by a single mother like Steve, Pityana was born and grew up in Port Elizabeth. Pityana's mother, unlike Steve's, received an education.

> I have no recollection of my upbringing as being in any way political or very religious. My mother was a churchgoer with a strong passion for education. Her parents had given up everything to send her to St Peter's College where she became one of the early black women to obtain a matric. She got very far with very little because of education.

Although the UCM was a movement of a great number of individuals, its inspirational leadership came from two priests, Colin Collins and Basil Moore. Collins was born in King William's Town and went to the prestigious local school, Dale College. Thereafter he studied theology at the University of Pretoria and was now the chaplain of the National Catholic Student Federation. Basil Moore was a Methodist minister and lecturer of theology at Rhodes University.

In an act of open defiance the UCM immediately affiliated to the World Student Christian Federation. Collins travelled extensively to world assemblies, linking up with radical student movements from as far afield as Czechoslovakia. He regularly attended meetings of the World Catholic Student Federation. On his return from the 1968 WSCF congress, he addressed a group of students at Wits University. He recounted the experience of other students around the world, and what they were doing to change not only their societies but world political culture in general. Careful not to fall foul of the country's stringent censorship laws, he paraphrased what other student movements were saying about the need for a social revolution to advance the interests of poor and oppressed people.

Religion for the student Christian movement was thus a matter of political commitment, and the role of students and intellectuals was to provide a radical critique of iniquitous social, political and economic arrangements wherever they prevailed in their societies. The rather eccentric Collins proposed a strategy for student political action that consisted of what he called the three C's: "cool criticism, cunning consistency and cute cells". This was the flamboyant Collins's play on the UCM's three C's: Contact, Criticism and Courage. By "cool criticism" Collins meant that protest had to be well informed, with a clear detail of priorities in educating white South Africans in particular. He warned, however, that white students ought not to think of themselves as the leaders of the revolution. This was a decidedly different attitude to that of NUSAS – prior to the Curtis years. There was in the UCM a sense of modesty and maturity that came out of the older leadership of the organisation. "Cunning consistency" was a warning against recklessness. The students needed to be made aware of what the state was willing to do to put down the revolution. "Some of you are going to get hurt, some of you might even be maimed and some of you may even die," he warned. Collins's "cute cells" were a reference to underground structures that needed to be set up for the leadership to be able to undertake detailed planning.

Steve Biko and the Making of SASO

Ironically, Collins failed to heed his own advice; his whole speech was being recorded by the security agents at the meeting. To be sure, he always suspected that he might be recorded, hence his careful use of language.

The UCM established an extensive international network and chapters around the world. The UCM also developed a strong local profile, building relationships with organisations such as the South African Council of Churches (SACC) and the Christian Institute, the South African Institute of Race Relations and NUSAS. And the organisation increasingly took on social concerns, providing literacy and other community development projects in poorer communities. At that point the secular movement was increasing its critique of the apartheid government. In 1968 the SACC issued the Message to the People of South Africa which described apartheid as "a false idol". It posed the question to white Christians: "to whom or to what are you truly giving your first loyalty, your primary commitment? Is it to a subsection of mankind, an ethnic group, a human tradition, a political idea; or to Christ"?[140]

Accompanying the SACC's critique was the work of the Christian Institute under the leadership of Beyers Naudé. Naudé came from a distinguished Afrikaner family – his father was a prominent cleric and a founding member of the Broederbond. However, Naudé became increasingly disenchanted with apartheid. After 1960 the Cottesloe Conference – where a World Council of Churches delegation met with leaders of the church in South Africa – Naudé set up the Christian Institute. The government put pressure on him

---

140 Cited in Magaziner, *The Law and the Prophets*, 66.

and he was forced to choose between the church and the Institute. What followed was a long and distinguished history of political leadership on the side of the oppressed. His last sermon to his Afrikaner congregation was along the same lines as those of the SACC's Message to the People: "We must obey God rather than men."[141]

One of the Christian Institute's most important interventions was the launch of Spro-Cas (the Study Project on Christianity in Apartheid Society), which spawned the Black Community Projects discussed in Chapter 8. Collins maintained that it was the church's duty to speak out against the persecution of UCM members by government through bannings and deportations. Collins's confrontation with the church ultimately led to his decision to ask to be laicised, i.e. released from all obligations of the priesthood. In a letter to the Vatican, he listed reasons that had to do with the church's policies on issues such as birth control and celibacy. The more important reason was the church's political conservatism. He wrote:

> ... in particular I would like to mention the fact that in South Africa the Church is more concerned with its preservation than with people; the fact that in South Africa it does very little to really assist the position of the oppressed majority; the fact that my Bishop has behaved in a somewhat unjust fashion towards me; and lastly the fact that the Church has taken a deprecatory attitude towards the ecumenical organisation I now work for.

---

141 Magaziner, *The Law and the Prophets*, 67.

Collins also wrote a trenchant critique of the racial imbalance within the church. Whites sympathetic to the status quo dominated the priesthood:

> It is particularly the attitude towards black people that I find repellent. Once more there are many wonderful exceptions but the ways in which black Catholics have in the past been threatened, bullied and excommunicated would have caused a national scandal had they been perpetrated within the white community. In general the pattern has been one that has been so patronising that very few African professional Catholics have remained within the Church.

With declining support from the church, the UCM started experiencing serious financial problems. By 1972 it could not finance its budget and was forced to get rid of its personnel, merely retaining the position of its travelling secretary, Basil Manning. Moore described some of the woes facing the UCM in a letter to Collins, referring in particular to the banning order served on UCM president, Justice Moloto. But this was not before the UCM would play a crucial support role for SASO – mainly through Steve's interventions.

The Stutterheim Meeting and the Origins of SASO

The relationship between the UCM and SASO has its origin at the UCM meeting Steve attended at the beginning of 1968, in the small town of Stutterheim, about 30 kilometres from King William's Town. The meeting took place at the local Catholic church in the "white" section of the town.

Prior to this meeting Steve had travelled to a number of

black campuses soliciting support for the formation of a blacks-only student organisation. The UCM conference presented an opportunity to consolidate and concretise the idea. It is indeed no coincidence that 60% of the students who attended that meeting were black university students.

The opportunity to openly canvass for a black student organisation presented itself when black students had to comply with one of the stipulations of apartheid legislation – that blacks could not continuously be in a white residential area for more than 72 hours. When the 72nd hour approached the black students would break from the conference, cross the boundary line, and come back to start a new 72-hour period, and "so came about one of the strangest occurences ever seen in South Africa. Far from the nearest town, only viewed by a few rural Africans and one passing car, 150 people marched over the municipal boundary line singing 'We Shall Overcome' (which is banned in South Africa) and wearing signs reading 'The Truth Shall Make Us Free'." [142]

Steve felt this approach was "hypocritical". He believed that the black students should be arrested if need be, and that white students should join in protest with them. But he then realised that the government wanted to use the 72-hour clause to stop the meeting, and so went along with going across the border, but purely for strategic reasons. To Steve this indignity confirmed the disparate experiences of black and white students, and further validated his call for a new blacks-only organisation. This is how he put it:

---

142 *Southern Africa Monthly Survey of News and Opinion*, vol. 1. no 8. Sept-Oct 1968, published by the Southern Africa Committee, University Christian Movement, New York.

> We have got no problems, we can walk across the border and come back for a further period, but the real thing that we should begin to talk about are problems affecting us Black students, which we feel are not given full treatment in organisations of that nature.[143]

Initially, Barney Pityana opposed the idea of a black caucus to discuss this matter because he thought this would be racially divisive. Steve called Pityana aside and urged him to reconsider and join this effort. He told Pityana that the black students at the conference were not strong enough to challenge the whites in the full meeting.

Pityana was persuaded by the power of Steve's argument, and joined the caucus meeting. They found an empty room in the church. First they discussed how they should respond to the 72-hour regulation, and agreed to comply for strategic reasons. Then it turned out Steve had more up his sleeve. He had planned to discuss much more at the meeting than he had let on to Pityana. It was time to make the call for a blacks-only national student organisation. Pityana was not really convinced: "I thought all of this was a bit too much, but Steve had extracted from me an unwritten pledge that I would support him in whatever he did."

And thus was formed one of the most important political partnerships in the history of the South African liberation struggle. If Steve Biko was the inspiration for the movement, then it fell on Barney Pityana to consolidate it, both as Steve's successor as president of the South African Students Organisa-

---

143 Arnold, *The Testimony of Steve Biko*, 10.

tion in 1970, and its full-time general secretary from 1971 to 1973. In Aelred Stubbs's words: "And so began that initial partnership of Steve and Barney which, though it lasted in physical form only two and a half years, seems to an outside observer to have been critically important for the stability of SASO." And when Steve moved into the Black Community Programmes, Pityana effectively became "the prime bearer" of the movement.

It is worth quoting at length the observations of the American chapter of the UCM on the historical significance of the black caucus and the march across the boundary in Stutterheim:

> This meeting and the resultant march were a watershed for the conference. From this point onwards, non-whites often took a leadership role, entertained us with their ability to find humor and irony in the tragedy of South Africa, blatantly confronted white liberals with their paternalism and non-involvement in suffering, and spent several hours in a black caucus. Yet throughout a spirit of unity and camaraderie prevailed. Addresses on theology, ecumenism, the present racial situation, and strategies for change (including a sharp look at the possible necessity of violence) were given in the evenings. Small groups met twice daily to discuss areas such as independent Africa, Black Power, New Theology, the Church and Social Change etc. Workshops on photography, folk singing, dance and drama punctuated the daily schedule.[144]

---

144 *Southern Africa Monthly Survey of News and Opinion*, 1968.

Top: Dr B Zondi, a former student of St Francis, handing prizes to current students Sizo Mazibuko (right) and Steve Biko (centre) at the Milk Festival in Lamontville in 1965. (St Francis College Archive)

Bottom: Steve Biko at the founding meeting of the Black People's Convention in Soweto in December 1971. Alf Kumalo, who took this photograph, said: "Steve was brilliant, but also down to earth. At this meeting, he wore a simple jersey which was slightly torn, yet he electrified the house." (Alf Kumalo Museum)

Top: Winifred Kgware (extreme left) and Mamphela Ramphele (standing) at the first Black People's Convention meeting at St Peter's Seminary, Hammanskraal in December 1972.
(UWC – Robben Island Museum Mayibuye Archives)

Bottom: Steve Biko at his meeting with United States Senator Dick Clark, chairman of the Senate Sub-Committee on Africa, on 1 December 1976. Politicians from around the

world visited Biko in his hometown, to which he was restricted by a banning order.
(Gallo Images/Daily Dispatch)

Above: Steve Biko and Mamphela Ramphele in January 1977 outside the magistrate's court in East London after another of Steve's many court appearances, a result of the many legal restrictions placed on him, which he often ignored. (Gallo Images/Daily Dispatch)

Top: Steve Biko with his son Samora. (BAHA Drum Photographer)

Bottom: A family photograph from 1977: From the left, family elder Nellyan Biko, with Nkosinathi, Ntsiki, Samora and Steve Biko's mother, Alice MamCethe Biko. (Daily Dispatch)

Ntsiki Biko at their house in Ginsberg township with Samora (left) and Nkosinathi (right). (KEYSTONE Pressedienst, HASPA, BLZ)

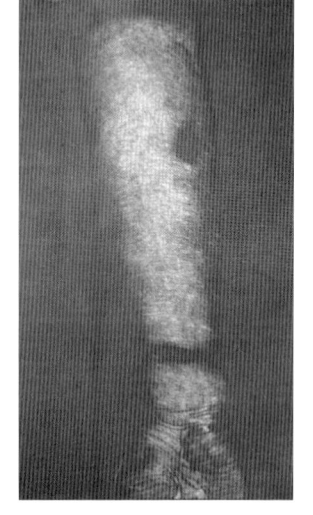

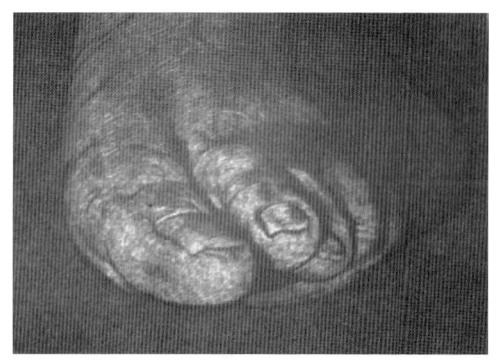

Top: The front page of the *Daily Dispatch* of 14 September 1977.

Bottom: Detail from an artwork by Paul Stopforth, entitled "Elegy for Steve Biko". (Paul Stopforth, in the Durban Art Gallery Collection)

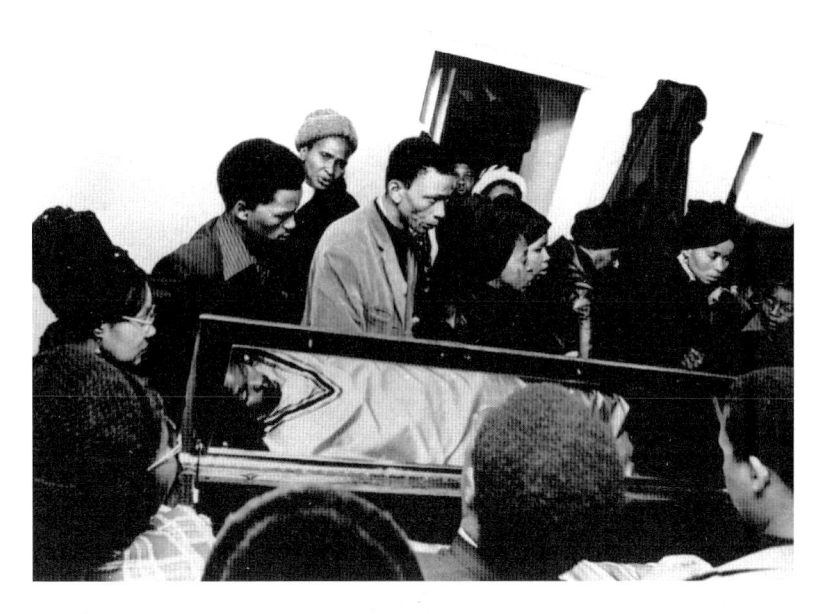

Top: Mourners at Steve Biko's funeral in 1977. A mirror on the raised lid of the coffin reflects his gold-robed body. The United States sent top diplomats to the funeral, which was the first of many highly charged political funerals in South Africa. (AP Photo/Franzola)

Bottom: Ntsiki Biko (second from the right) with (R-L) Steve Biko's mother Alice MamCethe, his sister Nobandile and his brother Khaya during the inquest into his death in November 1977. (Sahm Doherty/Time Life Pictures/Getty Images)

Steve Biko on the cover of *Drum* magazine in 1977 shortly after his death in September 1977. (BAHA, Drum Photographer)

The white participants had overcome the "resolutions complex" that had come to typify NUSAS – as witnessed at the Rhodes University congress in 1967. Interestingly, in his speech to NUSAS in early 1968 John Daniel was also quite critical of NUSAS's reactive politics:

> There has in the past few years been too great a tendency for NUSAS to react to a given situation. We have merely concentrated on staying alive and have reacted to such things as bannings and deportations with protests and then have settled back and waited for the next time we will have to protest. In short, we have reacted – not acted. This must be reversed. NUSAS must be more aggressive, positive and militant on the campuses.[145]

At the end of the Stutterheim caucus meeting a decision was made to call a national conference of black students for December that year. The students mandated Steve with the responsibility of visiting all the universities to garner support and recruit for the conference and potentially the new organisation. When the conference closed Steve invited Pityana to his home in Ginsberg, about 35 kilometres from Stutterheim. According to Pityana, "that is where a much more focused discussion on black consciousness took place, at Steve's home in Ginsberg".[146]

Subsequent to their stay in Ginsberg, the two of them at-

---

145 John Daniel's address to NUSAS, 1968.
146 While in our interview Pityana said Steve invited him to Ginsberg, Aelred Stubbs writes the opposite: "From Stutterheim, Steve went to Port Elizabeth to stay with Barney."

tended a meeting of all the black Christian student bodies on the Fort Hare campus, where Basil Moore was going to be the main speaker. The university had barred Moore from speaking, and the students asked Steve to be the main speaker instead. "We all really appreciated the leadership role he had played in Stutterheim," Pityana recalls. While the plan was to establish UCM at Fort Hare with this meeting, Pityana recalls that "Steve's presence got us beyond that, and instead led to the involvement of Fort Hare in the establishment of SASO". Steve found a debate raging at Fort Hare between students who wanted the Student Representative Council (SRC) to be re-established and those who were opposed to the idea. In 1959 the student body had abolished the SRC because they felt it was being used by the university authorities to spy on students. Barney Pityana belonged to those who opposed the idea of re-instituting the SRC while his antagonist Justice Moloto argued in favour of the SRC.

Moloto had come to Fort Hare from the University of the North where there was an SRC. Moloto naturally joined forces with the pro-SRC faction. His main contention was that the problem lay not with the principle of establishing an institution but more with the integrity and trustworthiness of the individuals elected to lead it. The difficulty Moloto faced in these debates was that he was a newcomer to the university, or what was known as a "fresher". The unspoken rule was that "freshers were to be seen, not heard". Moloto thus had to plead to be allowed to speak with senior students such as Master Tembeni, Mthetho Matanzima, Mbulelo Ntloko, Rams Ramogkopa and Feya Dwesi. Moloto argued that demand for an SRC was not peculiar to Fort Hare but was a fundamental principle of student life. By allowing him to speak, the student leadership uncovered an oratorical talent.

Because there was no SRC, the student body had to elect a chairman at every meeting. Moloto became the natural choice for the students, a remarkable feat for a first-year student. It became his task to report the proceedings of the meeting to the university principal, Johan Jurgens Ross. Ross was succeeded by a more reliable National Party sympathiser, Johannes Marthinus de Wet, in 1968. De Wet wasted no time in expelling the student leaders that same year. Among them were Pityana, Justice Moloto, Master Thembeni, Lester Peteni, Chris Mokoditoa, Mfundi Mvundla and Peter Vundla.

Ultimately the debate around the SRC was resolved in 1972 when a mass meeting voted in favour of re-establishing the SRC. However, this was thwarted by the rector, who argued that the students had not followed the proper procedures. At about the same time, the president of the Student Representative Council at the University of the North (Turfloop) and one of the leading lights of the Black Consciousness Movement, Abraham Onkgopotse Tiro, was expelled from the University of the North for giving a speech that was highly critical of the education system and the entire system of apartheid. Tiro concluded that brave and historic speech to the university community with the following words: "Let the Lord be praised for the day shall come when all shall be free to breathe the air of freedom which is theirs to breathe, and when the day shall have come, no man, no matter how many tanks he has, will reverse the course of events."

Tiro subsequently went to teach at the famous Morris Isaacson High School, where he taught the leaders of the 1976 uprising Tsietsi Mashinini and Murphy Morobe – the principal of the school, Legau Mathabatha, deliberately took on progressive teachers and students, and faced constant harassment by the police. The school was under the influence of Black Consciousness with the likes of Fanyana Mazibuko, who was also on the staff; and the famed Don Mattera, who frequented the school as a member of the Medupe Writers Association – Mashinini was also actively involved in this group. Tiro was ultimately killed by a parcel bomb after he went into exile in Botswana in 1974.

The events of the early 1970s – from the denial of student rights to the expulsion and killing of their leaders – contributed to the heightening of political consciousness among students at black universities. Black Consciousness had initially emerged as "a non-political politics"[147] and the apartheid government mistakenly welcomed the Black Consciousness Movement as a vindication of its policies of separate development. Once the government realised that the movement was more than it had bargained for, it embarked on a systematic process of eliminating its leadership.

This is how Steve described the government's mistaken assumptions: ". . . since we stressed Black Consciousness and the relationship of intellectuals with the real needs of the people, we were at first regarded as supporters of the system. The liberals criticized us and the conservatives supported us.

---

[147] Arnold, *The Testimony of Steve Biko*. There are striking parallels between this approach to resistance in South Africa and what happened in Eastern Europe during the Velvet Revolution, where artists and writers waged a mode of resistance that was initially not overtly political.

But this did not last very long. It took the government four years before taking measures against us."[148]

Justice Moloto recalls the more humorous side of the debates at Fort Hare. For example, each time he asked for the matter to be decided by a vote, the predominantly Xhosa-speaking "AbaThembu" would say "no, the matter is not ready for a vote", essentially buying time for the rest of the student body to give up and go to sleep. Then, in the very early hours of the morning, they would come back to the hall and demand the vote, knowing full well that most of the students in favour of the SRC had left. *Masivoteni, baThembu* – "Let's vote, Thembu nation", they would chant. Elements of this group had explicit tribal sentiments and wanted to keep Fort Hare Xhosa. Some were suspected of working for the "system".

Moloto also became increasingly involved with NUSAS. This was a risky gamble because NUSAS was not allowed to operate on black campuses. His membership of NUSAS was leaked and he was summarily expelled and barred from applying for admission in 1967. If he wanted to study further he had to apply for re-admission in 1968. He was elected chairman of the Catholic Students Association when he returned in 1968, right at the time of SASO's formal launch. He also became a member of the national executive committee of the umbrella body of Catholic students, the National Catholic Student Federation. He continued to attend NUSAS meetings but was now becoming more heavily involved with the newly formed University Christian Movement (UCM).

Moloto was expelled again, now with 20 others when the

---

148 Biko interview with Bernard Zylstra, 1977.

student body went on strike to protest the University of Cape Town's decision not to appoint Professor Archie Mafeje as an anthropology lecturer on racial grounds. This time around he was not allowed to return.

Moloto's close friend at Fort Hare was Chris Mokoditoa, who had tried to join the PAC shortly after finishing matric at PECS High School in 1958. He was refused membership because he was too young. He joined the Dube branch when he turned 21, and was one of a number of youths who boarded trains to bomb Johannesburg in 1963. This was in response to Potlako Leballo's abortive call on African people to attack enemy installations. Armed with petrol bombs the youths broke into two gun shops in downtown Johannesburg, Safrix and ME Stores. Someone was supposed to turn the city lights off at the mains in Soweto. However, when this did not happen the youths broke into Safrix, setting the alarm system off. In no time the police were on the scene and some of the youths were arrested. Mokoditoa was part of a group that ran to the Braamfontein train station, where they waited for the first train back to Soweto the following morning. Indeed, they boarded the train, only to be stopped by a police contingent at the next station at New Canada. Passengers coming from work in town were asked to step to one side. Luckily, the police mistook Mokoditoa for a worker. His friends were arrested but the police could not really build a case against them, and they were all released after two months in custody.

By the time he got to Fort Hare, Mokoditoa was a highly conscious student. In fact, for years he had refused to go to university on the grounds that the government was turning these institutions into little tribal colleges.

Steve prevailed on both Moloto and Mokoditoa to run for the presidency and publicity secretary positions of the UCM respectively. This was one of the most strategic moves Steve made as he tried to garner financial and logistical support for SASO. If they could take over the UCM, then they could provide a life-line for the proposed new black student organisation.

After the meeting in Stutterheim, Steve proposed that a follow-up meeting be held at the University of Natal, where he was still on the SRC. On 14 October 1968 Steve and the secretary of the SRC, DV Naidoo, sent out an invitation to all black colleges to attend the conference, which was to be held from the 1st to the 3rd of December that same year. They wrote: "The conference is intended to be an extension of dialogue among the non-white centres in Southern Africa. We intend to provide a platform for a more effective means of coordination and a strengthening of ties among the non-white centres."

They then enclosed with their correspondence a background document as to why the meeting was needed, referring to the earlier meeting in Stutterheim. The background document was mostly concerned with organisational questions such as establishing student societies, intervarsity sports and visits among the centres. The uppermost concern of the meeting was inter-collegiate communication – how to break the isolation of the "non-white" centres from each other so as to counter "the indoctrination and intimidation so effectively applied at all South African universities".

The conference also deliberated on the pros and cons of whether they should have an informal structure or a formal structure, and on whether it should be racially exclusive. Some students argued that it was potentially counterproductive to organise along separate racial lines at a time when students were on the move and probably the most powerful force in South African politics. They said, "any move that tends to divide the student population into separate laagers in terms of colour is in a way a tacit submission to having been defeated and apparently seems an agreement with apartheid". They further cautioned that this could be a ploy to divide the students and thus reduce the momentum of the student movement. Having considered the strategic limitations of a blacks-only organisation, the meeting felt it was nonetheless necessary to go ahead because contact among "non-white" students was viewed as of even greater concern because of their lack of political representation – the only black students who were allowed to participate in NUSAS were the handful at the white universities. And so the meeting concluded that "the alternative to meeting on a segregated platform is not meeting at all, which will be more welcome to the perpetrators of evil and detrimental to our course [sic]. This is the ultimate goal of 'divide et impera' policy." They also noted that "meeting on a segregated platform because we cannot help it does not mean we agree with segregation". Here one can sense Steve's not so "invisible hand", pushing for the new organisation.

Contrary to the idea of a seamless break from the multi-racialism of NUSAS to a well-defined position of black exclusivism, it is clear that there was a lot of soul-searching about the contradictions involved in pursuing the latter route. In 1968/9 Steve and his colleagues did not advocate the new organisation as a substitute for NUSAS, which they still regarded as the national student body. They also described their mandate as primarily that of promoting contact for "non-white" students who could not join NUSAS, even if they wanted to join a non-racial body. Hence the refrain that it was not out of choice but necessity that they formed a "non-white" organisation. The meeting concluded with a proposal for a follow-up meeting to formally launch the new organisation.

SASO's formal launch took place at the University College of the North in July 1969. Present at the conference were representatives from the University of the North, the University of Zululand (Ongoye), the University of Natal Non-European section, St Peter's Seminary and the University of South Africa. In reality, the meeting was no more than an endorsement of the earlier resolutions taken at the December 1968 conference. Steve was elected president, with PM Machaka as the vice-president, and Vuyelwa Mashalaba and Manana Kgware as the secretaries.

In a sign of deference to the newly elected leadership, the meeting resolved "that some unconstitutional functioning on the part of the Executive be condoned until the organisation is on a sound administrative and financial footing". The meeting repeated the emphasis on contact through sports, cultural activities and debate competitions. The intervarsity visits would provide cover for inter-SRC meetings and political discussions, which should all be recorded in minutes. The Executive of SASO was mandated with the task of distributing reading materials among the different centres. Indeed, some centres, particularly at white liberal institutions, were better resourced than others. The Executive was also asked to look into arranging "students exchange" through which "students from one centre shall attend lectures at some other centre". The members of the Executive were to play the role of roving envoys in their respective regions, so as to bring greater numbers of students into the new organisation.

One of the resolutions of the 1969 conference was that there should be a representative of SASO at NUSAS conferences. It was also resolved that the University of Natal Non-European section would host the next conference in 1970. The thing to bear in mind here is that while Steve and his comrades may have been ahead of the general student population – indeed, an incipient radicalism can be detected in some of Steve's own writing – the overall impetus is around the promotion of contact. In a communiqué sent out to all the major student bodies, formally informing them of the existence of SASO, Steve notes that SASO is "concerned primarily with black students, and with contact among students in general". In the communiqué he explains the initial focus on contact:

> ... too much caution has had to be taken at the beginning and the progress has been slow. We have reached a stage now where our existence has become an established fact and our way of seeing things has been adopted by a substantial number on the black campuses.[149]

Consequently, Steve's tenure as president was taken up with fundraising for SASO. In this regard he looked to the UCM for support. A couple of months after the SASO inaugural conference, Steve wrote to Justice Moloto, who had taken up the presidency of UCM, to ask for financial support for SASO. SASO had planned a formation school for December 1969 – mainly

---

149 SASO Communiqué, 1969/70.

to deal with the second challenge of leadership and philosophical development:

> We are having the proposed SASO formation school on the 1st to 5th December at this place [Alan Taylor Residence, University of Natal]. If you remember well, I raised the question of possible loans from UCM to meet some of the costs that shall arise from this and also other small organisational costs that have arised [sic] so far. I am therefore happy to learn from our secretary Miss Kgware that she has received R20 towards postage, stationery etc. This venture in December will probably cost us about R100. I am sure we shall need to raise about half of this from elsewhere other than the people attending. Please look into the possibility of lending us that much.[150]

And then on 27 February 1970 Steve wrote to Colin Collins:

> This is just to raise a few of the topics we discussed recently. Firstly, I shall ask you to look into the possibilities of forwarding an appeal to your Executive for the following loans:
>
> Stationery, Office Equipment etc R200 (needed immediately)
> Part-time Typist Salary – R20 a month
> Executive Tour of Centres – R75 (April)
> Central Contribution towards conference – R150
>
> In addition to the above we shall ask you guys to do some printing for us. We have a number of publications of very simple design that we may wish to design this year.[151]

---
150 Steve Biko's letter to Moloto, 12/09/1969.
151 Steve Biko's letter to Collins, 27/02/70.

On 2 April he wrote a further letter thanking Collins for the funds:

> Many thanks for your letter and cheque. Thanks also for seeing to it that the rest of the request was passed.[152]

Winkie Direko, who was president of UCM in 1971, would later tell me that: "When I was president of the UCM I gave R75 000 to SASO." Steve's decision to push for black leadership of UCM was paying off, and his relationship with Colin Collins was crucial to the formation of SASO. The issue was therefore not colour per se. For Steve, white people had to choose between the liberal humanism of NUSAS and the radical humanism of UCM. The turn towards radicalism would present its own challenges for Steve and the movement he founded.

The relationship between Steve and Collins should not be misconstrued to suggest there were no contradictions and tensions between their two organisations. First, the reliance on the UCM was viewed by SASO radicals as a negation of the organisation's own policy of going it alone.

The second tension was theological.

The Turn to Black Theology

By the end of the 1960s the UCM had been heavily influenced by the radical currents in the Christian world, particularly the arguments for a more secular religion that did not rely on a God out there who would perform miracles if people were patient enough. While not exactly embracing the more extreme denunciations of the idea of a God out there, and while

---

152 Steve Biko's letter to Collins, 02/04/70.

seeking out a more secular role for the church – particularly under the intellectual leadership of Basil Moore – the UCM got caught up in intellectual and theoretical debates that the black students found did not speak to the exigencies of the political situation. The black members of UCM began to pose the same critique that they had posed to NUSAS. In the same way that NUSAS looked at non-racialism as an end in itself, the white members of UCM were interested more in defining their theological identities than in addressing the broader political challenges of the day. Thus an anonymous contributor to a UCM newsletter poignantly noted that while "the white students within the UCM are primarily in search of a personal or theological identity ... the non-whites in UCM, more particularly the African group, feel a greater need for political identity in the wider sense".[153]

It is within this context of a search for a practical religion that Steve and his colleagues began to search for a theological framework that spoke to the practical needs of black people. Their critique of the secular theology as it was playing out within UCM and among white scholars did not lead them to the African Theology of people like John Mbiti, who were arguing for a return to a purist African religion. They also did not follow the road of their ancestors in the African independent churches by seeking to recover the rituals of lost African religious practices. This they could have done – but it surely would have had no meaning to the Coloured and Indian members of the movement.

The invention and growth of Black Theology under the leadership of James Cone in the United States came as a fortuitous

---

153 UCM Newsletter, "Creative Tensions", Third Semester, 1969.

blessing for Steve and his colleagues. An academic at Union Seminary in New York, Cone departed from the strictly secularist interpretation of Christ that had no meaning for many black people of faith – in that way he was a welcome ally to the Black Consciousness Movement (BCM). Cone departed from African Theology because of its apolitical and sometimes conservative stance. Indeed, John Mbiti, the leading theorist of African Theology castigated Black Theology as too preoccupied with liberation and an embarrassment to Christianity. Cone focused on the work of Christ (which appealed to the more traditional African Christians) as speaking to the conditions of the American ghetto (which appealed to those who wanted a practical Christianity). Magaziner argues that the genius of Steve Biko and the BCM lay in its ability to contextualise Black Theology by adapting African Theology's underlying logic – to plant it on South African soil. Or, as Magaziner puts it: "South Africans gave Black Theology an African twist ... Black Theology offered South Africans the possibility of restoring [a radical] Christ to African Theology" – so that the latter could speak to a broader black political constituency that included Coloureds and Indians. Thus Biko and his colleagues reframed both European and African Christianity into something more inclusive and relevant to the struggle.

Desmond Tutu, one of the leading voices of that struggle, would thus proclaim to John Mbiti: "I and others from South Africa do Black Theology, which is for us, at this point African Theology."[154] Yet another religious leader of the 1980s, Allan Boesak, spoke of a Black Messiah. The Black Messiah

---

154 Cited in Magaziner, *The Law and the Prophets*, 98.

was Black in the political sense of being on the side of the oppressed – which was indeed consistent with the BCM's conception of Blackness. Through this reframing of Christianity, Steve and his colleagues had put Christianity at the forefront of the struggle, and in the process gave the movement an entry point into the heartbeat of the community.

7
Strategic Leadership and "Losing Grip": The Black People's Convention

> "Gentlemen, this is what we want. This is where you are and this is where we are; and this is what we want."
> STEVE BIKO[155]

If Steve's presidency of SASO was characterised by organisation building, the end of his term in 1970 seems to have freed him to devote greater attention to developing the philosophical foundations of the movement. As a first step he visited the black campuses, mainly to recruit more students into SASO but also to deepen the ideological basis of the movement. He was surprised by the depth of intellectual and political leadership on these campuses. Less time was spent on what he calls "the morality argument", i.e. whether it was morally correct to organise along racial lines. There was:

> ... a growing awareness of the role the black students may be called to play in the emancipation of their community. The students realise that the isolation of the black intelligentsia from the rest of the black society is a disadvantage to black people as a whole.

Despite this assertiveness, there was always the question of "where to go from here", a lack of strategic direction he as-

---

155 Biko, *I Write What I Like*, 150.

cribed to the over-reliance on white students in bodies such as NUSAS: "Hence our originality and imagination have been dulled to the point where it takes a supreme effort to act logically even in order to follow one's beliefs and convictions."[156]

At this point, Steve was ready to move from the realm of tactical leadership to strategic leadership: "The blacks are tired of standing at the touchlines to witness a game that they should be playing. They want to do things for themselves, and all by themselves." While tactical leadership is preoccupied with the daily routines needed to make an organisation work, strategic leadership is about connecting the organisation to broader social goals and values.[157] The main vehicle for this new role was to be the SASO Newsletter. By this time SASO was renting offices in Beatrice Street, Durban. Again the church would prove a useful ally – the building was owned by the Congregational Church of Southern Africa. The treasurer of the church, Howard Trumbull, rented the upstairs of the church to SASO. It was from here that Steve worked as the head of publications for SASO. He penned a regular and influential column under the pseudonym Frank Talk.

The essays he wrote addressed a number of psychological, cultural, social and political issues from a Black Consciousness perspective. But, as Mamphela Ramphele and others have since pointed out, Steve and the Black Consciousness Movement failed to take note of gender in their analyses of the South African situation. The essays, later collected under the title *I Write*

---

156 Biko, *I Write What I Like*, 19.
157 Thomas Sergiovanni and John E. Corbally (1998). *Leadership and Organizational Culture: New Perspectives on Administrative Theory and Practice* (Urbana: University of Illinois Press).

What I Like, remain the most authoritative collection on Black Consciousness in South Africa[158] and yet remain devoid of analysis of the gender dimension of racial oppression. According to Kimberlé Crenshaw, both the mainstream feminist discourse (dominated by white women) and the black nationalist discourse (dominated by black men) tend to exclude the experiences of black women.[159] While gender was not part of the discourse of the movement, Nohle Mohapi argues that "women were mobilised as women to come together and do something for themselves instead of depending on their men," or, as Leslie Hadfield puts it: "If not for one male doctor, two male ambulance drivers and the political visitors, Zanempilo clinic would have been dominated by women."[160]

One of the most impressive aspects of Steve and Barney Pityana's leadership of the movement was their readiness to take their arguments to some of the most exalted academic forums. The two student leaders presented papers at a conference of the Abe Bailey Centre at the University of Cape Town (UCT).

---

[158] Although attributed to Steve, the idea to collect Steve's writings came from Hugh Lewin. Aelred Stubbs edited them and they were first published in 1978 by Bowerdean Press, London. The book was later republished by Pan Macmillan and remains a best-seller in South Africa to this day.

[159] Kimberlé Crenshaw, "Mapping the Margins: Intersectionality, Identity Politics and Violence Against Women of Color" in Dan Danielson and Karen Engle (eds). *After Identity: A Reader in Law and Culture* (New York: Routledge).

[160] Leslie Hadfield, "Biko, Black Consciousness and 'the System' e-Zinyoka: Oral History and Black Consciousness in Practice in a Rural Ciskei Village", *South African Historical Journal*, 62:1, 78-99. Zanempilo is discussed in Chapter 8. Suffice to say some of the women went on to leadership positions: Mohapi became mayor of Port Elizabeth and Thoko Mbaniswa commissioner at the Independent Electoral Commission.

Academics and student leaders from Stellenbosch University, and the University of the Western Cape (UWC) attended. At that conference Steve delivered the paper titled "White Racism and Black Consciousness". Steve was telling some of the most respected white academics about their own internalised notions of white supremacy. One can only imagine the atmosphere in the room as Steve read his paper:

> We now come to that group that has enjoyed the longest confidence from the Black world – the liberal establishment, including radical and leftist groups. The biggest mistake the Black world ever made was to assume that whoever opposed apartheid was an ally. For a long time the Black world has been looking only at the governing party and not so much at the whole power structure as the object of their rage. In a sense the very vocabulary the Blacks have used has been inherited from the liberals. Therefore it is not so surprising that alliances were established with the liberals. Who are the liberals in South Africa? It is that curious bunch of non-conformists who explain their participation in negative terms; that bunch of do-gooders that goes under all sorts of names – liberals, leftists etc. These are the people who argue they are not responsible for white racism and the country's "inhumanity to the Black man". These are the people who claim that they too feel the oppression just as acutely and therefore should be jointly involved in the Black man's struggle for a place under the sun. In short, these are the people who say they have black souls wrapped up in white skins.[161]

---

[161] Van der Merwe and Welsh, *Student Perspectives*, 192.

Steve then explained how this ultimately undermined the struggle:

> With this sort of influence behind them, most Black leaders tended to rely too much on the advice of liberals. For a long time, in fact, it became the occupation of the leadership to "calm the masses down", while they engaged in fruitless negotiation with the status quo. Their whole political action, in fact, was a programmed course in the art of gentle persuasion through protests and limited boycotts and they hoped the rest could be safely left to the troubled conscience of the fair-minded English folk.

Steve defined the non-racial, integrated circle of organisations such as NUSAS as a:

> ... soporific to the Blacks while salving the consciences of the guilt-stricken whites. It works from the false premise that because it is difficult to bring people from the different races together in this country, achievement of this is in itself a step towards the total liberation of the Blacks. Nothing could be more misleading.[162]

He argued that the guilt-stricken liberals were all too happy to live under the protection of the National Party (NP), even if they did not have to vote for it:

---

[162] Van der Merwe and Welsh, *Student Perspectives*, 193.

> Not only have the whites been guilty of being on the offensive but, by some skilful manoeuvres, they have managed to control the responses of the Blacks to the provocation. Not only have they kicked the Black but they have also told him how to react to the kick. For a long time the Black has been listening with patience to the advice he has been receiving on how best to respond to the kick. With painful slowness he is now beginning to show signs that it is his right and duty to respond to the kick *in the way he sees fit*.[163]

Barney Pityana gave a more scholarly paper titled "Power and Social Change in South Africa". He lamented the fact that many black people measured themselves according to white standards:

> This is true and it is to be regretted. It is a negative way of expressing one's values. It creates the unfortunate impression that all values are White-oriented and all standards are White-determined. This I cannot accept. I believe that we have values and standards which are bound to be different from those of the Whites simply because the Whites enjoy the privileges Blacks are robbed of. There cannot be much in common between the two peoples in that situation of imbalance. I am not aspiring to be equal to a White man but I am determined to establish my worth as a God-created being. I have to assert my BEING as a person.

Pityana traced this cultural imperialism to the arrival of the missionaries in the 19th century:

---

[163] Van der Merwe and Welsh, *Student Perspectives*, 195.

> The urgency of the moment would perhaps be that we ought to liberate the mind of the Black man. He must unlock himself from this vicious circle. He must determine his own goals and aspirations.[164]

In their turn of phrase we can already detect the Fanonian influence that Nigel Gibson, Percy More, Andile Mngxitama and others have so eloquently written about. In fact, Pityana quoted from Fanon's *Black Skin, White Masks*:

> I am not a potentiality of something. I am wholly what I am. I do not have to look for the universal. No probability has any place inside me. My negro consciousness does not hold itself out as Black. It IS. It is its own follower. This is all that we blacks are after. TO BE. We believe that we are quite efficient in handling our BE-ness and for this purpose we are self-sufficient.[165]

Against the argument that Black Consciousness was essentialist, Pityana was pointing out that it was the political situation that led to a particular culture in the black community:

> Culture is largely a social product which is imposed on each individual by the socialising process to which he is subjected in his particular society. Culture is a living tradition, a collection of ideas and beliefs which represent a people's collective way of life. The cultural orientation of the Black people is influenced by their lifestyle in the Black ghettos. They have

---

164 Van der Merwe and Welsh, *Student Perspectives*, 195.
165 Van der Merwe and Welsh, *Student Perspectives*, 180; see also Frantz Fanon (1952), *Black Skin, White Masks* (London: Pluto Press).

Strategic Leadership and "Losing Grip"

had to generate a soul-force which would enable them to remain human beings in these camps.[166]

Pityana concluded that to think that any of the existing political parties could bring about freedom for black people was a pipedream: "This is the reality of the South African situation. The Black person in South Africa must realise that he is on his own."[167] Although the slogan "Black man, you are on your own" has been attributed to Steve, it was Pityana's coinage. One of the most under-reported aspects of the formation of Black Consciousness was indeed the role that Pityana played as Steve's philosophical counterpart. According to some in the movement Steve was not necessarily the brightest member of their group although certainly the most influential. According to Malusi Mpumlwana, and according to Pityana himself, Steve had that overall edge in his force of persuasion, although he was not necessarily cleverer than everybody else. Mpumlwana puts it this way: "I'd think Barney was more analytical than Steve just in terms of careful analysis of things. Steve didn't do as much of that as I think he should have." As an adult Steve's leadership thus fitted MacGregor Burns's concept of peer leadership that he had shown in childhood. According to Mpumlwana:

> ... at those times Steve was very much a peer and he was a good listener, so what comes up in the end is not so much what he wanted but what he has facilitated to get discussed. With Steve you'd never differentiate between a party (jam

---

166 Van der Merwe and Welsh, *Student Perspectives*, 180.
167 Van der Merwe and Welsh, *Student Perspectives*, 183.

session) and a political meeting because they were all happening at the same time. There were no formal meetings and that in itself promoted peer structure of all communication and therefore his leadership emerged in that context.

However, peer leadership had its downside as well. It can also lead to problems of authority as there is no single figure to whom everyone can defer in times of crisis. This became acutely clear as Steve found it more and more difficult to get an increasingly assertive and militant leadership of the movement to listen to his counsel.

These leadership challenges played themselves out in the formation of the Black People's Convention (BPC). In answer to the question: "Where to from here?", Steve and his colleagues decided that they needed a community presence. In his paper at the Abe Bailey conference, Steve had stated that "the importance of the SASO stand is not really to be found in SASO per se – for SASO has the natural limitations of being a student organisation with an ever changing membership".[168] Indeed, the SASO leadership hatched the idea of reaching out beyond the student community at a meeting of the SASO Executive in Port Elizabeth in early 1971. A delegation consisting of Steve, Barney Pityana, Lindelwe Mabandla and Aubrey Mokoape fanned out across the country to meet with community organisations that could play this coordinative role – and it helped that there were relationships established through the discussions on Black Theology with organisations such as the Interdenominational African Ministers' Association of South Africa (IDAMASA) – which was one of the first to embrace Black Theology.

---

168 Van der Merwe and Welsh, *Student Perspectives*, 197.

Strategic Leadership and "Losing Grip"

IDAMASA was agreeable to the idea of a national coordinating body and asked for a further meeting on 24 April 1971 in Bloemfontein, to further thrash out what this new body might look like. At that meeting were other organisations, including ASSECA (the Association for the Educational and Cultural Advancement of the African People of South Africa, started by MT Moerane and PQ Vundla), the Old Boys Association of St Peter's Seminary and YWCA (the Young Womens Christian Association). SASO sent Barney Pityana and Vuyelwa Mashalaba as its delegates. The meeting resolved to call a bigger conference in August of the same year in Edendale, just outside of Pietermaritzburg. The conference, themed "The Development of the African Community", drew over 100 representatives.

The conference was organised in terms of presenters and respondents. Steve was asked to speak on African cultural concepts but he was also asked to respond to Gatsha Buthelezi's speech. Buthelezi used the occasion to justify the idea of working within the policy of separate development. Steve was scathing in his response.

That meeting elected an ad hoc committee under the leadership of the influential editor of the *The World* newspaper, MT Moerane. The committee was mandated to draw up a working paper from the proceedings of the conference and to organise a follow-up meeting. Immediately there was a difference of opinion among the members of the committee. Some people felt that whatever structure was going to emerge should be of a purely coordinative nature and limited to cultural and development issues, and others felt that a more political orientation was needed, given the political nature of the discussions at the Edendale conference.

The latter group were now insisting on what Steve would describe as "a vanguard movement ... to lead the entire Black consciousness thinking."[169] This position was in the minority in the drafting of the working paper. The majority of the committee, including Steve, favoured a cultural coordinating body. The follow-up meeting took place at the historic Donaldson Community Centre (DOCC) in Orlando, Soweto in December 1971,[170] chaired by Moerane.

Proceedings took a turn when the SASO delegation, led by Harry Nengwekhulu, walked out of the meeting, saying the preamble to the document was too apologetic. When they returned they insisted on a discussion of the rationale of the organisation. The SASO delegation then got into a stand-off with elders such as Moerane and Dr William Nkomo – a former ANC Youth League member who considered himself to have mellowed with time – on whether a political or a cultural coordinating body was needed. The younger people started getting support from respected elders such as Mrs Winnefred Kgware, who spoke in favour of the formation of a political organisation. The wife of the rector of the university, William Kgware, she was always supportive of students.

Steve was opposed to the idea or, as he put it: "I myself opposed the idea but finally voted with the resolution to form a political organisation."[171] Steve did not think that was the mandate of the Edendale meeting, and he also did not believe that there had been sufficient consultation with other groups, particularly in the Coloured and Indian communities, which is

---

169 Arnold, *The Testimony of Steve Biko*, 75.
170 This is the same venue where the PAC broke from the ANC in 1959, and a venue that was the site of many political gatherings in the 1980s.
171 Arnold, *The Testimony of Steve Biko*, 79.

why the BPC ended up co-opting individuals such as Saths Cooper into its leadership. This is how Steve phrased his reservations:

> When I had objected initially to the formation of a political organisation embracing the whole concept of Black consciousness, part of my line was that the platform which we had taken was not the right one, in the sense that we envisage forming a comprehensive Black organisation that involved everybody, and ... there had been no attempt by the organisers of that meeting to invite people from the Indian and Coloured communities within the Black world ... We should go out of our way to first of all get a venue where people can all come and make sure that invitations had been sent properly, to Indian and Coloured folk. [172]

Moerane was taken aback by the push for an overtly political organisation. According to Gail Gerhart, "what older participants seemed to fear was the gloves-off militancy of SASO, which appeared to lead the organisation and anyone associated with it into an early clash with the authorities".[173] Sipho Buthelezi argues that Gerhart is mistaken to see the division in terms of age, or even in terms of militants and conservatives: "This was a critical and complex debate which cannot simply be reduced to a division between militants and conservatives. It involved strategic choices about how to operate effectively in a tight political space."[174]

---

172 Arnold, *The Testimony of Steve Biko*, 79
173 Gail Gerhart (1978). *Black Power in South Africa: The Evolution of an Ideology* (Berkeley: University of California at Berkeley), 293.
174 Sipho Buthelezi (1986). "The Emergence of Black Consciousness", in Barney Pityana et al, *Bounds of Possibility*.

Yet another ad hoc committee was elected under the chairmanship of trade unionist Drake Koka. Koka announced the formation of the new organisation in the press in January 1972, emphasising its anti-ethnic stance. The organisation was formally launched in Pietermaritzburg in July 1972 under the leadership of A Mayatula (president); Mthuli ka Shezi (vice-president);[175] Drake Koka (secretary-general); Saths Cooper (public relations officer) and A Dlamini (national organiser).

At its congress in December 1972 the BPC elected a new executive under the leadership of Winnifred Kgware, making her the first woman president of a national liberation movement in South Africa. Other members of the Executive were Chris Mokoditoa (vice-president), Sipho Buthelezi (secretary-general), Mosibudi Mangena (national organiser) and Saths Cooper (public relations officer).[176]

What is worth noting is that Steve did not make himself available for the leadership of this national political organisation. One reason may well be that he was still a student at the University of Natal, and that the organisation had to be led by older community leaders. It also says something about his understanding of where to go to find leadership. As Ronald Heifetz puts it, strategy is about identifying the right group of stakeholders necessary to resolve a collective problem.[177] (Steve's ability to identify relevant stakeholders shall become even clearer later in our discussion of the Black Community Programmes.)

---

175 Shezi was pushed in front of a train by a white worker, and died shortly thereafter.
176 Unisa Archives: Accession 127, Communiqué 1/73, Saths Cooper: public relations officer.
177 Ronald Heifetz (1994). *Leadership Without Easy Answers* (Cambridge, MA: Belknap Press of Harvard University).

Strategic Leadership and "Losing Grip"

According to Alan Brooks and Jeremy Brickhill, by 1973 the BPC had 4 000 members in 41 branches across the country.[178] By that measure the BPC was too small to call itself a national political organisation. As Steve had suspected, it also suffered from the prevailing fear in the black community, especially in the midst of the harassment by the security forces and the killing of its leaders – starting with its own vice-president, Mthuli ka Shezi, who was pushed in front of a train by a white railway worker.

Another limitation was imposed by lack of funding for the BPC, resulting in the ironic situation of the national political organisation relying on the student organisation for material and intellectual leadership. There was indeed a great deal of cross-membership between members of SASO and the BPC. For example, one of the leaders of the BPC in the North was Pandelani Nefolovhodwe – and yet a future president of SASO. Harry Nengwekhulu was permanent organiser of SASO and a member of BPC. The president of the SRC at the University of Natal, Keith Mokoape, organised a function at which senior members of the BPC came to speak. It would have been stretching credibility for Steve to be the president of BPC and still maintain that the BPC was a community organisation.

Perhaps more important is that in 1972 Steve was excluded from the University of Natal on academic grounds. Six years into his studies, Steve was repeating third year. In the SASO/BPC Trial Steve testified that he had actually lost interest in studying medicine, and wanted to take up studies in law, which he subsequently did by long-distance correspondence with

---

178 Brooks, Alan and Brickhill, Jeremy (1980). *Whirlwind Before the Storm* (London: International Defence and Aid Fund for Southern Africa).

the University of South Africa (UNISA). Steve and his newly wedded wife Ntsiki – more about his relationship with his wife in Chapter 8 – then moved into Umlazi with Barney Pityana and his wife Dimza. Steve now worked full time for the Black Community Programmes but the apartheid government slapped him with a banning order in March 1973, together with Saths Cooper, Barney Pityana, Harry Nengwekhulu, Jerry Modisane and Bokwe Mafuna.

The banning order barred him from membership of political organisations and restricted him to the magisterial district of King William's Town. The fulcrum of the movement was thereby dismembered and dispersed throughout the country.

While the centre of gravity moved with Steve to King William's Town, he was hobbled from actively directing the activities of the movement, particularly the BPC. The BPC sought to get around this by making him its honorary president at its congress in Ginsberg in December 1975. This congress also elected Hlaku Rachidi as president, and it is the congress in which Keith Mokoape publicly made a call for a turn to armed struggle.

Since the BPC was organisationally weak, it is more useful to judge its legacy in strategic, qualitative terms as opposed to quantitative, organisational terms. A measure of its impact would be the extent to which it was able to spread the values of Black Consciousness throughout the country, and not necessarily only to the members of the organisation.

Thus Sipho Buthelezi notes that "although BPC failed to grow into a mass political organisation, its strategic use of the media, notably the regular weekly column in the *Daily Dispatch*, which appeared under Mapetla Mohapi's name, and the re-

Strategic Leadership and "Losing Grip"

lease of well-positioned press statements, established BPC as an important voice in South Africa".[179] According to the political scientist Sam Nolutshungu, "movement – emphasising sentiment and spontaneity and a diversity of ideological outlook – comes nearer to an apt description of both the popular mood and of the place of the organisation [BPC] with relation to it".[180] Or in Steve's own words, the BPC "certainly has a following. It probably has got much more following than it has got members in the country."[181]

Nolutshungu further argues that despite their student and middle-class status it was not the leadership's objective class position that mattered but whether their political aims were to advance the interest of a black middle class in opposition to that of the working people. In testimony to their commitment to the liberation struggle these students had by July 1976 "conjured a strong wind that poorly served the black middle class while increasing the number of those who sought a radical dissolution of the entire economic and social order".[182]

Steve Loses his Grip: The Viva Frelimo Rallies

In the vacuum caused by the 1973 bannings, a younger generation of leaders, or what Steve's peer Malusi Mpumlwana calls the second generation of leadership, emerged under the fiery leadership of Muntu Myeza and Saths Cooper. It is no coincidence that they emerged from Durban – Myeza was at the University of Zululand (Ongoye) and Cooper at the Uni-

---

179 Buthelezi, "The Emergence of Black Consciousness", 129.
180 Nolutshungu, *Changing South Africa*, 149.
181 Biko, *I Write What I Like*, 152.
182 Nolutshungu, *Changing South Africa*, 162.

versity of Durban-Westville. This, after all, was the "Durban Moment".

In 1974 Muntu Myeza, the secretary-general of SASO, came up with the idea of organising nationwide rallies in celebration of neighbouring Mozambique's independence from Portugal. Saths Cooper recalls receiving a telephone call from Muntu Myeza in September 1974, suggesting that they organise rallies throughout the country to celebrate Mozambique's independence. The biggest one was scheduled for Curries Fountain in Durban. Even though Saths Cooper was already banned and restricted to Durban, he played a behind-the-scenes role in organising the rally. He called the former president of the BPC, Reverend Mayathula, to speak at the proposed rally at Curries Fountain. When the latter was not available he got Dr Joel Matsipa to agree to speak.

The government immediately responded with a banning order of all rallies by SASO/BPC. When the newspapers reported that the rallies had been banned, Myeza organised a press conference and said: "We are not aware of any bannings. Even if we were, we couldn't care less. The will of the people shall not be suppressed by one white foreign minority regime." Myeza also prepared a press statement on the proposed rally at Curries Fountain: "This afternoon's rally will go ahead as scheduled." He then went down to address 5 000 people at Curries Fountain against police proscription. He was planning to disperse them, but got caught up in the energy of the crowd.

According to Mpumlwana, Steve was opposed to the rallies and made his views known to the new leadership. Mpumlwana remembers asking the new leaders in Durban if they had a plan in the event of arrests but no plan was forthcoming:

> Really, it was just a solidarity rally, it was not our cause. It's one thing to say we are campaigning for something ourselves, that we are prepared to die for in our country, but it's another to say we want our rights to die for other people who've got something. They killed people in Sharpeville but that was OK – people were standing up for their rights. It was our right to celebrate Mozambique's experience but was it right that we should lead our people to death at a time when our organisation is not that strong? We began to raise concerns, we started making calls just to be sure that they are not going to take this to the final point. Mapetla [Mohapi] got called I think by Nkwenkwe Nkomo, I can't remember, who said: are you chickening out too? And they went ahead right up to the last minute.

Mohapi, one of Steve's most trusted lieutenants, took offence at the insinuation that he was a coward. Mpumlwana says no one had ever called Mohapi a coward, let alone someone junior to him in the movement. He felt it was inappropriate for anyone to question his judgement.

As Steve had feared, the rallies were followed by a nationwide swoop on 200 Black Consciousness activists across the country, a process that culminated in the State vs. Cooper and eight others, otherwise known as the SASO/BPC Trial. In addition to Myeza and Cooper, trialists included Strini Moodley, Patrick Mosiuoa "Terror" Lekota, Nchaupe Mokoape, Pandelani Nefolovhodwe, Nkwenkwe Nkomo, Kaborane Sedibe and Zithulele Cindi. They were charged with contravening the Terrorism Act by fomenting racial hatred in the country. Mpumlwana was very unhappy that the group then asked Steve to appear in their defence:

> These are the people that undermined his leadership and authority right up to the last evening. Against his will he accepted summons from their lawyer. I think that in itself was very important because some of us felt so disgusted that we didn't think there was any point helping any further. But Steve said these are our folks, whether they are right or wrong, we can discipline them outside, but for as long as they are in the hands of the enemy we should get them out.

Steve then sought to use the trial as a platform for spreading the cause of Black Consciousness. Aelred Stubbs wrote that "this trial may have been for the Movement what the famous 'Treason Trial' was for the Congress Alliance of the 1950s".[183] That is probably true, but the 1950s trial did not have a spokesperson such as a Nelson Mandela in the Rivonia Trial of 1964 or a Steve Biko in this particular trial. A more appropriate parallel may well be between the SASO/BPC Trial and the Rivonia Trial – both in terms of the fearlessness of the leadership and the content of the message that both trials sent out to the black community and the world at large.

Stubbs shares what Steve's friend Ben Khoapa told him about the effect of the trial: "Overnight Steve became the toast of the Soweto shebeens. Here at last was the authentic voice of the people, not afraid to say openly what other blacks think but are too frightened to say."[184] Stubbs cites as an example Steve's response to a question about black policemen who worked for the government. Steve called them "traitors" without any equivocation – this to a roomful of police.

---

183 Biko, *I Write What I Like*, 109.
184 Biko, *I Write What I Like*, 135-136.

The trial gave Steve an opportunity to lay out the rationale and methodology of the movement without falling into the trap of incriminating either himself or his comrades. If the state could associate him in any way with the group, either by his words or actions, they could use that to put him away for a long time. Treason carried a death or a life sentence, or he could under the Suppression of Terrorism Act have suffered the same fate as his colleagues – all of whom were sentenced to at least six years in jail.

But this was not just a legal balancing act – it went to the core of the political balancing act that he had to manage as the leader of an aboveboard political organisation, i.e. how to bring about a revolution without falling foul of the state. While he appreciated the role that guerrilla war would play, he never saw himself leaving the country. In fact, during his testimony, he explained how people subjected to certain living conditions might indeed resort to violence – even if he did not advocate it himself. In the trial he turned the accusation of terrorism against the state itself:

> ... what we have to experience ... certainly is much more definite, much more physically depressing than the charge you are placing against these men for the few things they have said. I am talking about definite violence for instance ... actual forms of violence – people being baton charged by police, beaten up, like the people who were striking in March in Henneman. I am talking about the situation of police charging against people in places like Sharpeville without arms, and I am talking about the indirect violence that you get through starvation in townships ... I think put together all

> this is much more terrorism than what these guys have been saying. Now they stand charged. White society is not charged. This is what I mean. [185]

Steve walked a similar tightrope in response to a question about the ANC and the PAC:

> We must recognise that the ANC and the PAC were involved in the struggle, and not . . . for selfish purposes. It was certainly on behalf of Blacks and for the liberation of Blacks. We may or may not necessarily approve of their methods, but the fact is they exist in history as protagonists of our struggle. Without agreeing with them, we give them their due for existing in our history and for pushing the struggle forward.

There is a common thread running through from Steve's rethink about the 72-hour clause in Stutterheim in 1968 to his refusal to take the movement on a self-destructive path in 1974. He eschewed protest politics – which he described as "beggar tactics"– and the armed struggle, which would put him at risk of arrest and undermine above-board political organising. He eschewed armed struggle without counting it out, and that way is able to stay on this side of the law. The middle ground concept of bargaining was central to Steve's strategic thinking about how BPC should challenge the system while retaining its own organisational strength:

> . . . now has come the time when we as blacks must articulate what we want, and put it across to the white man, and from a position of strength begin to say: "Gentlemen, this is

---

[185] Arnold, *The Testimony of Steve Biko*, 139.

what we want. This is where you are and this is where we are, and this is what we want."[186]

Steve argued that the bargaining required careful organisation building and even tactical manoeuvres that could take as long as 20 years because "as you develop strength, you begin to pick up issue after issue and it is all over a course of time". The bargaining process could start "now when we take a resolution at a conference and we say we are going to communicate the contents of the resolution to the people, whether it is a university in the case of SASO or whether it is a sporting body or a governing body in the case of BPC, all of this is bargaining".

The judge in the case tried to pin him down on what he meant by building a powerful bloc against the white government. This is the closest that Steve came to what could have been classified as treasonous talk, and yet he pulled back only from the brink, so to speak. When his lawyer asks him whether building such a powerful bloc would not force him "to confront Mr Vorster and force on him the decision of war and peace", Steve answers: "Yes, I said to you we don't have an alternative." And then quickly turned around to say: "We are not interested in armed struggle."

Steve repeated this position in an interview with a journalist: "The line BPC adopts is to explore as much as possible non-violent means within the country, and that is why we exist." But then suggestively added, "there are people – there are many people – who have despaired of the efficacy of non-violence as a method":

---

186 Biko, *I Write What I Like*, 150.

> I don't believe for a moment that we are going to willingly drop our belief in the non-violent stance – as of now. But I can't predict what will happen in the future, inasmuch as I can't predict what the enemy is going to do in the future. [187]

On Violence and Death As Lived Experience

Steve's own cautionary stance on armed struggle notwithstanding, he could not ensure that everyone in the movement acted with the same restraint. There were militarists, like Keith Mokoape, who argued strongly for a turn to armed struggle. Harry Nengwekhulu, a senior leader of whom one would have expected greater caution, made an explicit call for a violent response to white oppression in a speech at Kajee Hall, Durban, in September 1974. In the speech he refers to Ahmed Timol's murder by the security police, and is angry at the fact that "you and I come here every day to try and mourn their death, and we don't do anything". And then he drops the bombshell:

> I am trying to say that we should kill them . . . I believe that if one man tries to take your eye, you must always try to take his eye. If one man tries to take your life, you must also try to take his life because it is the only life you can live here . . . try to protect your life right here on earth . . . the time is ripe that . . . we must carry the fight towards their camp . . . I'm not preaching violence; I only say we must react against this violent system . . . If we happen to destroy White racism, together with physical Whites, it is just damned unfortunate, but what we want to destroy is White racism.

---

187 Biko, *I Write What I Like*, 169.

He then urges violence against those collaborating with the system:

> We must guard against these Non-Whites, we must try to watch them and shun them, we must try to insulate them, and if possible try to destroy them, because even my mother or my father is a stumbling block to my freedom. I have every moral right to kill her and destroy her. That is a sign of determination. [188]

After Steve's death (see Chapter 9), the president of the BPC Kenny Rachidi raised his voice on death as the existential reality facing the movement:

> Since the formation of BPC in 1972, violence against the black man has grown intensively. A week before the first congress of the Convention in Hammanskraal our interim Vice-President Mthuli ka Shezi was pushed under a moving train at Germiston Station in the Transvaal . . . That was the beginning of onslaughts, attacks and executions on the movement. Steve Biko's tragic death is merely a continuation of the pattern of our experiences. [189]

In his book *The Law and the Prophets*, Daniel Magaziner sees the increasing militarisation of the language of Black Consciousness as a departure from its humanist beginnings in

---

[188] Unisa Archives: The State vs. Cooper and Eight Others, vol. 75, 4259-4260.
[189] Unisa Archives: Accession 127, Hlaku Kenneth Rachidi: Tribute to Steve Biko - King William's Town, 25th September, 1977.

SASO. He described the BPC as increasingly resembling a typical political party, "bound to orthodoxy and ideology". Magaziner describes his research on Black Consciousness as an attempt to reach back into those "early days" of SASO:

> ... when activists looked warily at post-colonies and called not only for political solutions but also for new ways of being human. To that end they thought about what makes people people at the most basic level ... In the mid-1970s the tide turned away from this vision of politics, however, and by the 1980s, what remained of Black Consciousness had joined the rest of the liberation movements in perhaps their greatest sin: pointing merely at a set of laws and saying, There, that is your enemy.

Ironically, Magaziner's critique is based on the very liberal humanism the movement rejected. Nigel Gibson argues that what it means to be human cannot be abstracted from the lived reality of black people in "an anti-black world". He argues that "philosophy is a product of the lived experience of social beings".[190] While Magaziner looks at black consciousness in ethical terms, a political approach lays bare the unique position occupied by black people in the world and in the South Africa of the 1970s. Whereas the ethical approach relies on the Hegelian self/other dialectic of mutual recognition between master and servant, black people were operating from what Frantz Fanon saw as a position of non-recognition. To be black was to be rendered invisible and illegitimate. Black Consciousness:

---

190 Gibson, *Fanonion Practices*, 46.

> ... demands an approach that addresses contradictions that are not of a dialectical kind. The liberal solution is to say at least the other is another – which is an ethical and not a political solution if that at all. But what to do when the place of discursive opposition has been closed?

Gibson argues that Black Consciousness asserts the humanity of black people in a world in which that assertion itself is viewed as "a contradiction". This conception of blacks as non-beings or lesser beings is exactly what led to the justification of slavery in the United States, colonialism in Africa and apartheid in South Africa. When they did not physically exterminate black people, white supremacist movements and ideologies systematically led to what Cornel West calls a form of social death. West is quick to add that this experience is inextricably linked to progressive action in that "tragedy can be an impetus, rather than an impediment, to oppositional activity". [191] In his book *Modern Tragedy*, Raymond Williams urges us to focus not only on the experience of suffering but also on what it generates:

> ... not only the evil but the men who have fought against evil; not only the crisis but the energy released by it, the spirit learned in it. We make the connections because that is the action of tragedy, and what we learn in action is again revolution, because we acknowledge others as men and such acknowledgement is the beginning of struggle, as the continuing reality of our lives. Then to see revolution in this tragic perspective is the only way to maintain it. [192]

---

191 Cornel West (1999). *Cornel West Reader* (New York: Basic Civitas Books), 168.
192 Raymond Williams (1966), *Modern Tragedy* (Stanford: Stanford University Press), 173.

Steve Biko prophetically brought this connection between tragedy and its possibilities to the South African situation in his essay "On Death":

> You are either alive and proud, or you are dead, and when you are dead you can't care anyway. And your method of death can itself be a politicising thing. So you die in the riots. For a hell of a lot of them, in fact, there is really nothing to lose – almost literally, given the kind of situations they come from. So if you can overcome the personal fear of death, which is a highly irrational thing, you know, then you are on the way.[193]

And, of course, here he can be interpreted as presciently referring to his own death but also to the death of many young students protesting apartheid education in June 1976. Tragic as the events of those days were, they also were a measure of the heightened level of consciousness and prefigured political activism in a way not seen since the 1950s. And thus when he was asked what he made of the events, Steve said:

> The response was in terms of their pride. They were not prepared to be calmed down, even at the point of a gun. And hence, what happened, happened. Some people were killed. These riots just continued and continued. Because at no stage were the students – nor for that matter their parents at some stage – prepared to be scared. Now this is the kind of lack of fear one is talking about which I see is a very important determinant in political action.[194]

---

193 Biko, *I Write What I Like*, 173.
194 Biko, *I Write What I Like*, 165.

It is, of course, this lack of fear that would lead to his own murder by the security police – with all the possibilities and energies that tragedy released for subsequent social and political movements. I will turn to the events leading to Steve's death in Chapter 9. But first, an examination of Steve's life back in Ginsberg after his banishment in 1973.

8
Banishment and Homecoming

> "Organisational development among blacks
> has only been low because we have allowed it to be."
> STEVE BIKO, *I Write What I Like*

Steve's return to Ginsberg after his banishment to the magisterial district of King William's Town in March 1973 was marked by a combination of personal and political difficulties.

Two years earlier, in Durban, Steve had met Nontsikelelo "Ntsiki" Mashalaba – a cousin of his comrade Vuyelwa Mashalaba. Ntsiki was then a nurse at King Edward Hospital in Durban. Vuyelwa would often visit Ntsiki, Steve in tow. Ntsiki remembers Steve as a not particularly attractive fellow. She was dating a guy from a well-off family, and all Steve could bring her was a bar of chocolate. Her boyfriend would find her with Steve but would not suspect anything because Steve was friends with Vuyelwa.

Steve grew on her, and they fell in love. But it was not a typical dating game. Sometimes they would have arranged a date but Steve would call to ask if they could meet at the railway station, because he was on his way to deliver a paper in Johannesburg. Ntsiki and Steve got married in December 1970 at the King Willliam's Town magistrates court. They held a little celebration at MamCethe's house, where my eldest brother Mzwandile proposed the toast to the newlyweds. "We were all still students then, and very close," Mzwandile recalls. Their first child Nkosinathi was born in 1971. Their young marriage was to experience many growing pains, and would ultimately tumble because of Steve's relationship with the other woman in his life, Mamphela Ramphele.

Life became harder for Steve after he was forced to return to Ginsberg early in 1973. Not only was he banned, but the restrictions were later strengthened to prevent him from working for the Black Community Programmes, from which he was earning a stipend. Ntsiki's income had sustained their family in Durban, but the government made sure that she could not get a job in King William's Town. This put additional pressures on their marriage. Ntsiki would have been justified in feeling that she was struggling for a man whose eyes were not only on political ideals, but on other women as well. She was not cut out for a life in politics, or as she put it: "Politics was not my line."[195]

Once they had moved to King William's Town, Steve was spending more of his time at Zanempilo Clinic where Mamphela Ramphele was the resident doctor. Ramphele became pregnant with Steve's child, Lerato, who died when she was only two months old in 1974. Steve's second son with Ntsiki was born in 1975 and Steve aptly named him after the Mozambican leader Samora Machel. Steve also had a relationship with Lorrain Tabane who bore his child, Motlatsi in 1977. Ntsiki eventually moved out of the matrimonial home and filed for divorce. By the time of his arrest Ntsiki and Steve were no longer living together. Hlumelo, his son with Ramphele, was born in 1978, after his death.

---

195 Ntsiki Biko, interview with Kyle Colston, 2008.

As stated in Chapter 5, Steve had met Ramphele when the two of them were studying medicine at the University of Natal. In her book *A Life*, Ramphele describes the dilemma she found herself in – she was in a long-standing relationship with her high school boyfriend, Dick Mmabane, from Soweto and yet found herself madly in love with Steve Biko:

> In the second half of 1969 it became increasingly difficult to resist Steve's advances. I fell hopelessly in love with him, but would not even admit this to myself. We conducted a semi-platonic friendship which frequently "degenerated" into passion. I became increasingly distressed at my dilemma. How could I desert Dick after all these years, particularly after his mother's death? I could not bear the thought of hurting him. But what of my passionate love for Steve? I was faced with a serious dilemma.[196]

Sensing the threat from Steve, Dick insisted that they should get married, which they did at the end of 1969, but the marriage was built on shaky grounds and they divorced at the end of 1970. In the interim Steve had accepted that Mamphela was married, had met Ntsiki, and had married her.

Ramphele remembers the butterflies in her tummy on meeting Steve again at a party – "that night was the happiest I had experienced in years". But then, "how were we to conduct our love affair in the light of Steve's marriage?"

This concern was shared by many in the movement, including Robert Sobukwe, who admonished Steve about the example

---

196 Mamphela Ramphele (1995). *A Life* (Cape Town: David Philip), 76.

he was setting as a national leader. Aelred Stubbs relayed Sobukwe's concern and the concern of others within the movement to Steve. Stubbs recalled that "while priding myself on my tolerant attitude towards student mores, I found distasteful the stories which clustered around him and his Durban colleagues of heavy drinking and excessive womanising. Such distaste had found expression after a long talk with Mr Robert Sobukwe in Kimberley on one of my visits to Stanley [Ntwasa]."[197]

Stubbs described Steve's response as "vigorous", claiming that "Prof"[Sobukwe] was out of date, and questioning why others with the same concerns, presumably Barney Pityana, had not raised the issue with him directly. Indeed, Steve and Pityana had contrasting personalities: "Steve was the outgoing, gregarious, party loving, sexually ebullient man, fertile in ideas, a voracious reader of anything relevant to his one consuming passion for liberation. Barney was more cautious, reserved, austere even, a committed Christian always, intellectual, a stickler for exactness in detail, a careful administrator."[198]

Bokwe Mafuna has expressed similar concerns in a recent article. He writes that while he had no doubt that Steve, if still alive, would have been a national leader, his "frankness about his love life might have led him to be seriously compromised in the jungle of politics, and could have become a weakness in the area of moral issues that are facing our people today. Truthful he was, but perhaps wise he was not." Mafuna says he was

---

[197] Aelred Stubbs, "Martyr of Hope: A Personal Memoir", in Biko, *I Write What I Like*, 194.
[198] Aelred Stubbs. "The Story of Nyameko Barney Pityana" in *South African Outlook*, vol. 110, no. 1300, October 1979.

not sure whether he "admired or envied his success with the ladies in those days, we were all caught up with the illusion of 'conquests'".[199]

If Stubbs's description of Steve's reaction to the criticism is anything to go by, the correct word is not so much "frankness" as it was "cavalier" and "defensive". Steve wrote a letter to Stubbs in which he complained about the manner in which he had raised the matter with him – as a parting shot after one of their meetings. He then invoked the right to privacy in defence:

> I thought our parting was not the best ever, and I felt like writing to you about the matter you raised just as you were going. First let me say I raised the matter with both parties concerned and with a mutual friend of ours in PE [Port Elizabeth].[200] I have assumed that your motives are completely altruistic – that you see a situation which is potentially explosive and you wish to share with your friend your fears about the possible outcome and if possible help in the formulation of some kind of solution. My response, of course, is that I regard topics of this nature as being extremely private. I am in many instances aware of the complexity that can be introduced by a willingness to accommodate the feelings of friends in a matter that is essentially private between the two – or, in this case – three parties. I have never, ever found it necessary

---

199 Bokwe Mafuna (2007), "The Impact of Steve on My Life", in Chris van Wyk (ed), *We Write What We Like* (Johannesburg: Wits University Press), 82.

200 This reference is to Barney Pityana, who told me Steve often spoke to him about his marital problems and at one point had asked him to ask Ntsiki to come back home.

to reflect on my friends' private activities except in so far as
I thought they affected at any one stage their political standing and their performance.[201]

Steve was being disingenious, for that is exactly the point that Sobukwe, Stubbs and the friend from Port Elizabeth were raising with him – that the relationships were causing political harm to the movement. Peter Jones also raised the issue with Steve on their fateful trip from Cape Town (see Chapter 9) but remembers the latter curtly telling him that this was a strictly private matter. Steve even invoked race in his defensive response to Stubbs:

> This brings me to your own contributions in discussions of this nature. There is a profound difference in the way Westerners basically believe in character analysis to that adopted by us here. In many discussions I used to have with David [Russell] here I agreed with him in comparing our attitude on the whole to that of the European working class approach to life. When you guys talk about a person, you tear him apart . . . you find a motive for everything he does; you categorise him politically, socially etc. In short, you are not satisfied until you have really torn him apart and have really parcelled off each and every aspect of his general behaviour and labelled it . . . Now most blacks do not indulge in reflection upon the self or others. They never form cut and dried opinions that thereafter guide their opinions with others. Of course this tendency is wrong in that on the whole for evaluation and redirection

---

201 Stubbs, "Martyr of Hope: A Personal Memoir", in Biko, *I Write What I Like*, 196.

> of oneself in life, a bit of reflection and self-analysis is necessary. But this has to be checked and not allowed to reach excess ... when you talk to me about my relationships do not assume that I am not aware of the dangers ... I would not like you to continue with any aspects of this debate as I believe there is nothing to be served by it and it remains a private matter. [202]

Steve, of course, realised that he was clutching at straws. The concerns were not coming from Europeans but from Sobukwe and Pityana and, obviously, his wife Ntsiki. And so he wrote back to apologise to Stubbs:

> I've been reflecting on the two letters I wrote to you – today's and the previous one – and cannot help feeling that I have been unkind to you ... a lot of friends of mine believe I am arrogant and they are partly right. Often what I call a critical frankness sounds much sharper than was intended and tends to assume holier than thou proportions. The problem with me is that I often take friends for granted and do not cater for the protective subjectivism that we all suffer from. I cannot say I do not mean what I say but I can point out the honest fact that whatever I've said is 100% devoid of malice or intention to hurt.[203]

And then he opened up to Stubbs about his loneliness:

---

202 Stubbs, "Martyr of Hope: A Personal Memoir", in Biko *I Write What I Like*, 199.
203 Stubbs, "Martyr of Hope: A Personal Memoir", in Biko *I Write What I Like*, 199.

> You know I am (so I think) a reasonably strong person, but quite often I find the going tough under the present restrictions. I am nowhere near despair or frustration but can understand only too well why the other guys are. I have been luckier than most blokes. I live with a very supportive family and one which is fully committed to my commitment if not to the cause itself. The township I am in is supportive and defensive . . . but in spite of all this, it's quite tough. [204]

In addition to the loneliness, he felt a certain guilt about the death of some of his comrades:

> My major problem at this moment is a strange kind of guilt. So many friends of mine have been arrested for activities in something that I was most instrumental in starting. A lot of them are blokes I spoke into the movement. And yet I am not with them. One does not think this way in political life of course. Casualties are expected and should be bargained for.[205]

In our interview, Barney Pityana maintained that Steve had been calling him, asking if he could intervene to get Ntsiki to come back. As it turned out she would come back only to become a widow.

Having condemned Steve's conduct, Stubbs provides a social explanation for women's attraction to him. He stood out even among the elite university students who gathered around him at conferences or on campus. He was their leader, daring, and incredibly articulate to boot. Steve was a hugely attractive man – in both the sexual and the social sense. Stubbs recalls:

---

204 Stubbs, "Martyr of Hope", 200.
205 Stubbs, "Martyr of Hope", 200.

> I remember so well the physical presence of Stephen at that time. Tall, and big in proportion, he brought to any gathering a sense of expectancy, a more than physical vitality and power ... He was even at that time, despite uncertainty about his choice of profession, to an unusual degree, whole. He was a proper man. No wonder the girls fell in love with him.[206]

The historian Noel Mostert expressed the same sentiment after meeting Steve for the first time in King William's Town in 1974:

> I found him as engaging as one could wish any human being to be. Touching thirty, tall, loose-limbed, with the graceful, unhurried movement so characteristic of the Xhosa, and which transmits so naturally to speech and tone and gesture, Steve Biko was an immensely attractive man.[207]

Mostert also made a rather prophetic observation about Steve: "It was Steve Biko who appeared to me to be the man with the key to the then immediate future."[208]

Organising in Ginsberg

On arrival in Ginsberg Steve moved into his mother's house in Leightonville, though he later moved into his own house. I remember vividly the visits by journalist Donald Woods and

---

206 Stubbs, "Martyr of Hope", 181.
207 Mostert, *Frontiers*, 1278. Mostert was not politically sensitive about using ethnic descriptions. I dissociate myself from any allusion that these are qualities that only the Xhosa possess.
208 Mostert, *Frontiers*, 1277.

his family to his house. The house had belonged to George Mangcu, and later to the very same man that Steve used to help with his studies in primary school – Major Sihunu. By this time Sihunu had become a prominent businessman and had built himself a mansion in nearby Zwelitsha. He had fallen out with Steve, claiming that Steve had instructed young boys from the township to steal petrol from his cars to burn Forbes Grant Secondary School in 1977. The boys – Lunga Lefume, Monde Mbekwa, Ace Lumnkwana, Thembile Duna (Steve's nephew) and Molepo Ramphele (Mamphela's brother) – were arrested. Steve organised legal defence for them but Mbekwa and Lumnkwana ended up spending five years on Robben Island.

In his memoir, *Martyr of Hope*, Aelred Stubbs raises the question of Steve's state of mind when he was forced to return to Ginsberg without a degree. Surely this must have been a source of great disappointment to him, to his family and his community? But the people who became part of his inner circle upon his return to Ginsberg said Steve showed no such regrets. Fikile Mlinda says that "if he felt any disappointment, he did a good job of hiding it. He just never showed it. It would be a joke among his fellow medical students who teased him for not having finished."

Steve registered with UNISA as a law student. At the time of his death he had passed Private Law 1, Constitutional Law I, Political Science II, and had scraped through with a 50% for Accounting. He repeatedly failed Praktiese Afrikaans, and was enrolled for private tutoring at the time of his death. His transcript shows that he had not been admitted for examinations in 1974 or 1975 and was absent from examinations in 1976. As a result, by 1977 he still had to pass Praktiese Afrikaans (1st year), Criminal Law in the second year and Private Law II, Mercantile Law I and Civil Procedure in his third year, as well as Private Law III, Roman Law I, Mercantile Law II and Evidence in his fourth year. This seems like a lot to accomplish when he had been absent from examinations for almost three years in a row. He was admitted to examinations on the basis of satisfactory work in 1977 – but who knows if he would have been able to attend examinations. What his poor academic performance at UNISA shows is that Steve was deluding himself in thinking that the reason for failure at medical school was his interest in law. No matter which field of study he was in, he simply would not have been able to prioritise his formal education – not with constant security police harassment and the demands on his time from the community and people from all around the world.

One of Steve's primary school classmates, Fikile Mlinda, remembers running into his old friend shortly after Steve's return from Natal. There was talk in the township that people should be careful not to associate with Steve because they might land up in jail. Initially, Steve cut a lonely figure walking to and from town carrying his attaché case. They would meet and talk "sweet nothings" and each would go on his way. And then one day Steve stopped Mlinda and said: "There is something I would like us to discuss". They agreed to meet later. Steve told Mlinda that he was not going back to university and that he wanted to start a branch of the BPC in Ginsberg. He needed help from the locals. He was upfront about the fact that this was a dangerous task that might land everyone in jail. Mlinda recalls:

I realised that this was trouble, but he kept on saying that this is for our children and their children and he pointed to the fact that people like Nelson Mandela were in prison for our sake. And so yes, there was the possibility of being jailed, but others were serving long-term sentences already for our freedom. Then somehow I put aside my fears about jail. But I was still worried that I could lose my job. But over time I put that fear aside as well.

The first BPC meeting took place at St Andrew's Church in Ginsberg – which, incidentally, was also where Steve had started school. David Russell preached from the same pulpit. Russell's presence in Ginsberg came at a crucial time for Steve. The apartheid government had sought to isolate Steve not only politically, but also spiritually and intellectually. Russell could provide him with the spiritual and intellectual stimulation he needed: "That was a fine friendship, which mitigated the hardship of the first month of banning."

In December 1973 Steve lamented David Russell's imminent departure from Ginsberg. "The evenings we spent together were very good palliatives to the mental decay which so easily sets in. Besides this he was a man full of life and always with something new to pursue. He was strong, reliable and made life purposeful."[209]

A number of people overcame their fear and turned up for the first BPC meeting at Russell's church. They were encouraged by the presence of people from all over the country. Mlinda remembers in particular the likes of Tom Manthata,

---

209 Stubbs, "Martyr of Hope", 185-189.

Mapetla Mohapi, Malusi Mpumlwana and Peter Jones. Mlinda says: ". . . and then I realised that this thing is big." Mlinda was elected on the branch executive which was to be chaired by Ray Magida. Other members of the executive were Thamsanqa Qambatha, Mzwandile Mbilini, Thami Zani and Siyolo Solombela.

The moment of reality came when Mlinda was arrested shortly afterwards. When I asked him the reason, he simply laughed: "What do you mean, for what reason? In those days you were simply arrested." Steve was particularly close to Mzwandile Mbilini, the man who, as described in Chapter 1, lived opposite my house and would always punch a clenched fist into the air whenever the police came to arrest him. According to Mlinda, "Mzwandile was truly fearless. He would say: *Siza kubadudula* – we are going to run over the whites. He was very stubborn and argumentative."

As always, there were moments of humour. To deal with some of the pressures of prison Thami Klaas for instance would refuse to wash and would smell so badly that the police would stay away from him. But this hardly helped the other prisoners, who had to put up with the smell. Thenjiwe Mthintso, who was apparently referred to as *u Ntombembi* – the ugly girl – was as tough as nails. As Mlinda puts it: "*Wayengelogwala* – she was not a coward." I can still see her in my mind's eye challenging and refusing to cooperate with the police. She later became a senior member of the ANC and South African ambassador to Cuba.

A sense of solidarity with Steve Biko began to develop. Everyone knew that he was restricted "*ngamabhulu*" – by the whites – because he was fighting for them and their rights. It was only a matter of time before almost everyone in the community joined the BPC branch. "Ginsberg was all BPC – even a dog was BPC here", Mlinda recalls. The solidarity also came from the fact that Steve was working with the community through the Black Community Programmes. Mlinda says the people of Ginsberg supported Steve because "he was within their reach. Steve had a big heart for his people."

Ginsberg was also where Steve was to engage deeply for the first time with Aelred Stubbs, who had come to South Africa from the Community of the Resurrection in England. He taught at St Peter's in Rosettenville in Johannesburg. The college was later moved and became part of the Federal Seminary in Alice, which is where Stubbs met Steve and his colleagues – Stanley Ntwasa, Lindelwe Mabandla and Barney Pityana. He would spend the next four years in the Eastern Cape before he was moved back to Rosettenville in 1972, and there began what he describes as his long-distance "ministry to the banned", as he criss-crossed the country visiting people like Ntwasa, who was restricted to Kimberley, and Steve, restricted to King William's Town. For the most part, though, Stubbs and Steve now communicated by letter. In one of his letters to Stubbs, Steve spoke about how much he enjoyed the work he was doing for the Black Community Programmes (BCP). He notes his intention of "finding expression for my skills in the context of the present job".[210] He further told Stubbs that "I am of the opinion I should raise as much support for these projects as possible from South African sources".[211]

Steve was easily touched by the suffering around him, and

---

210 Biko, *I Write What I Like*, 188.
211 Biko, *I Write What I Like*, 190.

I suspect this had something to do with his mother's own suffering. This is how he reacted to the destitution of people resettled by the government in Dimbaza, one of the poorest areas just outside King William's Town:

> . . . a peculiar situation of families who have been moved, in most instances from the Northern Cape, North Western Cape and Western Cape, who are settled in Dimbaza. And in most instances the man is not in a state to work; the woman of the family does not immediately get work when she arrives there. They are given by the government rations, and of course they are given a house. Their rations in most instances last for sometimes two weeks, three weeks, but they are supposedly monthly rations. The church has had to move in. I went there once with the minister of the Anglican Church, visited about three, four houses. I could not take it anymore. In all the houses there was no furniture except perhaps a chair or a *bank* or some old bedstead, some a stove and some pots, and there was clear evidence of utmost suffering on the part of the kids there. That is what I mean by starvation.

Steve decided to do everything in his power to change the situation. He embarked on community projects and developmental activities with great passion. These projects included the Zanempilo Health Clinic, Njwaxa Home Industries, the Ginsberg Education Fund and the Ginsberg Crèche.

Zanempilo Health Clinic

According to Steve, there were three dimensions to the work of the BCP. First, there was the community clinic (Zanempilo

Health Clinic) they had started in Zinyoka village, just outside King William's Town. The funding came from a German citizen whose inheritance was frozen in South Africa, and she was persuaded by BCP director Ben Khoapa to donate it for the construction of the clinic.[212]

There is also a family connection to the Zanempilo story which has to do with B ka T Tyamzashe – the same B ka T who had negotiated with the King William's Town municipality for Steve to be buried at the Victoria Stadium. Woods tells that B ka T was Steve's "beloved Xhosa composer. Steve often visited the old man, and particularly like his choral work."[213] B ka T used to own a big farm in Zinyoka – there is a controversy over this because some members of the family still contend that the farm belonged to his older brother James. Steve approached B ka T for help in securing land for the proposed new clinic. He had been to every village around King William's Town, but local headmen and community leaders were afraid to be associated with him. B ka T approached Reverend James Gawe, who was willing to rent church land in Zinyoka to the Black Community Programmes for a clinic. But there was a problem with access to water. On 3 December 1974 B ka T and his sons Wonga – who became a prominent medical doctor in the Transkei – and Nganga – who ran a store in Zinyoka – signed a memorandum of agreement for B ka T to erect a pipeline from a borehole on their farm to the new clinic. The Tyamzashes undertook to "supply a minimum of 60 kilolitres

---

212 Leslie Hadfield (2010). "Biko, Black Consciousness and 'the System' e-Zinyoka: Oral History and Black Consciousness in Practice in a Rural Ciskei Village", *South African Historical Journal* 62:1, 78-99.
213 Donald Woods (1978). *Biko* (New York: Penguin) 90.

of water per month to the clinic to the purchaser through the pipeline". Meters would be erected on both the farm and the clinic, and the BCP would pay 30c per kilolitre of water consumed. The agreement was for 10 years with the option of extension.

In charge of the clinic was Mamphela Ramphele. Other doctors were Sydney Moletsane, Dubs Msauli, Siyolo Solombela and Ralph Mgijima. Nurses such as Nontobeko Moletsane and professional staff such as Nohle Mohapi and Pumla Sangotsha were employed. Steve described the ambitious nature of the Zanempilo project:

> The creation of Zanempilo Community Health Clinic is part of a wider and more general health project introduced by the Black Community Programmes in the Eastern Cape. The aim of this project is to provide the Black Community with essential services of a medical nature, both curative and preventative, which are often sadly lacking in the "resettlement areas".[214]

I visited Zinyoka recently to talk with some of the residents who had worked with Steve on the project in the late 1970s and early 1980s. I found my aunt Mbeki Tyamzashe sitting with one of the women who had started as cleaner at the clinic with Steve – Nonezile Nondalana. Mrs Nondalana described Steve in the most endearing words – which I found repeatedly to be the description provided by people from the villages who had known Steve. The trouble with writing in English is that it is impossible to convey the depth of meaning

---

214 Biko, *I Write What I Like*, 190.

contained in some of the words people use to describe Steve. She described him as "*umntana ka mama*" – that was my mother's child.

She also spoke of how Steve transformed that community. People came from far and wide because this was the only primary health care centre in the region. People who did not have jobs suddenly found themselves with something to do at the clinic, whether in the construction or, as in Nonezile's case, as cooks or cleaners. According to Ramphele, Zanempilo "could be said to have been one of the earliest primary health care projects in South Africa".[215] The BCP replicated the Zanempilo model on the Durban South Coast – the clinic there was called Solempilo (which, roughly translated, means looking out for the health of the community).

But Zanempilo was more than just a clinic. It soon became the place where the nucleus of the movement would converge to discuss important matters. Steve would steal away from his home in the dark of night to be part of these crucial discussions. Mlinda says that Zanempilo was ideal for discussing BCP matters but also those matters that could not really be discussed at a BCP branch meeting because of their sensitivity. For example, Steve's trip to Cape Town was discussed by a handful of individuals in Zanempilo. Ramphele writes that Zanempilo became "a guest house for visitors from far and wide who came to see the project or consult with Steve Biko over a range of issues. These visits increased as Biko's stature increased both nationally and internationally."[216]

---

215 Ramphele, *Black Consciousness and Development*, 165.
216 Ibid.

Njwaxa Home Industries

The second dimension of BCP had to do with home industries and employment creation. BCP sponsored home industries that manufactured leather goods and cloth garments – belts, purses, handbags and upholstery. According to *Black Review* – a publication of the BCP – these industries employed 50 people in 1974. Seventy more people were employed by projects of the Border Council of Churches, a close collaborator of the BCP. Unemployed women were taught sewing skills and encouraged to produce articles for which they were paid according to their production. The BCP subsidised the purchase of materials and machines.

I also visited Njwaxa village where some of this work took place, and found there an old lady who had made beadwork for the project. Her name is Nofenisi. She refused to provide a last name and she would spit whenever I mentioned the word surname: "*Asiyibizi thina loo nto apha, siyayitshicela. NdingowakwaNdanga emaQwathini!*" – We don't mention that word here, we spit at it. I am of the Ndanga homestead of the amaQwathi clan!

So we shall stick with Nofenisi.

When I mentioned Steve Biko to her, she almost charged at me, saying: "*Umazela phi uSteve Biko wena. Wayesebenza nam ndiliqaba ndinje lomntwana. Ndandisenza iintsimbi kaloku mna. Kwakumiwe kum apha ngeentsimbi.*" – Who are you to say his name? He worked with me, uneducated child as I was. I was doing the beadwork. I was the main person here when it came to beadwork.

And she continues to say: "*Siyalamba ngoku kulo rhulumente. Ukuba wayekhona uBiko ngekutheth' ukuba siyase-*

benza ngoku. Mhla wasweleka kumhla saqala khona ke ukulamba." – We are poor now under this government. If Biko was alive we would be working for ourselves. The day he died is the day we started going hungry.

She remembers Steve saying: "*'Mam' uNofenisi, masifumane omnye umntu azokuncedisa.' Wangena njalo uNtombomhlaba lo. Sasibaninzi pha, kukho noMncedisi Xaphe, uEsther Mpupha, uNolulamile Phupha, noNtombomhlaba James.*" – Then one day he said: "Mam' Nofenisi, let us get a second person to help you with the load of work." That's how Ntombomhlaba got a job here. There were others such as Mncedisi Xaphe, Esther Mpupha, Nolulamile Mpupha and Ntombomhlaba James.

And she spits with each surname coming out of her mouth. But she is angry that no one came to tell them when Steve died: "*Kutheni sasingaxelelwa nje ukuba uXhamela uswelekile?*" – Why were we not told that Xhamela [Steve's clan name] had died, why?

As I leave she says: "*Ndiyakupha isimilo sikaBiko, mntanam*" – and this one is not only difficult to translate but seems rather profound, for she seems to be saying: "I wish on you Steve Biko's humility, my child."

This is yet another word that keeps cropping up in my discussions with Steve's friends in Ginsberg, and this is one of the things that turned so many in the community into BPC supporters. Steve had humbled himself to his community. He was doing things in the community – all the way from sending young people to university to making sure that the community had a functioning crèche.

The Ginsberg Education Fund

In 1975 Steve set up the Ginsberg Education Fund. When I was growing up there were no university graduates in Ginsberg other than my two elder brothers, Mzwandile and Mthobi, and my sister Pumeza – all of whom graduated from Fort Hare. Mthobi's story is instructive because he was directly assisted by Steve to get a university education.

Mthobi's parents died when he was very young. My mother took him in and so we grew up as brothers. Mthobi graduated from the prestigious St John's College in Umtata, and was admitted to the University of Fort Hare for a Bachelor of Computer Science degree, which was an academic novelty in our community. However, money was increasingly becoming a problem for my single-parent mother. Mthobi approached Steve to see if he could help with his university education. Steve listened to him between telephone calls he was making, and then picked up the phone: "Frank, it's Bantu here. There is a young man who is coming to see you for fees at Fort Hare, please help him."

Frank was Mapetla Mohapi.

Indeed, Mthobi went to see Mohapi, who gave him a letter to take to Reverend Stanley Mogoba at the Federal Seminary in Alice. Mogoba later became a prominent Methodist Church bishop and the president of the Pan Africanist Congress in democratic South Africa. Reverend Mogoba gave Mthobi a cheque for R125 made out to Fort Hare. "That is how I got into Fort Hare because of Steve," Mthobi recalls.

With the help of the Ginsberg Education Fund, he completed his BSc degree in Computer Science and proceeded to obtain an MBA from Ohio State University. Later he would become the first director-general of sport in Nelson Mandela's government, and a senior executive at the cellphone company Vodacom.

At Fort Hare, Mthobi became close friends with the famous boxer Mzukisi Skweyiya, who asked to be introduced to Steve. Skweyiya is one of the most interesting figures in South African history whose story remains to be told. He was for many years the national bantamweight boxing champion from Mdantsane township, the second largest township in South Africa. None of his adoring fans suspected that he was also an underground ANC activist and hardcore Marxist. Skweyiya used his boxing gym to recruit township youth into the ANC, and vehemently disagreed with the nationalism of the Black Consciousness Movement. And so one day Mthobi took Skweyiya to Steve's house. Skweyiya came out steaming with his Marxist arguments, and Steve kept deflecting him by asking about his boxing achievements. Skweyiya emerged from that meeting bowled over by Steve, calling him "a genius".

Because of the Ginsberg Education Fund, a new group of students was able to go to Fort Hare. Siphetho Mlonyeni studied law at Fort Hare and is now a practising attorney. Vuyisani Piliso and Nomalungelo Gcilishe also graduated with education degrees from Fort Hare. Sindisile Maclean graduated from Fort Hare and went on to become an ANC activist and ultimately executive mayor of Buffalo City Municipality. The brightest star of them all was Monde Keke, who was completing his legal degree when he died in a car accident in 1985.

The Ginsberg Education Fund grew with time and expanded beyond Ginsberg to the Border and the Eastern Cape region after Steve's death. It was then run by some of his closest colleagues – Malusi and Thoko Mpumlwana, Mapetla Mohapi's wife, Nohle and Charles Nqakula. (Mapetla had been killed in detention in August 1976.)

While I did not financially benefit from Zingisa, many young people in the Eastern Cape benefited from its programmes, and obtained the elusive university education. I benefited indirectly from the educational programmes that Zingisa ran in our community, mostly through winter school programmes. In 1981 Zingisa organised a winter school to which it invited some of the leading black intellectuals and professionals in the country to teach us for a few weeks. The guest teachers included Neville Alexander – who had spent ten years on Robben Island for his underground activities in the Unity Movement. Guest speakers were Lester Peteni, one of the first black architects in the country, the Reverend Sigqibo Dwane and Francis Wilson, an economist at UCT, and one of Steve's trusted white friends. The climax of the winter school was a series of debates, with the finals taking place in the presence of these distinguished figures. I emerged as the overall winner of the debate, and Charles Nqakula, who later became a cabinet minister under both presidents Thabo Mbeki and Jacob Zuma, presented me with the winning prize, a box of chocolates. To my chagrin I was obliged to share them with the rest of the contestants.

This is how Steve's wife, Ntsiki, described his impact on Ginsberg:

> His main concern was that in Ginsberg at that time there was only one graduate; that was a certain Mr Mangcu, who happens to be the brother to Dr Mangcu [the author of this

book]. So he was the only graduate here, and that was worrying Steve a lot, so he raised money and established the Ginsberg Educational Trust Fund. From that Trust, I am glad to say, most of the people who got bursaries are well-off now in that they are well-educated. He produced mayors and some of them are working in government.[217]

Reviving the Ginsberg Crèche

Steve was just as concerned with early childhood education. He worked with community members such as Chris Soka and long-serving teacher Nozipho Bisholo to revive the local crèche. Here is how he described his own work with the crèche:

> Where I stay in King William's Town we revived a community crèche, which was serving a basic need for the community in that a number of mothers could not go to work because they had to look after their babies and toddlers. Or if they go to work it implies that kids who are supposed to be school-going must stay behind looking after the toddlers. It became clear to us that there was a strong community need to provide a crèche to that community. And we revived a crèche – which I had attended, actually, when I was young – but it had gone defunct... we call it the Ginsberg Crèche.[218]

Even more important was the rationale behind Steve's community work:

---

217 Interview with Kyle Coston, August 2008.
218 Biko in Arnold, *The Testimony of Steve Biko*, 94.

> We believe that black people, as they rub shoulders with the particular project, as they benefit from that project, with their perception of it, they begin to ask themselves questions, and we surely believe that they are going to give themselves answers, and they understand . . . this kind of lesson has been a lesson for me: I must have hope. In most of the projects we tend to pass over the maintenance to the community.[219]

The head of the BCP in the Transkei, Reverend Mcebisi Xundu, described the rationale behind their community work in similar terms when I interviewed him in Port Elizabeth. He argued that the projects gave people a sense of ownership, which in turn meant that they would be more willing to resist the government's encroachment on these projects. The size of the assets involved did not matter as much as the deep sense of injustice when they were confiscated. This explains the sense of injustice that the people of Ginsberg felt as they saw Steve being harassed by the police on a daily basis. This was not just a passive sense of injustice. People actively protected Steve.

Ginsberg was a very rough township and it did not lack in young men willing to fight with the police. The group of youths known as the Cubans were on hand to protect Steve at every turn, including when the police came to harass him at Skweyi's shebeen.

Steve's other favourite shebeen was Getty's Place in the Tsolo section of Ginsberg township. The police would get wind that Steve was out drinking and would rush to Getty's place. Upon arriving they would meet a wall of resistance from the Cubans

---

219 Arnold, *The Testimony of Steve Biko*, 94.

who would simply refuse them entry until Steve had disappeared through the back door and gone back to his home. One of the young people who worked with Steve, Lunga Lefume, describes his experience:

> I remember one day when Bra Steve was at a local shebeen, Sis' Getty's place, and the police had surrounded the place and he had to escape. A pseudo wedding was organised on the spot between Ponki Qilo and Kholeka Mbilini. This was done to confuse the police so as to allow Bra Steve to escape and enter a nearby house through the window. But the owner of the house knew Steve's mother. [220]

As it happens, this was one of the poorest homes in Ginsberg – a one-room house where the residents were selling traditional brew. Steve jumped in through the window, fell on the bed and fell asleep. The elders just let him sleep until the following day. But the fact that he had not slept at home would present a problem with his wife. Embarrassed, Steve got up early and walked over to the Mbilini shebeen where he got a few drinks before setting off home – he had the perfect excuse: he had been up all night drinking with friends. This is an aspect of Steve that deserves special mention – that despite all the hardship and the harassment he had told himself he would not allow himself to be isolated from the community, whether this was through community work or through socialising with his friends.

Steve's best friend at this point was Sonwabo Yengo, who also lived on Zaula Street with his wife Beth. This is where all

---

220 Interview with Lunga Lefume.

the fun happened. Beth was a nurse at Frere Hospital, and she would invite her nursing colleagues over to Ginsberg for parties with Steve. Steve was besotted with women and had a special word for them – he called them *Toto* – a colloquial word for baby or young one in isiXhosa. Sonwabo Yengo remembers that one day Steve was harassing a woman, and she kept running to him to ask him to stop Steve. But Steve kept asking: "*Yiz' apha man, Toto*" – Come here, baby, please.

Beth Yengo agreed with Nonezile and Nofenisi about Steve's humility: "*Wayenentliziyo entle uBantu, wayezithobile, kodwa wayethuka yho xa sishusha pha kum.*" – Bantu had a good heart and he was very humble. But Sonwabo quickly adds: "He could be quite foul-mouthed too when we were drinking in my house."

Steve was certainly no saint. At the Yengos' house they would have *gumbas* – parties – until the morning, with Steve often singing at the top of his voice. He loved Donny Hathaway's song "To Be Young, Gifted and Black". And then in isiXhosa he would sing along with Hathaway's "Be Real Black For Me" – "*Ndimnyamele mna!*"

Sonwabo Yengo recalls that they would sometimes turn the radio off and sing church songs and freedom songs and songs from playwright Gibson Kente. Steve loved the Anglican Church's *IMvana kaThixo* in particular. His favourite freedom song had the lyrics: *Nqo, sithi nqo. Siziinkokheli thina. Ezalapha, zalapha eAfrika. Phakamani! Phakamani, zinkokheli, siqonde phambili* – We are the leaders of Africa. Rise up, leaders, and let us move forward.

After hours of singing, they might change venues and go to Zanempilo. Sonwabo recalls:

> There would be ten of us in that car – Steve's green Passat CD 655 – and we would be singing and singing. One day we ran into a roadblock and Mamphela kept on complaining: "*Ndicaphukele le nto besilayita.*" – I hate the fact they shine those torches in our faces.

For some reason that Yengo does not recall, he and Steve called each other Tshawe – even though that is not their clan name. (The Tshawe are the ruling clan among the Xhosa.) Yengo remembers well the last time he ever saw Steve. The latter was coming out of Dr Marais's quarters in King William's Town. He had a swollen eye and a limp. "*Heyi, ayandibetha la ma-Bhulu, Tshawe. Kodw' andizi kubayeka. Ndiyalwa nam. Aza kundibulala ngale ndlela*" – These whites are really beating me now, Tshawe. But I am not going to let them just do that to me. I am fighting back. But they are going to kill me at the rate they are going.

And then Yengo reminisces rather wistfully: "Steve got us all into politics here in Ginsberg. He got everyone into politics. He would say people must read and he would smuggle pamphlets and publications such as *Staffrider* and young boys like Sithethi Keke, Fumbathile Mbilini and Mabrukhwe Marai would be giving people these documents, calling themselves Cubans."

Beth Yengo remembers her mother's reaction to the news of Steve's death: "It was a blow. My mother cried and cried and cried. Ginsberg was devastated." But Beth also recalls the humorous side of Steve: "One day he found my sister Mido's daughter in our house and said I must buy her both a black and a white doll. And then the black and the white doll must fight and the black doll must beat up the white doll."[221]

---

221 Interview with Sonwabo and Beth Yengo.

Drawing On the Lived Experience of His People

Writings about Steve Biko tend to over-theorise why he did what he did. Marxists such as Baruch Hirson argue that Black Consciousness was limited by what he regards as "the petty bourgeois outlook" of a student organisation.[222] This neglects the sacrifice and suffering these students went through – including the biggest sacrifice, death.

Sam Nolutshungu gives a more accurate description of the Black Consciousness movement as a revolutionary movement, with its projects an exercise in "class suicide". Nolutshungu argues that despite their student and middle-class status, it was not the leaders' objective class position, but rather their political aims that mattered. Were they advancing the interest of a black middle class or those of the working people.[223]

Saleem Badat places Black Consciousness within the lived experience of black people. He writes that the Black Consciousness experience:

> . . . was sharpened by the insights offered by Fanon, Nkrumah, Nyerere and various black American Black Power activists. While these were formative influences, on balance the lived experiences were pivotal in the construction and elaboration of an alternative ideology and strategy of liberation.

His perceptive analysis notwithstanding, Badat still views the movement's community development work as "voluntaris-

---

[222] Cited in Saleem Badat, (2009). *Black Man, You Are On Your Own* (Johannesburg: STE); see also Baruch Hirson (1979). *Year of Fire, Year of Ash: The Soweto Revolt: Roots of a Revolution?* (London: Zed Press).
[223] Badat, *Black Man, You Are On Your Own*, 162.

tic" (i.e. unplanned or not properly thought through) because they underestimated not only the might of the state, but also what it would take to implement their community development projects:

> First, project after project was adopted willy-nilly without any attempt to prioritise in terms of political objectives, strategy and resources. Second, SASO was completely unrealistic about its ability to run some of its projects. Third, it also seriously underestimated what the projects would entail in practice.

Consequently, Badat rejects the idea that the community projects were vehicles for long-term organisation as far-fetched. However, the tendency to over-theorise the projects fails to appreciate the subjective response to suffering that led someone like Steve to say "I could not take it anymore" when he saw the suffering in Dimbaza. The critical difference is that even if that was a voluntaristic response this impelled him to action, and to draw on the resources of the community instead of pretending that SASO or the BCP would be solving the people's problems after a rational planning process.

Also, while Badat argues that Steve was working from "lived experience", it is important to specify what lived experience he was talking about. The concept of self-reliant development which Steve espoused has a long history among African people, and in Steve's case in the history of the Eastern Cape. It goes back to the contrasting experiences of early African intellectuals such as John Tengo Jabavu and WB Rubusana.

While Jabavu relied on white financiers for his initiatives – which were no less historically important for that – Rubusana used the influence he had among the black intellectual and political elite. He had been a teacher and subsequently the head of the Peelton Missionary School, from where he became a member of the Native Educational Association and a founder of the Native Vigilance Association. He is credited with establishing more than ten schools in East London. SJ Ngqongqo credits Rubusana with an important shift in black politics: "A founder member of the Native Vigilance Association, Rubusana was part of the very first generation of African leaders that formed political organisations to represent Africans. The shift to organised politics moved political agitation away from the personal."

Ngqongqo observes that:

> ... hitherto Africans in the Eastern Cape had lacked political organisations and relied on the influential personality of John Tengo Jabavu, the towering editor of *Imvo Zabantsundu*, to speak on their behalf.

Even though his community-organising efforts could not match the power of Jabavu and his white financiers, Ngqongqo argues that:

> Rubusana's legacy lives not only in memory but in the schools and churches he set up in the area of East London. Almost all of these schools and churches were demolished during the apartheid programme of forced removals in the 1960s and 1970s, when thousands of African inhabitants from East London were uprooted to Mdantsane, a township in the Ciskei homeland, thirty miles away.[224]

---

224 SJ Ngqongqo (1996). "Mpilo Walter Benjamin Rubusana, 1858-1910: The Making of the New Elite in the Eastern Cape", Master of Arts thesis, University of Fort Hare, Alice.

From this perspective Rubusana was the progenitor of a tradition of community organising that characterised teachers in particular – through organisations such as the Teachers League of South Africa, the Cape African Teachers Association, the Transvaal Teachers Association and many others.

This tradition was extended into the emergent townships in the 20th century. Belinda Bozzoli explains the Black Consciousness Movement's efficacy in terms of its ability to draw from what she calls "syncretic movements" in the townships, with syncretism meaning people's ability to create hybrid identities out of their interactions with the social and cultural world:

> In most townships, both language and cultural forms were an expression of a syncretic [hybrid] rather than an ethnic, racial or class identity. Mixed street languages emerged; township music, style, churchgoing, dance, marriage patterns and the arts were all created from elements drawn from a variety of cultural sources. In spite of complaints by some that "cultural imperialism" had introduced "foreign customs" (in the form of say youth clubs, or ballroom dancing), nothing entered townships without being given local meaning.[225]

The Ginsberg of Steve's childhood was not only characterised by social activism; it was also culturally diverse with Coloureds and Africans living together, making it possible for Steve to imagine an expansive Black identity that included Coloureds and Indians.

---

225 Belinda Bozzoli, "The Difference of Social Capital and the Mobilizing and Demobilizing Powers of Nationalism: The South African Case", unpublished manuscript.

Bozzoli argues that in societies of racial or colonial domination, the rulers use space as a means of controlling their subjects. They then invest the educated elite with the authority to be the mediators with the communities. Space thus becomes the physical terrain for contestations of power between the dominant and the dominated groups.

Bozzoli also cautions against a dualistic conception of the relationship between the dominant and the dominated: As argued in Chapter 2, in real life things do not work out as neatly, as Fanon consistently pointed out.[226] It is out of this "zone of occult instability" of the struggle that new identities are formed. Or as Martin Bernal put it at a lecture on the diversity of early Egyptian society, which provided the foundations of Western civilisation: "I am the enemy of purity." [227]

Sometimes the dominated groups move into spaces where there is less control by the dominant group. Thus space becomes a multidimensional terrain of struggle. Townships developed as spaces with great similarity to the sub-worlds of the poor in many other Third World settings where states are incompletely formed, and strata of urban society remain "uncaptured, and authority is unstable". These spaces became the basis for the creation of new cultural meanings by township residents, and also oppositional spaces to the state. Memory is yet another crucial element in this process of "culture making" – as people draw on previous experiences in charting out solutions for how to cope and survive in an adverse world.[228]

---

226 Fanon, *Black Skin, White Masks*, and *The Wretched of the Earth*.
227 Martin Bernal, Platform for Public Deliberation, Wits University, 2006.
228 Harry Boyte, "Constructive Politics as Public Work: Organizing the Literature", in *Political Theory*, vol. 39. no. 5. (2011), 630-660.

Living in the township – particularly the older ones [like Ginsberg] – meant becoming (or seeking to become) an insider, one who knew the terrain, who could attach memories to places, whose neighbours had been schoolmates, or fellow church-goers, or football teammates; whose aunts and uncles had lived a block or two away; whose grandparents, in some cases, had been buried in the local cemetery, whose mother ran the local shebeen in a tin shack, or whose parents had suffered the indignity of having their homes demolished, their liquor stock confiscated or their residence permits demanded at 3 a.m. by the overzealous policeman who may even have lived next door.[229]

These are the memories and networks upon which Steve drew not only in building the Black Consciousness Movement, but also in the cover and support given voluntarily by networks of people who protected him from security police harassment – not only because he had done so much for the community, but also because he was "*umntana ka MamCethe*" – MamCethe's child. MamCethe's fellow church-goer, Mrs Bhisholo, told me that Steve's political activities were always a great worry to his mother but the other women in the church were the first to provide her with support – reassuring her about the leadership role her son had been chosen by God to perform, very much like Jesus had been sent to this earth to change the world. Steve described Ginsberg as a closely knit community where politics were frequently discussed by residents as part of their everyday existence.

---

229 Bozzoli, "The Difference of Social Capital", 6.

In one of his court appearances, Steve was asked by defence lawyer David Soggot to explain life in his hometown of Ginsberg:

> SOGGOT: And you yourself have lived for example in Ginsberg Location in King William's Town, is that right?
> BIKO: Yes, I have.
> SOGGOT: And is that a rather poor rural location?
> BIKO: Yes, it is a small township of about a thousand houses, very poor.
> SOGGOT: So you are familiar with life there?
> BIKO: That is correct.
> SOGGOT: Now the echoing of this sentiment [of condemnation of white people], is that common there?
> BIKO: Oh yes, very common.
> SOGGOT: And you people speak of psychological and physical oppression, is there reference to oppression at all in any shape or form by people in their ordinary thinking?
> BIKO: Yes, often.

In South Africa's townships culture-making was led by the intelligentsia all the way from Soga to Rubusana to Biko: the teachers, priests, writers, musicians, painters etc. While government-enforced segregation enabled political control of townships, it disabled social and cultural interference or any form of complete hegemony. Those were the spaces and networks that Steve Biko and his colleagues built upon in creating a new political and cultural movement, despite the harsh political system that sought to eviscerate life itself in the townships through arrests, bannings and killings. Thus, according to Bozzoli,

… a striking response to the resulting vacuum was the rise of the Black Consciousness Movement in the 1970's, one of whose main platforms was the creation of a revitalized urban culture and a series of systems of community activism and self-improvement. While it was unsurprising that the imposition of "blackness" led to its discovery from below, the BCM, unlike many other ethnic fundamentalisms, and in sharp contrast to the tone of black consciousness-influenced discussions today, did not confine itself to matters of identity, but addressed civil society as well.

The civil society projects of the movement "drew from the syncretic [hybrid] and memory-saturated culture of African communities and created a visionary emancipatory ideology around which they could be mobilised and organised, while paying specific and quite detailed attention to the inner working of the projects themselves".[230]

Curiously, Saleem Badat argues that "the SASO generation had not witnessed the harsh repression of the early 1960s and the suppression of the ANC and the PAC". But to which extent individual Black Consciousness leaders were exposed to repression is an empirical question. As discussed earlier, Steve was traumatised by what the apartheid system did to his brother Khaya, and Barney Pityana came from a strong ANC background in Port Elizabeth; Aubrey Mokoape and Keith Mokoape had been in the PAC. This argument underestimates the courage of the conscious decision to take an active part in the struggle, knowing full well what had happened to earlier genera-

---

230 Bozzoli, "*The Difference of Social Capital*", 8.

tions. Black Consciousness leaders may not have been formally well organised, but they changed the consciousness of a generation in organising them through these community projects.

Steve Biko's Theory of Action

While most scholars tend to reduce Biko to Fanon, there are striking parallels between the lives of Steve Biko and the Guinea-Bissau revolutionary Amilcar Cabral, and similarly in their theory of action. They shared a belief that it was the role of the revolutionary *petite bourgeoisie* to lead the struggle. But for the *petite bourgeoisie* to carry out its historical mandate, it had to commit what Cabral called "class suicide". To begin with, both Steve and Cabral would have rejected a class-based analysis as appropriate for their societies. This is how Cabral refuted the calls for a class-based approach:

> Does history begin only from the moment of class and, consequently, of class struggle? To reply in the affirmative would be to place outside history the whole period of life of human groups from the discovery of hunting, and later sedentary and nomadic agriculture, to cattle raising and to the private appropriation of land. It would also be to consider – and this we refuse to accept – that various human groups in Africa, Asia and Latin America were living without history or outside history at the moment they were subjected to the yoke of imperialism. [231]

For Cabral it was the colonial state – not class – that was the primary mover of society. Steve would have defined this in

---

231 Amilcar Cabral (1979). *Unity and Struggle: Speeches and Writings*, (New York: Monthly Review Press) 124-125.

South Africa as white racism. Arrayed against the colonial state, Cabral saw a broad anti-colonial alliance, the equivalent of Biko's antithesis. And indeed, like Steve, Cabral was quite vague about the exact nature of the society or the synthesis that came out of the struggle. There could be no blueprint for the future of society; the results would result from the action of the progressive forces. It was sufficient that the outcomes would be generally socialistic in direction but not founded on any model. This was because "national liberation and social revolution are not exportable; they are, and increasingly so, the outcome of local and national elaboration".[232]

Cabral further believed that the *petite bourgeoisie* were best placed to lead the revolution because of the central contradiction of colonialism: the promise of entry into European modernity and the denial of its rights and privileges. Their marginal existence is what increasingly turned the *petite bourgeoisie* into revolutionary nationalists. There were of course, no guarantees that the *petite bourgeoisie* would play this role. The revolutionary consciousness had to be gained through action – by identifying with the political experiences of their people. This was the only way that the *petite bourgeoisie* would be persuaded to act against its own class interests, and commit class suicide.

The projects of the Black Community Programmes were for Steve one way of ensuring a real cross-class alliance between black students and their communities. Steve shared with Cabral the idea of politics as action, and the need to develop a theory of action, not as a speculative exercise but as a response to reality, to what Badat calls "lived experience". As Badat himself argues, "for Biko there had to be some agitation . . . action

---

[232] Patrick Chabal (2003). *Revolutionary Leadership and People's War*, (Trenton, New Jersey: Africa World Press), 181.

rather than sophisticated theory and detailed social analysis . . . was more urgent and important".[233] Or as Steve put it, "it doesn't matter if the action does not take a fully directed form immediately, or a fully supported form".[234]

Patrick Chabal's summation of Cabral's life could just as easily be applied to Steve Biko. For Chabal, the essential features of Cabral's approach were "creativity and independence of thought; a careful link of ideas to reality; and an internal coherence and consistency over time". Chabal then concludes with a flourish:

> What emerges then is the picture of a leader who was reluctant to engage in theoretic speculation, who preferred political analysis to ideology, who valued independence of thought more than adherence to an accepted political doctrine and who was determined to create an original body of ideas which would both reflect and inspire the development of the revolution in Guinea. [235]

Nigel Gibson has described Steve Biko in similar terms as "the greatest liberation theorist in the history of South Africa". His death on 12 September 1977 was not only a body blow to him but also to our body politic as a whole. In Chapters 9 and 10 I deal with Steve's elusive quest for unity among the liberation movements, the manner of his death, and its implications for our democracy today.

---

233 Badat, *Black Man, You Are On Your Own*, 100.
234 Gerhart, *Black Power in South Africa*, 288-9.
235 Chabal, *Amilcar Cabral*, 187.

9
How Steve was Killed

"Who did it? How did it happen? What is the bastard's name? What does he look like? Come on Steve! Answer Stevo! Heh-Stivana? He mnta ka Biko – Biko's child, answer me!"
DONALD WOODS on hearing of Steve's death[236]

While Steve believed that the Black People's Convention could be the instrument for black solidarity in the same way that the National Party represented the majority of whites, he also articulated a desire for unity among the various black liberation movements. "I would like to see groups such as the ANC, PAC and Black Consciousness deciding to form one liberation group. It is only, I think, when black people are so dedicated and so united in their cause that we can effect the greatest results,"[237] he wrote. According to Steve's contemporary Malusi Mpumlwana:

> It is here that you begin the process of looking out to negotiate with other organisations. It is here that you begin to see the need of having some kind of central figure. That's why we decided to make Steve the honorary president of the BPC. Before that he had no formal authority, it was all about charisma and the influence he had as an individual.

---

236 Woods, *Biko*, 228.
237 Biko, *I Write What I Like*, 169.

This forms the backdrop to Steve's decision to begin a process of reaching out to the ANC, the PAC and the Unity Movement. He was talking with the ANC through Griffiths Mxenge, who had studied at Ginsberg's Forbes Grant Secondary School. There Mxenge had also met his future wife, Victoria. Mxenge was very fond of Steve, their relationship going back to the formative years of the Black Consciousness Movement in Durban. He also acted as defence counsel for movement activists. Both Mxenge and the militant ANC stalwart Harry Gwala were attracted to the militancy of the BCM and saw it as a counterweight to the reactionary politics of homeland leader Mangosuthu Buthelezi. Biko's scathing criticism of the homeland system, "Let's Talk About the Bantustans," was in part directed at Buthelezi. He described the Bantustans as "the greatest single fraud ever invented by white politicians". The system, Steve observed, was designed to:

> ... create a false sense of hope among the black people so that any attempt by blacks to collectively enunciate their aspirations should be dampened ... to boost up as much as possible the intertribal competition and hostility that is bound to come up so that the collective strength and resistance of the black people can be fragmented.

Steve was disappointed in Buthelezi. Although he does not mention Buthelezi by name, one can sense that is the homeland leader he is referring to: "We have some men in these Bantustans who would make extremely fine leaders if they had not decided to throw in their lot with their oppressors." And then, more pointedly, he writes: "For me as a black person it is extremely painful to see a man who could easily have been my leader being so misused by the cruel and exploitative white world." For Steve the Bantustans were nothing more than toy telephones:

> Matanzima and Buthelezi can shout their lungs out through the phony telephone. No one is listening in Pretoria because the telephone is a toy. The real lines between Pretoria and Zululand, between Pretoria and Transkei are very busy day and night with [commissioners] Torlage and Abrahams telling their system every step Matanzima and Buthelezi are likely to take three months hence and how best the system should respond to such stances.[238]

While Steve wanted unity above all, this was not a viable proposition with Buthelezi, given the latter's decision to participate in the homeland system. One of the co-founders of the Black Consciousness Movement, Harry Nengwekhulu, had left the country after his banning in 1973. He was tasked with the job of securing a meeting between Steve and ANC leader Oliver Tambo. The question was how to spring Steve out of the country to meet Tambo. One possibility was to organise an invitation for Steve from a European country, most likely the Netherlands. The other alternative was to drive him to meet Tambo in Botswana. The latter option was rejected as being too dangerous. Steve was also worried that the fractious nature of the relationship among Black Consciousness leaders in exile might pose a security risk. Movement activists had moved in differ-

---

238 Biko, *I Write What I Like*, 92-93.

ent directions when they reached exile. Some joined the ANC, others the PAC and others formed the Black Consciousness Movement of Azania (BCMA) under the leadership of Mosibudi Mangena, who had been national organiser of the Black People's Convention in 1972.[239] The BCMA also had a military wing – the Azanian National Liberation Army (AZANLA).

Steve was also having clandestine discussions with the PAC, mainly through its revered leader Robert Sobukwe. The last time Steve had seen "Prof" – as Sobukwe was called because of his work as a lecturer at Wits before his incarceration – was when Steve had visited him in Kimberley with Stanley Ntwasa and others as students. It was arranged for Sobukwe to meet Steve in King William's Town on his way from his mother's funeral in the Transkei.

Moki Cekisani, the fiery activist from Port Elizabeth, remembers getting wind of the upcoming meeting, and deciding to gate-crash. Cekisani recalls a clearly annoyed Steve asking him what he was doing there: "It's my country you people are talking about," Cekisani replied. Cekisani would later join the PAC. He was one of the people who were severely injured through beatings and electrocution by the security police, leading to a serious loss of hearing in his case.

Further discussions with Sobukwe were conducted through Mpumlwana and Mapetla Mohapi. Mpumlwana recalls the meetings with Sobukwe:

---

239 Mangena would later become deputy minister of education and minister of science and technology in President Thabo Mbeki's cabinet.

> We used to meet with him at the graveyard in Galeshewe [outside Kimberley]. There was an Indian who was a friend of his – I can't remember his name, we used to go and get a van from him. One day the van wouldn't start and we were there at the cemetery. Sobukwe could not drive and therefore he had to push. It felt very awkward to have him push a van.

The problem, of course, was that Sobukwe was isolated from the mainstream of the PAC leadership because of his banishment. The PAC's leadership now revolved around the more militant Zephania Mothopeng. Mothopeng and his colleagues were less compromising in their attitude to the ANC. The unity discussions suffered a setback when the entire leadership of the PAC was arrested in 1975. Mpumlwana recalls how the arrests, and the subsequent June 16 uprisings, upset the process of the unity talks:

> This is December 1975. Now we've got these position papers, and documents we had prepared to present as a common platform to these organisations. We've had enough preliminary discussions, and then this happens. Mapetla [Mohapi] got arrested and killed and we all stayed in detention.

Mohapi's death in detention was a devastating blow to Steve. He had been entirely dependent on Mohapi, and it seemed a part of him had literally been severed from him – these are some of the stresses that led to his excessive drinking in Ginsberg in the years before his death.

Steve was also pursuing another track – unity talks with the Unity Movement in Cape Town. He had met activist (and later judge) Fikile Bam when the latter visited him at his home in Ginsberg in 1974. Bam (aka "Bra Fiks") had just come from a ten-year spell on Robben Island and was restricted to the Transkei. He requested Francis Wilson, his former classmate at the University of Cape Town and now a friend of Steve's, to spring him out of the Transkei. Wilson recalls that they took a back road to avoid police surveillance and spent a night at his family home in the Hogsback mountains, just outside Alice, before proceeding to Ginsberg the following day.

At the meeting with Bam, Steve had expressed his desire to meet the leading figure of the Unity Movement, Neville Alexander, from Cape Town. Alexander had also come back from serving a ten-year prison sentence on Robben Island. He started a study group at his home with about 15 or so like-minded comrades from both the Unity Movement and the BCM in Cape Town. Alexander was concerned that the Unity Movement had failed to make connections with the black community, and asked his comrade Nicki Westcott, who had strong relations with BC people in Cape Town, to facilitate connections. Alexander felt that this could be forged through joint action. One of the collaborative projects planned by the two movements was a nationwide protest against the granting of independence to the Transkei on 26 October 1976. ANC people, such as Winnie Mandela and Joe Gqabi, were also contacted, and joint committees of the BCM, the Unity Movement and the ANC were set up. Alexander recalls:

> We all realised that this would be the beginning of public mass politics. What none of us foresaw, however, was 16 June 1976. We immediately set up committees to facilitate the

protests in the Western Cape. We produced pamphlets and other materials, including materials on how to make weapons. And then 1976 came up and everyone got caught up with that.

There was yet another reason for Steve's risky trip – in violation of his banning order – to Cape Town. A rebellion was brewing in the Western Cape branch of the Black Consciousness Movement. This had to do with the position papers that the movement had developed as the basis for the discussions with the ANC and PAC. The Western Cape branch felt that the proposed positions were not radical enough. This was the most Marxist-oriented branch of the movement, and they rejected anything short of a socialist/communist vision for the country. They were strongly opposed to the concept of black communalism proposed in the position papers as the basis for future economic policy.

The Cape Town "rebellion" was led by Johnny Issel, who questioned what he saw as a turn towards economic conservatism. Some in the group also questioned Steve's earlier decision to meet with American Senator Dick Clark in December 1976. Clark chaired the powerful Senate Subcommittee on African Affairs and was well placed to influence the direction of events in South Africa and Africa. In Lesotho to attend a meeting of the African Institute, Clark thought it important to come to South Africa to consult with Steve Biko – an "elder statesman" of the movement, although only in his twenties. At this point Steve was regularly consulted by representatives of countries from far and wide. The militants stood their ground, arguing that they had always refused to meet members of the

American government, and had even rejected a request for a meeting from US Ambassador to the United Nations Andrew Young.

When the request for a meeting with Clark came, Steve had just been released from 101 days in prison. He consulted his comrades, who were still in jail in King William's Town, and arranged for them to see the memorandum he would present to Clark. The memorandum was smuggled in and out through a prison warder who lived in Ginsberg.

The memorandum was indeed presented to Clark and published in *I Write What I Like*. In it Steve was quite scathing in his criticism of the United States, describing its role as "shameful in the history of our country". The memorandum pointed to America's collusion in the oppression of black people through its bilateral trade and cultural exchanges with South Africa: "Otherwise so far [America's] role has been that of bolstering the minority regime all at the expense of the black man." The memorandum called for America to boycott trading links with South Africa: "Whilst it is illegal for us to call for trade boycotts, arms embargo, withdrawal of investment etc., America herself is quite free to decide what price South Africa must pay for maintaining obnoxious policies."

He was critical of the US decision to meet homeland leaders instead of the authentic leaders. He also called for "the release of political prisoners and banned people such as Nelson Mandela, Robert Sobukwe, Steve Biko, Govan Mbeki, Barney Pityana and the integration of these people in the political process that shall shape things to come". Steve concluded with the following prophetic words:

> Mr Carter will therefore no doubt be aware that he takes up power at a time when American influence in Africa has become of particular significance. If he stands with those whose righteousness may not be doubted – he shall have used the tremendous influence that America has legitimately and usefully. If, on the other hand, he assists those who are trying to keep the clock still, then America will have irreparably tarnished her name in the eyes of black people in this country.[240]

According to Danile Landingwe even Steve's use of the term "egalitarian" was viewed as too liberal by the Marxists in Cape Town. The fact that he had consulted with his comrades before the meeting did not satisfy the Cape Town lot. Behind all of this was also a feeling among some in Cape Town that the King William's Town group had centralised the movement around its resources. They thought that "the guys in King" who were working for the BCP were better paid because of their proximity to the movement's funding.

Steve felt he could not address these problems without physically meeting with the Cape Town group – even if this meant violating his banning order and risking jail.

On the evening of 16 August 1977 Steve met with colleagues at Zanempilo Clinic to brief them about the meeting. He agreed to leave his car with one of the drivers to create the impression that he was around town, and took a car that belonged to BCP executive member Rams Ramokgopa, who was visiting Steve to brief him about the activities of the BCP in Johannesburg.

---

240 Biko, *I Write What I Like*, 160.

Around midnight Steve and Peter Cyril Jones (aka "PC") packed their bags in the car and set out on the long drive to Cape Town. Peter was an activist from King William's Town and a friend of Steve's. They arrived in the Cape at around 10 am on August 17. They drove straight to Jones' home in Strand, a town outside Cape Town. Steve took a nap, and Jones went out to see the people they would meet. Those were the days before cellular telephones or e-mail. Communication was mainly by public phones and sometimes it would have to be coded. This was part of the problem with this trip – they could not forewarn everyone that they were coming because of the security risk. And so it was often a matter of just showing up at the door.

Jones immediately went to see Ronnie Crotz, and the two then went to fetch Johnny Issel. Issel was not home, and so they left a message with his wife that Steve was around. Jones dropped Crotz back at his home and proceeded to fetch Steve for their meeting with Alexander. They could always catch up with the Black Consciousness guys later. The priority was Neville Alexander. They first had to link up with Fikile Bam so he could connect them to Alexander.

"Fiks" Bam was staying in a mansion in the posh suburb of Crawford. The house belonged to Ishmail Mahomed, a mathematics professor at UCT. Mahomed was away at the time but he had asked one of Alexander's friends, Armien Abrams, to look after his house. Abrams was also the manager of a community-based factory that had been set up by the Black Community Programmes in Cape Town, which fell under Peter Jones's portfolio within the movement. Jones and Abrams were thus always in touch and Abrams would be the perfect conduit for communicating to Alexander that they were driving down to see him.

There is some confusion about whether Jones had actually communicated to Abrams that he was coming to Cape Town with Steve. While Jones insists that he did, Abrams and Alexander say he never did. In any event, on their way to the professor's house Jones decided to stop and make a phone call from a public telephone booth to the professor's house. "Fiks, it's PC, we're coming to see you," Jones told Bam.

Bam recalls that he could not recognise the two when they walked in because they were heavily disguised. Steve wore a heavy overcoat and a balaclava that partially covered his face. "I am in Cape Town to see a couple of people but Neville [Alexander] is my first prize," Steve said. Jones in the meanwhile drove over to Alexander's house in Grassy Park – "to check if the coast was clear" – before he brought Steve over. To Jones' surprise Alexander said he would not see Steve. "But Neville, the man drove eleven hours outside of his restriction area, and you can't see him for a few minutes?"

Alexander was unyielding. Jones returned shortly afterwards to the professor's mansion with the news. This infuriated Bam. He called Alexander and said he could not really speak on the phone but was coming over to see him. Without waiting for an answer Bam dropped the phone and asked Steve to come along. Off they went to Alexander's home in Grassy Park in Bam's yellow Volkswagen Beetle. They drove around to the back of the house, and Bam jumped out to knock at the door, leaving Steve behind in the car. Thirty minutes went by without Bam emerging from the house. Steve would later tell Jones that he would have walked back to the professor's mansion if he knew his way around Cape Town. He was stuck and trapped in the car while these men argued inside, and the clock was ticking. Alexander recalls the altercation with Bam:

> Fiks tried every trick in the book to convince me to meet with Steve. But I would not budge. In order to put pressure on me he said Steve was sitting in the car in the backyard. But I was instructed by my guys not to meet Steve because of problems within the Black Consciousness Movement in Cape Town. I did not want to be caught in the crossfire. [241]

Seeing that it was going nowhere, Bam stormed out and they left for Crawford. Steve was deeply disappointed. He had looked up to Alexander as a fearless revolutionary intellectual. As soon as they got back to the professor's house, Steve insisted that they should "immediately get back to base". They left for King William's Town in the early evening of August 17. It was largely quiet in the car as they set out.

They had a torturous twelve-hour journey ahead of them, and they did not have sufficient rest coming down to Cape Town. And although they had taken measures to keep the King William's Town police from being suspicious, every hour away increased the chances of the security branch finding Steve missing. There could be no resting on the way. Steve had a small radio on his lap, and spent the better part of the return journey just listening to the radio. He was heartbroken, and Jones was bitterly angry. Bam only had damning words for Alexander: "The guy was a coward, man." Alexander saw it differently:

---

241 Interview with Alexander.

It was a clash of political cultures. We were a disciplined underground movement. On their side they were carried away by their own spontaneity. They thought if they just showed up I would see them. But my house was literally besieged by the cops for weeks on end. We were sent to prison because of such little mistakes.

Ntsiki Biko described her husband's attitude towards the restrictions that were placed on him:

> Well, that didn't affect him. As far as he was concerned he was not banned. I mean, he was going to do whatever he wanted to do; of course the police surveillance was preventing him from doing most of the things he would have loved to do. For example, he was not allowed to go to church where there's a group of people or go to schools, because they were saying he was going to teach students politics. He was not allowed to have more than two people at a time, but the advantage about us being here at home was that we were living here with the rest of the family, so nobody would say those visitors were coming to him, per se. So he just took a banning order as if it's nothing existing.[242]

Neville Alexander speaks of the heavy heart this incident has left him with over the years: "It was one of the most tragic moments of my life. There was a contradiction between commitment to organisational discipline and my own wish to meet a person I really should have spoken to that evening."[243]

---

242 Ntsiki Biko, Interview with Colston, 2008.
243 Interview with Alexander.

In the early hours of August 18 and about an hour away from King William's Town, on the Grahamstown-King William's Town road, Steve and Jones ran into a police roadblock. Whether this was a routine roadblock or was set up to apprehend them has been a subject of great speculation. A member of the security branch, GA Fourie, claimed in an affidavit submitted to the Truth and Reconciliation Commission that they had a spy who operated in Alexander's circles. This spy allegedly got wind of Biko's abortive visit and informed the police that Biko and Jones were driving back to King William's Town that same evening. When I revealed the name of the alleged spy to Alexander, he vehemently rejected the allegation, and said that this person was still hurt by the false accusation. The Investigative Unit of the Truth and Reconciliation Commission dismissed the allegation as unreliable at best. The Unit's report stated that there was no record of the existence of the security policeman who made the allegation, and that the alleged informer could not have known some of the information contained in the allegation.[244] That's at least one theory about the roadblock.

The other theory is that the notorious spy Craig Williamson ordered the roadblock. This is based on the theory that Williamson, an undercover agent for the apartheid government, was the conduit for the meeting between Tambo and Biko that was meant to take place in Botswana. Mac Maharaj testified to the Truth and Reconciliation Commission that "the South African security forces saw this (the meeting between

---

244 Investigative Unit Report of the Truth and Reconciliation Commission, 1 April 1998.

How Steve was Killed

Tambo and Biko) as too dangerous to allow and therefore there is a possibility that Biko was murdered while in detention."[245]

Williamson had worked as the vice-president of the International University Exchange Fund, which provided funding to the various liberation movements, while secretly in the employ of the security police. Barney Pityana and Ben Khoapa tell a story of how they were almost trapped by Williamson. They had left the country in 1978 to pursue unity discussions with the ANC leadership. At one point they asked Williamson to fund a trip for them to meet with Oliver Tambo in Lusaka. Pityana was to come from New York and Khoapa from London. When they got to Lusaka they learned that Oliver Tambo was in Lesotho, and arrangements were made for them to fly to Bloemfontein. They had already checked in and were approaching the gate when Pityana said to his friend, "Ben, I don't feel good about this, something fishy is going on here." Indeed, the police entered the plane in Bloemfontein, not knowing the two men had not boarded at the very last minute. Apparently, some newspapers even published that the two had been arrested. That's when Williamson's cover as a spy was blown. He was immediately airlifted out of Botswana by the South African government. It is one of the travesties of justice that a man whose hands are dripping with the blood of so many people was let off the hook by the Truth and Reconciliation Commission.

Another explanation for the roadblock is that the police were on the alert for external "agitators" stoking the ongoing

---

[245] Mac Maharaj's testimony to the Truth and Reconciliation Commission. Mac Maharaj was a member of the ANC High Command and served as a cabinet minister in President Mandela's government and as spokesperson for President Jacob Zuma.

youth and student boycotts in Port Elizabeth. Thus in their interrogation they wanted to tie Steve to a pamphlet that had been circulating in Port Elizabeth about commemoration services for June 16.

And yet another theory is that the police had realised that Steve was not in the King William's Town area as he was meant to be, and had put out a call to block off all the major entrances to the town.

I am not in a position to decide which of these theories is true; suffice to say that it is not unlikely that Steve was being monitored by the security police. The Amnesty Committee of the Truth and Reconciliation Commission was, however, correct in denying amnesty to the five policemen who murdered Steve. What remains unclear is why they were never prosecuted by the democratic government. It is abundantly clear that they had acted out of ill will – as will be evident in the discussion that follows.

The Arrest

At the roadblock the police asked Steve and Jones to step out and open the boot. Jones, who was driving, followed their orders but struggled to open the boot. The car's boot had to be opened in a special way, known only to Rams Ramokgopa, back at Zanempilo. Apparently, the car had been in a minor accident resulting in a small dent above the left tail-light that jammed the lid. Whilst Jones tugged at the boot, the police kept accusing him of being a terrorist on his way to see Steve Biko, while Steve sat quietly in the passenger seat. Jones tried to make light of his struggle with the boot and invited one of the policemen to have a try. After a while the senior officer, Colonel Alf Oosthuizen, ordered the unit to clear the roadblock

How Steve was Killed

and to take Steve and Jones to the nearby police station in Grahamstown.

Oosthuizen drove with Steve in Ramokgopa's car while Jones drove with the other officers. The police searched the car thoroughly at the police station. Jones recalls that "they even went through the ash in the ash-tray. It was now clear that this was not a joke." They found Jones's wallet, which, apart from an amount of R43, contained his identity document. And then Oosthuizen bellowed in Afrikaans: *"As jy Peter Cyril Jones is, dan wie is daai groot man?"* – If you are Peter Cyril Jones, then who is that big man?

Steve realised how awkward the situation was for his friend. On principle, Jones would not reveal Steve's identity, exposing himself to torture and imprisonment. Yet in the end the police would find out anyway. Steve interjected: "I am Bantu Steve Biko."

And then there was silence.

"Biko?" retorted Oosthuizen, mispronouncing the B.

"No, Bantu Steve Biko," retorted Biko, pronouncing the Bs in his name silently.

The two men were separated. Jones was taken to Algoa Police Station and Steve to Walmer Police Station, both in Port Elizabeth, about 250 km from King William's Town.

> I was in front and Steve was a couple of paces behind me. My entourage stopped at a Kombi and I was told to enter and lie face down on the floor between the seats. I turned to look at Steve who had just passed us and I called his name out loud. He stopped to look at me and called my name and we smiled a greeting which was interrupted when I was slapped

259

> violently into the Kombi. This was the last time I ever saw my comrade – alive or dead.[246]

Over the next months Jones was repeatedly interrogated and tortured. He was detained for nearly eighteen months.

> During the height of my interrogation there wasn't a spot on my body that wasn't either swollen, bruised or sensitive. At times, I struggled to find a comfortable sleeping position, resorting to sleeping in a kneeling position with my forehead resting on the floor.[247]

How Steve Was Killed

At Walmer Police Station Steve was kept naked and manacled for 20 days before being transferred to the notorious Sanlam Building in Port Elizabeth. The security police there resented the respect Steve enjoyed from the King William's Town security police. Stories had reached them that Steve had, in a previous stint in detention, even fought back and had punched one of the senior officers in King William's Town, Warrant Officer Hattingh. When he arrived at the Sanlam Building the security police told him to remain standing. After a while he sat down. That was when one of the policemen, Captain Siebert, grabbed him and pulled him back onto his feet. A "scuffle" ensued, and true to what he had told Sonwabo Yengo, Steve would defend himself.

On 6 September Steve sustained a massive brain haemorrhage. The cause of his death was not disputed: complications

---

246 Interview with Peter Jones.
247 Interview with Peter Jones.

resulting from a brain injury. Steve suffered at least three brain lesions occasioned by the application of force to his head; the injury was suffered between the night of 6 September and 7.30 a.m. on 7 September. In their amnesty application the policemen who killed Steve tried to evade spelling out what exactly had happened in the same way that they had during the original Biko Inquest in 1977. The details are not fully known. However, they admitted that after Steve had suffered a brain injury, they still kept him in a standing position. They shackled his hands and feet to the metal grille of the cell door. The police noticed that he was speaking with a slur but would not relent and continued with their interrogation.

Equally complicit in Steve's murder were three doctors involved in the case, the district surgeon Dr Ivor Lang, the chief district surgeon Dr Benjamin Tucker and Dr Colin Hersch, a specialist from Port Elizabeth.

On September 7, one day after Steve suffered the brain haemorrhage, the police called in Dr Lang. Lang could find nothing wrong with Steve, despite the fact that he found him in a daze with a badly swollen face, hands and feet. Instead the doctor alleged that Steve was "shamming". Lang's more senior colleague, Dr Benjamin Tucker, was called in for his opinion on what should be done. Tucker suggested that Steve be taken to hospital, but the police strongly objected, and Tucker subordinated his Hippocratic oath to their wishes. Lang, even though he was acutely aware of Steve's condition, recommended that Steve be driven 700 kilometres to the prison hospital in Pretoria. By 10 September Steve's condition had deteriorated alarmingly. The following day, September 11, the police put Steve in the back of a Land Rover and drove him for more than twelve hours from Port Elizabeth to Pretoria – naked, manacled and unconscious.

On September 12 Steve Biko died, in the words of Sydney Kentridge, "a miserable and lonely death on a mat on a stone floor in a prison cell".

The minister of justice and the police, Jimmy Kruger, issued a statement that Biko had died from a hunger strike. Addressing a National Party Congress, Kruger proclaimed to laughter: "I am not saddened by Biko's death and I am not mad. His death leaves me cold." Kruger's remark reverberated around the world.[248] Speaking at the first Steve Biko Memorial Lecture 23 years later, UCT Vice-Chancellor Njabulo Ndebele described this callous event as:

> ... a continuum of indescribable insensitivity that begins as soon as Steve Biko and Peter Jones are arrested at a roadblock near Grahamstown on 18 August 1977. It starts with lowly police officers who make the arrest in the relative secrecy of a remote setting and ends with a remarkable public flourish, when a minister of government declares that Biko's death leaves him cold. This situation lets us deep into the ethical and moral condition of Afrikanerdom, which not only shaped apartheid, but also was itself deeply shaped by it. [249]

---

248 Pik Botha says he was alarmed by Kruger's remark and he called him aside to ask if he realised the damage that his remark would cause the country. Kruger simply said: "That is how I feel, he's a terrorist". Quoted in Theresa Papenfus (2011). *Pik Botha and His Times* (Pretoria: Litera), 213.

249 Njabulo Ndebele, Steve Biko Memorial Lecture, 2000.

Here is how Barney Pityana describes his friend's last hours:

> On the night of 11 September Biko, evidently a seriously ill patient, was driven to Pretoria, naked and manacled to the floor of a Land Rover. Eleven hours later he was carried into the hospital at Pretoria Central Prison and left on the floor of a cell. Several hours later he was given an intravenous drip by a newly qualified doctor who had no information about him other than that he was refusing to eat. Sometime during the night of 12 September Steve Biko died, unattended.[250]

News of Steve's death instantly reverberated around the world. While there had been deaths in detention before, no one thought that, in their savage madness, the security police would kill someone with the stature of Steve Biko.

The Gaping Wound

The South African artist Paul Stopforth attended the autopsy of Steve's body, took several photographs and later made a series of drawings that vividly display the injuries he sustained.[251] Stopforth depicts how Steve's body was cut in the process of the autopsy but in his artistic representation he had sewn it back together – to restore his wholeness.

This process of restoration was denied to the Biko family – despite a cash payout to the family and to the South African

---

250 Barney Pityana in Barney Pityana, Mamphela Ramphele, Malusi Mpumlwana and Lindy Wilson (eds) (1992). *Bounds of Possibility* (Cape Town: David Philip), 80.
251 Paul Stopforth's depictions of Steve Biko's body is among the most dramatic representations of the inhumanity of the killing of political detainees in South Africa.

public at large. In an attempt to pretend to the world that there was some element of justice in South Africa, the Nationalist government established an inquest into Steve's death. After 14 days of testimony, which incontrovertibly demonstrated the assaults on Steve, the presiding magistrate of the Biko Inquest concluded that "no act or omission by any person involving an offence by any person" was responsible for the death of Steve Biko – not the police who brutally assaulted him, not the doctors who covered up for the police, and certainly not the government.

With his judgement the magistrate confirmed what black people already knew and what many white South Africans pretended not to know – that South Africa was a police state. When asked under what statute the police had arrested Steve, the head of the security branch in Port Elizabeth Colonel Goosen answered: "We don't work under statutes."

South Africa was presented with yet another opportunity to restore Steve's soul when the democratic government set up the Truth and Reconciliation Commission (TRC). The TRC promised amnesty to apartheid perpetrators who were willing to disclose the full truth of what happened to their victims. Steve's killers were forced to testify, but were denied amnesty because they failed this test.

However, the government failed to prosecute them for Steve's murder until they either died or the statute of limitations meant they could no longer be prosecuted.

Steve's death, and the manner in which it was dealt with by those in positions of power both during and after apartheid, left a gaping wound in our body politic. This wound continues in the failure of white South Africans to own up to their collusion in a political system that allowed the police to murder government opponents at will. Benedict Anderson describes the crucial role of shame in the life of any society as follows:

> If we are not capable of being ashamed of our country, then we do not love it. It is a shame that can be valuably mobilised. What comes to mind are the mothers in Buenos Aires who, year by year, held quiet demonstrations at the Plaza de Mayo on behalf of all the young people who were disappeared in their thousands by the military regime of General Videla. These mothers wanted justice, of course, but what they tried to arouse was a general shame among their fellow Argentineans, a shame in the face of unborn Argentineans. Hence a good nationalist slogan is always: "Long Live Shame."[252]

The unity that Steve had cherished and pursued as essential was dealt a heavy blow by his death, followed as it was by the bannings of the Black Consciousness organisations and black newspapers on 19 October 1977 – Black Wednesday. As Steve had feared, the second generation of Black Consciousness leaders – Saths Cooper, Strini Moodley, Muntu Myeza, Pandelani Nefolovhodwe – were locked away for several years on Robben Island. Those who came after them left the country by the thousands to join the liberation movements in exile, or to set up their own movements. Their leaders Tsietsi Mashinini and Khotso Seathlolo died lonely deaths – Tsietsi in exile and Khotso after he had already returned. But in the end they were largely forgotten.

---

252 Benedict Anderson (2010). "The Goodness of Nations" in Xolela Mangcu (ed.), *Becoming Worthy Ancestors* (Johannesburg: Wits University Press), 112.

Even as a new organisation, the Azanian People's Organisation (AZAPO), was set up to continue this tradition, there was hardly any solidarity in the black political community. The ANC – which had been absent from the political stage since 1960 – saw in the vacuum an opportunity to reclaim the political initiative through organisations such as the United Democratic Front, trade unions and civic organisations in the townships. And there ensued a bitter conflict for political hegemony in the black community, with AZAPO and the United Democratic Front railing against each other. The former claimed to be the custodians of Steve Biko's legacy, the latter boasted that they had outgrown it. The gaping wound remained and continued to fester.

The 1980s were to prefigure a new political culture in the community. Whereas the BCM had concentrated on patient institution building – Badat's reservations notwithstanding – the "young lions" of the 1980s brought a dizzying urgency to the situation, and often turned on community institutions and destroyed them. They took Oliver Tambo's message to South Africans to make apartheid South Africa ungovernable as a licence for destroying community institutions and community life. In no time the liberators became the predators. This would have long-term effects on our political culture ...

10
Steve Biko's "Extraordinary Gift of Leadership"

> "We have in us the will to live through these trying times"
> STEVE BIKO[253]

Steve Biko's murder by the apartheid police recalls that of 19th-century Xhosa chief Hintsa (1789-1835). The similarities between their circumstances – and the way in which they died – could not be more striking. As pointed out in Chapter 2, anti-colonial resistance was waged first by the Khoikhoi and the San people, and after them by those Xhosa who had moved west of the Kei River – amaRharhabe, imiDange, amaNtinde and amaGqunukhwebe. This meant that the descendants of Gcaleka (from the Great House) on the east of the Kei River were relatively removed from the war front. Gcaleka's grandson, Hintsa, took over from his father Khawuta in the 1820s, and was from the beginning very cynical and suspicious of the colonial government and the missionary establishment set up by the Wesleyans in his territory in Butterworth. He saw the latter as nothing more than agents of the colonial government.

In the historical divide among the Xhosa – between Ndlambe and Ngqika – Hintsa weighed in on the side of the former

---

253 Biko, *I Write What I Like*.

in resisting the whites, fighting alongside Nxele in the Battle of Amalinde before withdrawing back to his territory. He refused to eat or even have tea with whites.

Hintsa is reported to have turned down a request to have tea with the missionary Stephen Kay by saying: "The sugar I know to be sweet, and the tea is doubtless good, seeing that you drink it. But they say, Hintsa must eat alone."[254]

When presented with a red British uniform as a gift, he remarked: "I will wear this when I go to my cattle kraal and the oxen will come out to look at me." He turned down an invitation to visit the British colonial government by saying he was busy with his people, and noted that the British governor was not in the habit of visiting other people.

The other historical parallel between Biko and Hintsa has to do with the period in their respective histories in which they assumed leadership of their people. As a young man Hintsa had seen how the British had brutally suppressed his uncle Ndlambe and how they had imprisoned Nxele on Robben Island, where he died trying to escape. He was in his late thirties when Ndlambe and Ngqika died, in 1828 and 1829 respectively. According to Mostert "the end of the dramatic transitional decade of the 1820s thus seemed to come on a highly symbolic note, of the passing of the two men who had dominated the initial contact period and interaction between white men and Xhosa people".[255]

Holding the fort among the Rharhabe on the west side of the Kei was Hintsa's warrior nephew Maqoma. After his father Ngqika's death, Maqoma took over as regent for the Great Son,

---

254 Mostert, *Frontiers*, 610.
255 Mostert, *Frontiers*, 608.

Sandile (even though Maqoma was older, Sandile was in the direct line of accession to inherit the chieftaincy once he came of age). Maqoma thus assumed the leadership of the Rharhabe on the west side of the Kei during this moment of leadership transition among the Xhosa – the 1820s. The Xhosa were all but defeated after the Fifth Frontier War. They had suffered another bloody experience of dispossession of their lands, and been pushed back still further eastwards into Hintsa's territory. Most of their cattle had been taken from them and they were homeless and starving.[256]

While there was a total of five wars between 1799 and 1818, it was the Sixth Frontier War (1834-1835) under Maqoma's command that routed the British. After an unexpected rebellion – even against the admonishment of their chiefs – the Xhosa spontaneously took the battle to the British as a response to yet another cattle-raiding and hut-burning campaign by the colonial soldiers.

While the first five wars were skirmishes, this was the first full-scale war that involved almost all of the Xhosa people. The British were used to traditional warfare and did not understand the new method of fighting adopted by the Xhosa – close to guerilla warfare, as Maqoma's men lured the British deep into the thicket of the Amathole Mountains. Benjamin D'Urban, the colonial governor wanted to pursue the Xhosa into the Amathole and drive them to the east of the Kei, thereby clearing the fertile lands of the western side for themselves. When the British realised they could not put down the Xhosa warriors – despite using heavy artillery and shooting ran-

---

256 Mostert, *Frontiers*, 490.

domly into the thick bush of the Amathole Mountains – they set their sights on the source of the Xhosa strength – the east of the Kei. Despite his apparent removal from the fighting, Hintsa was the one giving sanction for Maqoma and the other chiefs to coordinate the war efforts.[257] And thus we come to the tragic similarity between Hintsa and Biko's deaths.

The British Commander Harry Smith and one of his guides George Southey decided to invade Hintsa's territory and instructed the chief to go with them in search of the cattle. Hintsa asked them, in his characteristic sarcastic fashion: "What have the cattle done that you want them? Why must I see my subjects deprived of them?"[258]

Hintsa's subsequent murder as he was fleeing his captors was an early precursor of the brutality that would befall African leaders from Zulu chief and warrior Bambatha to Steve Biko and ANC soldier Solomon Mahlangu. Mostert describes how Smith and Southey chased Hintsa to his death:

> Smith's own horse at that point was racing too wildly to round easily, but George Southey and the other Guides had caught up. "Shoot George, and be damned to you!" Smith shouted back. Southey fired and hit Hintsa in the left leg. The chief tumbled, but got to his feet again. Smith, galloping back, yelled, "Be damned to you, shoot again!" Southey fired, and Hintsa pitched forward. But once more he struggled to his feet, and managed to reach thick cover along the banks of the river ... A Khoikhoi trooper wading through the river had also spotted the Chief, who then stood up and called out

---

257 Peires, *The House of Phalo*, 166.
258 Mostert, *Frontiers*, 724.

several times in Xhosa, "Mercy." George Southey, who spoke Xhosa fluently, took aim and fired, shattering Hintsa's head and scattering his brains and skull fragments over the bank. Southey was first beside the body and quickly took Hintsa's brass ornaments for himself. As the others gathered around, they grabbed for what was left of Hintsa's beads and bracelets. George Southey or his brother William cut off one of Hintsa's ears and someone else took the other ear. Assistant Surgeon Ford of the 72nd Highlanders took the teeth. [259]

If, in Njabulo Ndebele's words Biko's death "lets us deep into the ethical and moral condition of Afrikanerdom",[260] Hintsa's death leads us into the ethical and moral condition of the British in the 19th century.

On the day of the news of Steve's death, the people in my community carried placards saying "Martyr of Hope" – this is the hope that sustained the next phase of the struggle for freedom in South Africa. The usual response among activists to the killing of struggle heroes was that their deaths would not halt the struggle. The struggle, we argued, was larger than the individual.

However, now that we are free and perhaps can be more reflective about our history, we should also be able to admit that the removal of certain individuals had damaging effects on the course of the struggle. We are now living with the consequences of Steve Biko's death and with the consequences of the subsequent destruction of the movement he started.

Something which that movement represented is today

---

[259] Mostert, *Frontiers*, 725-726.
[260] Njabulo Ndebele, Steve Biko Memorial Lecture, 2000.

sorely missing in our public life. That "something" is often expressed in the form of a question: "What would Biko have done if he was still alive?" Or: "Would things have turned out this way if Steve was alive?"

I used to get irritated by these questions because they were impossible to answer – how can anyone really know how a dead person might have turned out? – until I realised that they were rhetorical questions. Put differently, they are an expression of what Njabulo Ndebele described to me as "a social wish".[261] The more familiar articulation of this "social wish" is in the now archaic, patriarchal formulation "*aphi amadoda?*" – literally "where are the real men?" but as a figure of speech: "Where are our leaders?"

And so I wish to draw this book to a conclusion by reflecting on Steve's leadership legacy for South Africa. Aelred Stubbs called it his "extraordinary gift of leadership".[262]

Steve Biko and the Quest for a Higher Consciousness

Biko and Black Consciousness practised a politics of "psychological empowerment", according to Millard Arnold. This empowerment proved to be the *sine qua non* for the resumption and further continuation of the struggle in the 1980s. As a leader, Steve Biko challenged black and white people to confront their inner fears head-on. His unique contribution lay in his vision, on a wide scale, of the interrelationship between consciousness and culture, on the one hand, and develop-

---

261 I ran into Njabulo Ndebele in a mall in Cape Town, and he used this phrase in our conversation. The phrase obviously stuck in my head. So here it is, Prof.
262 Biko, *I Write What I Like*, 211.

mental and political action, on the other. This stands in sharp contrast to South Africa's recent leaders who, in the creation of a democratic society, have concentrated on the latter without sufficient attention to the former.

To be sure, as detractors have pointed out, Steve was not the first person to discover the centrality of culture as a tool for self-empowerment and political action. The term "culture" itself entered mainstream political thought in the 18th century – it is actually a derivation from the German word *Kultur*. Feeling victimised and held in contempt by countries such as France (the French spoke of civilisation), 19th-century Germans looked to culture as a form of defence. Isaiah Berlin describes the antecedents of this turn towards culture among Germany's intellectuals and clergy:

> By the end of the eighteenth century some among the spiritual leaders in the devout, inward-looking German principalities began to counter-attack. This took the form of pouring contempt on the worldly success of the French ... The inner life, the life of the spirit, concerned with the relation of man to man, to himself, to God – that alone was of supreme importance; the empty materialistic French wiseacres had no sense of true values – of what men alone lived by. Let them have their arts, their sciences, their salons, their wealth and their vaunted glory. All this was, in the end, dross – the perishable goods of the corruptible flesh.[263]

Steve could well be playing out a similar cultural reaction to the one Berlin describes when he says "the great powers of

---

263 Biko, *I Write What I Like*, 36.

the world may have done wonders in giving the world an industrial and military look but the great gift still has to come from Africa – giving the world a more human face,"[264] or when he wrote:

> We have in us the will to live through these trying times; over the years we have attained moral superiority over the white man; we shall watch as time destroys his paper castles and know that all these little pranks were but frantic attempts of frightened little people to convince each other that they can control the minds and bodies of indigenous people of Africa indefinitely. [265]

Berlin argues that throughout recorded history "great waves of rationalism" have been accompanied by this kind of cultural backlash. The flowering of rationalism in Greece in the 4th century BC was followed by an equal flowering of cults and mysticisms. The achievement of Roman law and the legal structure of Judaism were followed by the rise of Christianity. It is no surprise, then, that by the end of the 19th century a number of scholars, many of them of German descent, questioned the foundations of Enlightenment rationality. They rejected the idea that people were simply calculating, rational beings who looked out only for their individual, material interests. If that is how people lived, then it should be seen more as an aberration than as a practice that is to be assumed as a standard – which is unfortunately what those in positions of leadership have assumed in South Africa today.

---
264 Biko, *I Write What I Like*, 51.
265 Biko, *I Write What I Like*, 78-79.

The "social wish" is for a return to the kind of leadership that is underpinned by solidarity with the people. By bringing culture into the public discourse, the German writers were bringing about a corrective to a culture that had turned completely rationalistic and materialistic in the half-century after the Industrial Revolution. South Africa faces a similar challenge since the dawn of a new democracy.

In *Consciousness and Society*, H Stuart Hughes describes the German thinkers as "a cluster of genius" that emerged at a time of political and institutional lethargy in Europe: "Now, rather suddenly, a number of thinkers independently began to wonder whether these emotional involvements, far from being merely extraneous, might not be the central element in the story [of freedom]." Hughes argues further:

> ... in this sense the new doctrines were manifestly subjective. Psychological process had replaced external reality as the most pressing topic for investigation. It was no longer what actually existed that seemed most important: it was what men thought existed. And what they felt on the unconscious level had become rather more interesting than what they consciously rationalised. [266]

A prime example of the turn towards interiority as the basis of political action was the Romantic movement, which in turn inspired the Populist movements among farmers in the United States and peasants in Russia. Rejecting Enlightenment formalism and the idea, promoted by the likes of Jeremy Bentham,

---

266 H Stuart Hughes (1976). *Consciousness and Society* (New York: Octagon Books), 66.

that human beings were naturally selfish, the Romantics looked to poetry, folklore and the arts to plumb deeper into people's consciousness and capacity for solidarity.

The turn to consciousness had an impact on the emerging black nationalist movements of the 20th century, particularly the Negritude movement. According to Lewis Nkosi, the Romantic rebellion against Western formalism and rationalism suited the black militants' desire to liberate themselves from a similar rationalism that saw people as objects. Restoring psychological subjective consciousness became the duty of black intellectuals:

> ... the instruments that lay close at hand were no different for the black writer than those which the Western artist, in his accumulating frustrations with the proprieties of Western bourgeois society, had fashioned out of a conglomeration of ideas and techniques, from Marxist economic theories to Freudian interpretation of dreams, from free association to verbal non sequiturs or surrealist techniques.[267]

Ngugi wa Thiong'o argues that "in a situation of the coloniser and the colonised, the question of consciousness is vital. In fact, it becomes a site of intense struggle".[268] Should they lose the struggle for consciousness, the colonised will not only be unable to rise up to claim their rights but will also be unable to redefine the world in their own image.

For Steve Biko racism was founded on the internalisation of

---

267 Lewis Nkosi, "Negritude: Old and New Perspectives", 284.
268 Ngugi wa Thiong'o (2009). *Something New and Torn: An African Renaissance* (New York: Basic Civitas Books), 109.

white superiority, and the institutionalisation of those attitudes in the society at large – through political and economic process:

> First of all I accept that in our analysis, the cardinal point is the existence in our society of white racism, which has been institutionalised, and also cushioned with a backing of the majority of whites. In other words, a white child does not have to choose whether or not he wants to live with the white, he is born into it. He is brought up within white schools, institutions, and the whole process of racism somehow greets him at various levels and he attempts to have an attitude against blacks, so whites are together around the privileges that they hold, and they monopolise this away from black society. [269]

Steve believed that it was primarily because of the institutionalisation of these privileges that white people were unlikely to listen to moral suasion. I have elsewhere argued that although Nelson Mandela played a pivotal role in ensuring our transition to democracy, he nonetheless left us the unfinished business of racism.[270] Biko's challenge of the psychological freedom from racism was therefore left unaddressed by even the greatest political icon of the 20th century.

In the effort to bring white people on board the project of democratisation, Mandela stopped short of challenging whites to change the attitudes that underpinned their privileged position in our society. Because of his emphasis on reconciliation,

---

269 Biko, *I Write What I Like*, 149.
270 Xolela Mangcu, "Nelson Mandela and the Unfinished Business of Racism", Nelson Mandela Foundation, 7 April 2009.

Mandela had "a rather generous interpretation of racism in South Africa". Thus, to paraphrase Aelred Stubbs, South Africa's transition was founded on forgiveness without repentance.

Stubbs reflected on whether he could forgive those who killed Steve: "I personally cannot pray for the forgiveness of those responsible for his death. I can and do pray for their repentance, which will then make possible and efficacious their forgiveness. The real miracle of the Gospel, Coleridge wrote, is not forgiveness but repentance."[271]

To be sure, Steve did not face the challenge of building a fractured society on the brink of a racial conflagration, and there is no way of knowing that he would not have reached out to whites in the same manner that Mandela did. However, something about their political backgrounds tells me that Biko might have been more challenging. He came of age and became the midwife of a much more cultural nationalist stage of our revolution.

Having defined white racism as the totality of the white power structure in South Africa, Steve feared that black people in the 1960s were on the brink of giving in to the apartheid behemoth. Just as standing up to the bully requires reaching within and overcoming one's innermost fears, he believed that what black people needed to do, was to affirm their humanity by overcoming their fears. This was nothing less than a psycho-cultural challenge that needed to be faced head-on. Steve saw that black people needed to believe that they were worthy of freedom and its responsibilities. This required an affirmation by themselves of their own humanity:

---

271 Biko, *I Write What I Like*, 242.

> We try to get blacks in conscientisation to grapple realistically with their problems, to attempt to find solutions to their problems, to develop what one might call an awareness, a physical awareness of their situation, to be able to analyse it, and to provide answers for themselves. The purpose behind it really being to provide some kind of hope; I think the central theme about black society is that it has got elements of a defeated society; people look like they have given up the struggle . . . now this sense of defeat is basically what we are fighting against; people must not just give in to the hardship of life, people must develop a hope, people must develop some kind of security to be together to look at their problems, and people must in this way build up their humanity. This is the point about conscientisation and Black Consciousness.[272]

He expressed the same sentiment as follows:

> It becomes more necessary to see the truth as it is if you realise that the only vehicle for change are these people who have lost their personality. The first step therefore is to make the black man come to himself; to pump back life into his empty shell; to infuse him with pride and dignity, to remind him of his complicity in the crime of allowing himself to be misused and therefore letting evil reign supreme in the land of his birth. This is what we mean by an inward-looking process. This is the definition of Black Consciousness.[273]

---

272 Biko, *I Write What I Like*, 127.
273 Biko, *I Write What I Like*, 31.

Consciousness and Nation Building

Given the events of the first two decades of freedom, I would modify Ngugi's observation about consciousness as vital in the fight between the coloniser and the colonised. I would argue that consciousness is vital in the relationship between the leadership and the citizenry.

Our country is ripe for a leadership that puts the community and the nation first – not a leadership that is bent on stealing from the future of its own children. Conversely, we already see growing insurgent citizenship movements popping up all over the country. The people are saying "enough is enough". That constitutes the beginning of a new consciousness.

Steve's work also had relevance to how we see ourselves as a nation – after all, consciousness is the first step towards defining oneself. Increasingly our public discourse and the discourse of the ruling party is peppered with displays of racial and ethnic nativism. The ANC's deputy president Kgalema Motlanthe cautioned his own party for this descent into nativism at the 2012 commemoration of the June 16 uprisings at the Lilliesleaf Farm in Rivonia.[274]

South Africans find themselves stuck between the Scylla of racial nativism among some in the black community and the Charybdis of racial denialism among some in the white community. This is certainly no way of building what Steve called the "joint culture". Hybridity was at the heart of his approach to politics: nothing was pure, and those who make claims to pure blackness have no understanding of what Steve stood for.

---

[274] Kgalema Motlanthe in a speech in commemoration of the June 16 uprisings at Lilliesleaf Farm in Rivonia – the hideout where prominent ANC leaders were arrested before they were sent to Robben Island, together with Nelson Mandela in 1964.

Steve rejected essentialist categories – from his inclusive definition of blackness embracing Coloureds and Indians to this concept of a joint culture, a new culture crafted by blacks and whites from their best respective experiences. The open society of Steve's dreams was one that allowed for cultural fusion:

> . . . cultures affect each other, you know like fashions, and you cannot avoid rubbing against someone else's culture. But you must have the right to reject or not anything that is given to you. At the moment we exist sort of as a limb of white culture.[275]

He described South African culture under apartheid as so European that the country might as well have been "a province of Europe": "We don't behave like Africans, we behave like Europeans who live in Africa."[276] To Steve it was obvious that the "joint culture" would have aspects of European experience, "because we have whites here who are descended from Europe. We don't dispute that. But for God's sake, it must have African experience as well."[277]

Steve thus avoided an either/or racial politics and advocated a both/and accommodative political culture and a mature citizenship that was not afraid to confront the contradictions involved in building a national identity. He believed that black people were sufficiently "innovative" to build what he constantly referred to as "the open society": "I think what we need in our society is the power by us blacks to innovate – we have

---

275 Biko, *I Write What I Like*, 147.
276 Biko, *I Write What I Like*, 148.
277 Biko, *I Write What I Like*, 148.

the very system from which we can expand, from which we can innovate, to say this is what we believe, accept or not accept."[278]

He was always unequivocal about the place of race in the electoral system of the open society, which he envisaged as based on "one man, one vote, no reference to colour". And that is because "we do not need any artificial majorities, any artificial laws to entrench ourselves in power because we believe that once we come into power, our sheer numbers will maintain us there".[279] Elsewhere he was asked: "Do you see a country in which black and white can live amicably on equal terms together?" And he answers:

> That is correct. We see a completely non-racial society. We don't believe, for instance, in the so-called guarantees for minority rights, because guaranteeing minority rights implies the recognition of portions of the community on a race basis. We believe that in our country there shall be no minority, there shall be no majority, just the people. And those people will have the same status before the law. So in a sense it will be a completely non-racial society.[280]

And what about concerns for a racial backlash against white people? Here he speaks as a prophet of the reconciliation that would indeed come to take place under Nelson Mandela and Desmond Tutu's leadership, drawing on his knowledge of *ubuntu* in the black community, but always with that radical edge:

---
278 Biko, *I Write What I Like*, 146-147.
279 Biko, *I Write What I Like*, 170-171.
280 Biko, *I Write What I Like*, 170.

> And I know people in terms of my own background, where I stay, are not necessarily revengeful, nor are they sadistic in outlook. The black man has got no ill-intentions for the white man. The black man is only incensed at the white man to the extent that he wants to entrench himself in a position of power to exploit the black man. But beyond that, nothing more.[281]

In his argument for a "joint culture" in a reconciled society, Steve is not far from Frantz Fanon, who wanted to liberate the process of nation building from some of the more crass, nativist claims to racial authenticity by the post-colonial elite. While he appreciated the importance of history in the lives of black people, Fanon also cautioned that "this historical obligation in which men of African culture racialise their claims and speak more of African culture than national culture leads these men down a cul de sac".[282] Fanon cautions against a ready reliance on past racial identities:

> During the struggle for liberation, the leader awakened the people and promised them a forward march, heroic and unmitigated. Today, he uses every means to put them to sleep, and three or four times a year asks them to remember the colonial period and to look back on the long way they have come since then.[283]

---

281 Biko, *I Write What I Like*, 170
282 Fanon, *The Wretched of the Earth*, 152.
283 Fanon, *The Wretched of the Earth*, 169.

The challenge for Frantz Fanon -- and for Steve Biko – was how to achieve an "actional" racial moral identity as opposed to a reactional identity. Reactional existence was when black people defined themselves only in relation to white people:

> . . . when the Negro makes contact with the white world, a certain sensitising action takes place. If his psychic structure is weak, one observes a collapse of the ego. The black man stops behaving as an actional person. The goal of his behaviour will be the Other (in the guise of the white man), for the Other alone can give him worth.[284]

Conversely, the white also has no existence outside of the black, for it is the black that gives him a sense of superiority. What was needed, Fanon argued, was a new humanity that rejected the assumptions of white superiority without generating what Berlin called "the bent twig" – which is the ferocious response that comes out of the experience of oppression – among black people. Thus, Fanon continued: "One does not endure massive oppression or witness the disappearance of one's entire family in order for hatred or racism to triumph."[285]

Steve expressed the same caution as follows:

> Blacks have had enough experiences as objects of racism not to wish to turn the tables. While it may be relevant now to speak of black in relation to white, we must not make this our preoccupation, for it can be a negative exercise. As we proceed further towards the achievement of our goals, let us

---
[284] Fanon, *The Wretched of the Earth*, 119.
[285] Fanon, *The Wretched of the Earth*, 119.

talk more about ourselves and our struggle and less about whites.[286]

The big obstacle in building a national culture, however, was that both blacks and whites were locked in a world with no "reciprocal recognitions" and no "authentic communication". Fanon insisted that:

> ... both must turn their backs on the inhuman voices which were those of their respective ancestors in order that authentic communication be possible.[287]

This is why, Fanon felt, it was necessary to move from a racialised conception of culture (culture writ small) to a new national culture (culture writ large). And that could mean taking the best from the former to contribute to the latter. In the case of South Africa, this was the culture of self-assertion "that is responsible for the restoration of our faith in ourselves and therefore offers a hope in the direction we are taking".[288]

Kwame Anthony Appiah describes the process necessary for this cross-cultural dialogue as "soul making". Steve, borrowing from Paulo Freire, called it "conscientisation". Just as children are not born with a certain set of values or orientations, people do not just become self-reliant. They need to be conscientised to think and act as subjective agents and not objects of other people's sympathy and largesse. And that too requires leadership that speaks and engages with the people – instead

---

286 Biko, *I Write What I Like*, 108.
287 Fanon, *The Wretched of the Earth*, 180.
288 Biko, *I Write What I Like*, 50.

of seeing them merely as racial voting cattle. Appiah believes it is the duty of the state to provide the educational "soul making". Steve believed that:

> ... it is the duty of the vanguard movement which brings change to educate people's outlook. In the same way that blacks have never lived in a socialist economic system, they've got to live in one. And in the same way that they've always lived in a racially divided society, they've got to live in a non-racial society. They've got many things to learn. All these must be brought to them and explained to the people by the vanguard movement which is leading the revolution.[289]

Unfortunately, the leaders of the vanguard movement seem to have neither the patience nor the time to engage with the people – they are busy chasing the next government tender while social institutions are falling all around them. While the Black Consciousness movement created a solidarity based on a political definition of blackness, we have seen the resurgence of a crude conception of blackness as nothing more than the colour of one's skin – to be flaunted as justification of economic claims made by the elite in the name of black people. To be sure, I support initiatives such as affirmative action but when applied within the context of party political allegiances, they do more harm than good to national institutions. Blackness in this context is misused as an indication of political loyalty and economic greed.

Frantz Fanon warned about this development among the

---

289 Biko, *I Write What I Like*, 170.

post-colonial elite: "These men, who have sung the praises of their race, who have taken upon themselves the whole burden of the past, complete with cannibalism and degeneracy, find themselves today, alas, at the head of a team of administrators which turns its back on the jungle and which proclaims that the vocation of the people is to obey, to go on obeying, and to be obedient till the end of time."[290]

To quote the Harvard scholar Michael Sandel: "The public philosophy by which we live cannot secure the liberty it promises, because it cannot inspire the sense of community and civic engagement that liberty requires".[291] In place of a public philosophy of community building, South Africans live under a cult of leadership that exemplifies and inspires self-interest.

The Decline of Black Consciousness

Steve Biko's death, and the crackdown on the movement he spawned, was followed by new directions in the liberation struggle. While it is true that most of the leaders of the 1980s had been through what Barney Pityana called the Black Consciousness mill, the environment in which they were now operating was rapidly changing. This was mainly due to the resurgence of the ANC as the dominant force in South African politics for the first time in 30 years, through its proxy organisations such as the United Democratic Front (UDF), the Congress of South African Trade Unions (COSATU) and the

---

290 Fanon, *The Wretched of the Earth*, 168.
291 Michael Sandel (1996). *Democracy's Discontent: America in Search of a Public Philosophy* (Cambridge: The Belknap Press of Harvard University), 6.

Azanian Student Organisation. This also meant a shift from the radical black nationalism that had been associated with the Pan Africanist Congress (PAC) and the BCM. Perhaps most important in the ideological resurgence of the ANC was the shift from the politics of community organising of the 1970s to the mass mobilisation of the 1980s. Whereas community organising was focussed inward – both on the individual and the community – the mass mobilisation of the 1980s was explicitly outer-directed – aimed at making unworkable apartheid-created institutions such as the Black Local Authorities introduced as part of PW Botha's reformist initiatives in the 1980s. After his election as prime minister in 1978, Botha issued a warning to white South Africans to "adapt or die". The adaptation meant doing away with or relaxing certain apartheid restrictions, including abolishing the pass laws and allowing mixed restaurants and inter-racial relationships.

As part of these concessions, Botha also proposed a modification to the idea that black people permanently belonged in the homelands. New legislation was introduced to recognise the permanence of urban blacks, and new local authority structures were meant to serve their political interests. Concurrent with those reforms, Botha introduced the Tricameral Parliament, which sought to introduce parliamentary representation for Coloureds and Indians in two different houses of parliament. Their remit, however, was limited to passing legislation on their "own affairs". The whole thing was rejected by the Coloured and Indian communities, and the Black Local Authorities came under attack – through petrol bombing of their offices and sometimes the killing of those who served on these structures. There were calls for "liberation before education", as youth and some community leaders called on students to stay away from school, and as the schools were themselves burned to the ground. The youth were reacting – and rather overzealously – to ANC president Oliver Tambo's call to make the country "ungovernable". The ensuing violence against government structures extended from the streets of Soweto to what became the killing fields of KwaZulu-Natal – where the ANC and the apartheid government-backed Inkatha Freedom Party (IFP) battled it out for political dominance.

Of relevance to this book were the attacks on the name of Steve Biko. It is hard to know when the denigration of Steve Biko's name started within the ANC. Right up to his death, there were efforts to arrange meetings between him and Tambo. One can only conclude that those attacks were not from within Tambo's faction of the ANC in exile – that it came mostly from the communists who were threatened by the influx of the post-1976 nationalistic leadership that was swelling the ranks of the organisation in exile. According to Moeletsi Mbeki the Black Consciousness influx saved the ANC from a communist takeover in the 1970s.

Neville Alexander told me that he ran into Mac Maharaj in Europe during this time. He remembered how contemptuous Maharaj was of the Black Consciousness Movement, describing Biko as "CIA". This only served to fuel the hostility towards the BCM inside the country – although by the 1980s the animosity was generalised beyond divisions between nationalists or communists. In the words of Charles Dickens in *The Tale of Two Cities*, the 1980s were:

> . . . the best of times, it was the worst of times, it was the age of wisdom, it was the age of foolishness, it was the epoch of belief, it was the epoch of incredulity, it was the season of Light, it was the season of Darkness, it was the spring of hope, it was the winter of despair, we had everything before us, we had nothing before us, we were all going direct to heaven, we were all going direct the other way, in short, the period was so much like the present period . . .

The 1980s were indeed the best of times as the struggle advanced sharply forward; but also the worst, as the black community tore itself apart. There was a breakdown in respect for adult authority, a loss of interest in education, and a turn towards the militarisation of our society. Aggrey Klaaste captured the mood of the times in typically Dickensian language:

> Blacks lost many things. Worst of all, we lost the innocence of our children. We also lost their respect for us. It took the security forces a longish time to deal with the violence unleashed in 1984 and onwards. They looked on with sadistic fascination as the black community was tearing itself apart. That hurt as well, and the scars are still raw. Some of that insanity is still being played out in the shades of the lovely hillsides of Natal. As if we are a nation accursed there has been a swing to the right in white politics which is perhaps as frightening as the necklace phenomenon of the 1980s. It is in its own appalling crudity fanning racial hatred. Apartheid is not dead at all. No, it is about to stalk the streets of our townships in all its dreadful menace. There is therefore a holding of the breath in the black community. It is proba-

bly unconscious but I can feel it in my bones. There is the silent preparation by blacks for the next inevitable explosion. Quite clearly somebody has to do something to stop this madness.[292]

AZAPO and the UDF: The Turf Wars

On completing matric I enrolled at Wits University in Johannesburg in 1983. I had hardly unpacked my bags when the charismatic student leader of the Azanian Student Organisation, Tiego Moseneke came knocking on my door. He wanted to know if he could put up a poster announcing one of their meetings on my door. "Sure," I said. That was soon followed by a series of visits by other members of AZASO, urging me to join the organisation. Given my own history in high school, it was logical for me to join a student organisation. And then one day a close friend, Kwezi Kobus, came to me fuming, asking how it was that a boy from Ginsberg had an AZASO poster on his door. Kobus was joined by others: Moreilane Moreilane and Linda Mtshizana.[293] Did I have no loyalty to Steve Biko? Unbeknownst to me AZASO was the breakaway student wing of the Azanian People's Organisation (AZAPO).

AZAPO was formed in 1978 by, among others, Ishmael Mkhabela, Sam Tloubatla and Lybon Mabasa as the successor to the banned BPC. AZASO was consequently formed as the

---

[292] Aggrey Klaaste's speech at the launch of the *Sowetan*'s Nation Building programme, Shareworld, Johannesburg, 21 October 1988.

[293] Linda Mtshizana was the son of the famous struggle lawyer, Louis Mtshizana, who for a very long time was the only person willing to defend political prisoners in the Eastern Cape. This landed him on Robben Island. Linda took after his father and also became a lawyer. Sadly he passed away at a young age in 1993.

student wing of AZAPO in much the same way that SASO was the student wing of the BPC. What infuriated Kobus and the other Black Consciousness activists was that in 1981, AZASO had broken away from AZAPO and substituting Black Consciousness with the non-racialism of the ANC, aligned itself with NUSAS. AZASO in turn, took over the Black Students Society (BSS) at Wits, which was the equivalent of a student representative council for black students. The irony, of course, is that the AZASO-NUSAS alliance was founded on two racially segregated organisations.

Hot on the heels of the AZASO breakaway from AZAPO, the fiery cleric and former Black Consciousness and Black Theology exponent Allan Boesak called for the formation of the United Democratic Front (UDF). At the UDF's helm were leading ANC-aligned figures such as Albertina Sisulu, Frank Chikane, Winnie Mandela and many others.

At about the same time, AZAPO was involved in the formation of organisations sympathetic to Black Consciousness under the banner of the National Forum. Some of the leading lights outside of AZAPO were Neville Alexander, Frank van der Horst of the South African Council on Sport and many other left-leaning organisations. And thus was institutionalised the ideological faultline of the 1980s, with the National Forum-aligned organisations claiming Biko as their inspiration, and the UDF claiming Mandela as theirs.

My own history – and the arguments made by Kwezi Kobus and Linda Mtshizana – led me towards the Black Consciousness side. I became particularly close to the leaders of that group. Saths Cooper was released from Robben Island and registered at Wits and came to live in our residence. Muntu

Myeza, also released, lived in nearby Diepkloof in Soweto and visited frequently. Over piña coladas and Romany Cream biscuits, they would regale us with stories from "the island" – Robben Island. Myeza always had a dangerous mission that needed to be undertaken – which made me avoid him as much as possible. And I began to reconnect – now as an adult activist in my own right – with the likes of Peter Jones, or, as we often said, "the last man to see Biko alive" – as if that were a measure of our own or his authenticity. We would have heated debates at the Glyn Thomas House Lecture Theatre with AZAPO speakers such as Cooper, Myeza, Lybon Mabasa and Khehla Shubane debating some of their former Black Consciousness colleagues who were now prominent UDF leaders: Terror Lekota, Aubrey Mokoena, Murphy Morobe and Sydney Mufamadi. More often than not these meetings would end in scuffles, in which I played no small part, either by howling someone down or saying something really annoying.

Because AZASO had broken away from AZAPO, a new student movement was formed, spearheaded by students at the University of the North (Turfloop), prominent among whom was a charismatic law student, Kabelo Lengane. Lengane was our answer to Moseneke in both the charisma and intellectual stakes. Their rivalry merited a *Sowetan* article, comparing them as if they were comparing the two rival soccer clubs, Kaizer Chiefs and Orlando Pirates. I was elected projects coordinator of the Wits University branch of AZASM (the Azanian Students Movement) in 1983, and ultimately chairman between 1984 and 1986. Before I knew it, I was the leading exponent of Black Consciousness at Wits.

Things took a terrible turn when AZASM leaders Kabelo

Lengane, Kenny Mosime and others were attacked in the Alan Taylor Residence at the University of Natal by leaders of AZASO. It was indeed ironic that Black Consciousness student leaders were assaulted at the birthplace of the movement. The violence spread to the townships, particularly to Soweto. In the face of the violent attacks on its members, AZASM aligned itself with the notorious gangster group ama-Kabasa. The Lengane home was attacked in Soweto and Kabelo's father was murdered by a group of youth aligned to the UDF. AZAPO leader George Wauchope retaliated and was alleged to have been behind the murder of some youths. He fled the country to Zimbabwe, never to return. He died in London in 2011.

After receiving threats to my own life I also moved out of Glyn Thomas House to find a place in a newly established university residence in town, Braamfontein Centre. The violence reached all corners of the country but became most intense in the Eastern Cape, particularly in Port Elizabeth. AZAPO activists stayed at Reverend Maqhina's home, which they used as a fortress against UDF attacks. A number of my fellow AZASM comrades were killed in those attacks, and AZAPO leader Reverend Maqhina was in turn accused of working with "the system".

The UDF also established a foothold in our township but we were determined that Ginsberg was the last place in which the memory of Steve would be discarded. We were a core group who also made up the AZAPO executive in Ginsberg – Lunga Lefume, Thembile Duna, Ace Lumnkwana, Ndoda Keyisi, and yes they are the culprits who stole Major Sihunu's petrol to burn down Forbes Grant in 1977. I was later elevated to the position of publicity secretary of AZAPO for the Border region.

Ace Lumnkwana still prides himself for having chaired the meeting on Robben Island that expelled "Terror" Lekota from the BCM. By that stage Lekota had been convinced by the likes of Nelson Mandela to join the ANC. Our leadership was in turn succeeded by people such as Andile M-Afrika, Mncedi Ngoloyi, Vusumzi Ntenteni and Linda Nyakathi.

This is not to say there were no fights in Ginsberg. Typically a fight would break out in a shebeen, and we would attack each other mostly with our bare hands, although one of my comrades was not shy to pull out an Okapi (a notoriously dangerous knife popular among township *tsotsis*). Sometimes the UDF crowds would in their hundreds go and sing in front of Steve Biko's house: *U-Steve Biko, I –CIA!* – alleging Steve had worked for the CIA. We would confront the crowds to defend Steve's name, at the risk of our lives.

The decline of Black Consciousness was, however, not just the making of "the system", or the result of the attacks in the 1980s. The decline was also self-inflicted.

While the UDF and the mass democratic movement drove mass mobilisation, AZAPO became obsessed with intellectual dispositions. Increasingly we were dismissed as "armchair revolutionaries". AZAPO also fell into the habit of opposing anything the UDF did. Sometimes this backfired badly. We won the hearts and minds of our community by opposing UDF calls for students to boycott schools for lengthy periods of time, sometimes for a whole year. But sometimes AZAPO would oppose worker "stayaways" that had the support of trade union federations such as COSATU – which was growing in strength. This would leave us with egg on our face. The most embarrassing political act was AZAPO's opposition to Edward Kennedy's visit as a guest of Archbishop Desmond Tutu. Some of our comrades went to the airport with placards reading: "Yankee, go home." And yet Kennedy was one of the staunchest supporters of the struggle in the US Senate, and one of the most influential Senators.

It was this "boycottist" frame of mind that led AZAPO, now under the leadership of the exile wing, to oppose the negotiations with the apartheid government and to stay out of the first democratic elections. AZAPO never really recovered from the lost opportunity to define itself right at the start of the democratic journey. This organisation, that had set itself up as the inheritor and custodian of Biko's vision, split into various factions – the Socialist Party of Azania under Lybon Mabasa, and the Black People's Convention under the leadership of Nkosi Molala. In what would be the death knell for the movement, AZAPO president Mosibudi Mangena was invited to join Thabo Mbeki's government as deputy minister of first education and later science and technology. After that he was hardly visible as the leader of an opposition party. AZAPO and the PAC would be reduced to one seat each of the 400-odd seats in parliament.

The Technocratic Turn

The politics of consciousness raising and cultural empowerment that inspired the Black Consciousness Movement have all but disappeared in contemporary South Africa.[294] I have written elsewhere about the emergence of "technocratic creep" as

---

294 Xolela Mangcu (2003). "Johannesburg in Flight from Itself" in Richard Tomlinson, Robert Beauregard, Lindsay Bremner, Xolela Mangcu (eds), *Emerging Johannesburg*, (New York: Routledge), 286.

the philosophy of rule in South Africa. I first recognised this drift – from culture as a resource for development towards a modernist technocratic outlook – during a discussion with my good friend Martin Bernal at Cornell University. This was shortly after the government had announced the Reconstruction and Development Programme as the policy blueprint for the new South Africa. Bernal commented, half-jokingly, that South Africa had leapfrogged her way back to the 1950s, as if the 1970s had nothing to teach us.

The concept of "service delivery" had its origins in this period when civic organisations were demanding services in the townships, and in the intellectual role played by white academics advising the civics and subsequently the new government. The most glaring example of this consumerist orientation came when then president Nelson Mandela announced that the government would deliver three million houses by the end of the decade. Poor people below a certain income level would receive housing subsidies, but the subsidies would be given to developers who would then construct the houses, and the people would get them for free. Indeed, the government's record in terms of the number of houses built for the poor is unparalleled in the world. But it was just a matter of time before the government realised that giving poor and unemployed people free houses on such a large scale was a recipe for disaster. Not only were the houses shoddily built by developers who saw in this a bonanza to make a quick buck, but the people also began to rent the houses out while they returned to their former shacks. Many houses were built in far-flung places with no economic opportunity. In terms of quality they were worse than the matchbox houses of the apartheid era, and the government had to demolish many of them at huge cost. A staggering 87% of these houses were found to have had one building flaw or the other. It took ten years for the government to adopt a new housing policy that sought to develop homes closer to places of economic opportunity, with greater recognition of different modes of housing delivery – from mutual assistance to upgrading of informal settlements.

The Mandela government was faced with the challenge of demonstrating not only to a sceptical white world that it could undertake development on a large scale, but also to black people that the struggle had indeed been worthwhile. Housing delivery was seen as democracy's most immediate and visible dividend. But in doing so the government forgot Julius Nyerere's injunction that "people cannot be developed; they can only develop themselves. For, while it is possible for an outsider to build a man's house, an outsider cannot give the man pride and self-confidence in himself as a human being. Those things a man has to create in himself by his own actions."[295] Steve Biko and the BCM understood this insight well. How tragic that this insight was not extended to the reconstruction of our society. As I write, South Africa has established a National Planning Commission. Its initial rhetoric about promoting citizenship is encouraging, although its leadership is often too timid in preaching the philosophy of self-reliant development that was the hallmark of Black Consciousness.

---

295 Julius K Nyerere (1973). *Freedom and Development* (New York: Oxford University Press), 27.

The "Big Chief Syndrome" in South Africa's Leadership

Along with the technocratic, consumerist conception of development, a "big chief" approach to leadership started to develop. This was a departure from the peer leadership of the Black Consciousness Movement. As previously mentioned, Steve was known for his bad temper and he could be arrogant at times. But this cannot negate the fact that the movement he led was more or less a movement of equals. They were all university students and were not going to be steam-rollered into blindly following any one leader.

This egalitarian culture had its drawbacks, however. The decision to go ahead with the Frelimo rallies despite Steve's opposition is an example of what can happen when there is no balance. And yet Steve's approach to leadership has lessons for contemporary discussions on leadership and succession. Stubbs has described Steve's "extraordinary gift of leadership"[296] as consisting of his ability to develop layers of leadership under him. This empowering of leaders started from the very beginning of the movement when he insisted on Barney Pityana taking over as president of SASO. According to Stubbs, "it was an integral part of Steve's greatness as a leader that he could step down and give loyal service to someone as yet very little known outside the Eastern Cape".[297] Stubbs made a similar observation in his memoir, *Martyr of Hope*:

> One of the most impressive features of the BCP [Black Community Programmes] was its capacity to survive the removal

---

296 Stubbs, "Martyr of Hope", in Biko, *I Write What I Like*, 211.
297 Aelred Stubbs, "The Story of Nyameko Barney Pityana" in *South African Outlook*, no.1300, 1979.

> of key personnel, and to continue to function with a minimum loss of effectiveness, and no loss at all of spirit . . . if Steve had been the kind of leader who kept everything in his own hands, the whole thing would have collapsed. But full scope was given to every individual for initiative, and the supportive spirit of the King [William's Town] community buttressed the shortcomings an individual might be afraid of in him- or herself.[298]

Stubbs gets dangerously close to Thomas Carlyle's "great man" theory of leadership in explaining Steve's care for those under him. "But I would have to go to Jesus himself to find a parallel to this extraordinary pastoral care which Steve had for his own. I suppose this is why I was prepared to commit myself so whole-heartedly to the care of his leadership. In this particular area I trusted him with the same kind of trust I have in Jesus." And then this man of the cloth self-consciously realises he may be crossing the line of "great man" worship, especially regarding a man who was at best an unconventional Christian and who was critical of organised religion and denominationalism:

> I know this sounds idolatrous to a Christian believer, but there was nothing idolatrous in my attitude to him . . . the main points here are the freedom Steve gave to his followers, a freedom to be themselves; and the actual rightness of his judgements and dispositions, rightness which flowed from his intelligence and from his essential revolutionary selfless-

---

[298] Stubbs, "The Story of Nyameko Barney Pityana", 210-211.

ness. Whereas other leaders tend almost insensibly to become Leaders with a capital L, I never saw any sign at all of this happening with Steve. He remained to the end on all fours with us, an example of what we all could be, above and beyond us only in his vision, and in the depths of his commitment as his death in detention showed.[299]

Stubbs perceptively adds that strong organisation was important to prevent the emergence of the "big man syndrome" in the movement. He writes that even at the time of the formation of SASO, Steve had "an extraordinary magnetism. His hold on his all-black audiences was almost frightening, it was as if they were listening to a messiah. Yet the organisation was not only democratic but from the outset set its face against a leadership cult."[300]

Steve's wife, Ntsiki, also describes Steve's leadership in semi-religious terms:

> Steve was, I think, just a gifted person. I always say even the name he was given by his parents, Bantu – meaning people – was apt because he was able to reach out to the older people, and also able to reach out to the younger people. He was able to mingle with different ages. He was able to sit down and talk sense. If he was with younger kids, he would behave like young kids. So that was the gift, I think, he got from God, so he would be able to work with all sorts of people.[301]

---

[299] Stubbs, "Martyr of Hope" in Biko, *I Write What I Like*, 218.
[300] Stubbs, "Martyr of Hope", 180.
[301] Ntsiki Biko, interview with Colson, 2008.

Ntsiki Biko also provides a more earthly account of Steve's leadership:

> I married a guy not knowing he was a leader, he was just like any man to me. But I could see that there was something driving him to want to work with and for the people. So much that, most of the time, you would find that even the family was not coming first. I'll give you an example of what I am saying. Sometimes, you know, when we were staying here [Ginsberg] when he got banned in 1973, people would come with problems. There's money problems or family problems. Somebody would come and say "I don't have money to send my child to school", or "I haven't got food at home". You know what he used to do? He would take our bags and actually empty our bags so that he gets whatever he wants to help that person. So he was always wanting to do something for people. [302]

Bokwe Mafuna describes the atmosphere when Steve was around. He remembers the day of their first encounter:

> So there I was, in front of this hovering black man, with an unbelievable presence. Steve shone in any gathering because of his deep interest in people, his sharp intellect and eloquence. He was a gifted speaker and could spellbind any audience – black or white, intellectuals, working class or rural folk, young or old. I was immediately attracted to his intellectual handling of our main preoccupation, the evils of apart-

---

[302] Ntsiki Biko, interview with Colson, 2008.

heid and the challenges to our community. But he could also talk about economics, literature, jazz or Marabi music. He was knowledgeable about African traditions and the history of our people. I was amazed at the range of his abilities.[303]

Stubbs similarly remembers walking into a room at St Peter's College at the Federal Seminary in Alice:

> During my last year at the seminary I did not see much of Stephen, but I remember entering the students' common room at St Peter's one day and seeing him sprawled in an armchair, as usual the centre of attention. He looked like one of the large feline animals – a tiger maybe – with an animal grace and an insolent ease and a sense of immense latent power. "Hallo there," he greeted me, not rising from his chair, but with a relaxed friendliness that was virtually irresistible. It was only much later that I learned that this spontaneous informality masked his deep respect for me as his "dear priest".[304]

Donald Woods wrote that Steve "more than any other person I have encountered had the most impressive array of qualities and abilities in that sphere of life which determines the fates of people – politics."[305] As the sociologist Max Weber said, revolutionary movements do require charismatic leaders such as Steve Biko and Nelson Mandela. And as Ronald Heifetz puts it,

---

303 Bokwe Mafuna, "The Impact of Steve Biko on My Life" in Chris van Wyk, *We Write What We Like*, 80.
304 Stubbs, "Martyr of Hope", in Biko, *I Write What I Like*, 182.
305 Woods, *Biko*, 85.

from time to time people need to rest the weight of their burden on someone's shoulders.[306] However, the challenge of democratic societies is the ability to institutionalise their values – this is what Weber called rational-legal authority based on impersonal administration and rule-following. This was necessary if democracy was to be bigger than the sum of its parts – bigger than the individuals who make up its leadership. Mandela was acutely aware of the dangers of charismatic leadership and stepped down after one term in office, even though the presidency was his for the taking for another term.

Mandela was succeeded by Thabo Mbeki – who started out as a mix between charismatic and rational-legal authority. Mbeki sounded hopeful notes of a return to the cultural themes of empowerment that were the hallmark of the Black Consciousness and Pan Africanist movements. My former Black Consciousness comrade, Mojanku Gumbi, became one of Mbeki's closest advisors. Richard Calland described Gumbi as the most important person in the country after Mbeki.[307] Mbeki advocated the idea of the African Renaissance as the leitmotif for Africa's cultural, political and economic revival. The African Renaissance could become part of what the American literary critic Van Wyck Brooks called the "usable past", which is really nothing more than the idea that in re-imagining themselves, societies ought to turn to the treasure trove of their collective memory, and selectively choose that which they think can be useful in the making of a new political, eco-

---

306 Ronald Heifetz (1994). *Leadership Without Easy Answers* (Cambridge: Harvard University Press), 251.
307 Richard Calland (2006). *Anatomy of South Africa: Who Holds The Power?* (Cape Town: Zebra Press).

nomic and cultural order. Just as memory is needed to avoid the mistakes of the past, it is equally needed to adapt what has worked in the past to meet the challenges of the present.

The African Renaissance held the promise of a new public philosophy. Unfortunately, the African Renaissance became no more than what Cabral called "a cultural renaissance [that] was expressed in European languages, which the indigenous people could not understand".[308] What was supposed to be a public philosophy became a measure of private loyalty to the leader and an instrument of economic gain for the politically well-connected. A couple of conferences were organised in Sandton, and nothing has been heard of the renaissance ever since. A Centre for African Renaissance Studies is attached to the University of South Africa, but it is a far cry from the mobilising leitmotif that some of us had hoped for. The Renaissance lacked the organic link to communities that was the central tenet of Black Consciousness philosophy. I shall not dwell on Mbeki's other shortcomings, such as his disastrous stance towards HIV/AIDS. Suffice to say that Mbeki, in the words of Achille Mbembe:

> ... made enemies of people who could have been his friends and of those he could have easily won over by charm, persuasion, or simply by carefully listening to them ... he never really achieved the kind of inner peace and inner joy that could have set him on the path towards authentic freedom – freedom from past wounds, pettiness, paranoia, vindictiveness and lack of generosity.[309]

---

308 Patrick Chabal (2003). *Amilcar Cabral: Revolutionary Leadership and People's War* (Trenton, NJ: Africa World Press), 185.

309 Achille Mbembe, "When the dust settles South Africa will note his good work", *The Star*, 1 October 2008.

A leader who does not have "inner peace" is unlikely to help his followers achieve what Stubbs argues Steve gave to his fellow leaders and followers: "inner freedom". Mbeki was unceremoniously kicked out of office by his fellow party members in the famous Polokwane ANC leadership elections in December 2007, and was subsequently recalled from the presidency of the country in September 2008. He was replaced by Kgalema Motlanthe who did nothing much in government other than warm the seat for the real contender for the throne – Jacob Zuma.

Zuma emerged as the classic charismatic hero, representing the interests of the alienated masses and many of those who had been hurt by Mbeki. That is how Zuma was able to put together one of the most remarkable political alliances of the post-democratic era – from pimps and hooligans to stripe-suited businessmen to trade unionists and opinion makers. And, as Ernesto Laclau puts it: "Since any kind of institutional system is inevitably at least partially limiting and frustrating, there is something appealing about any figure who challenges it, whatever the reasons and forms of the challenge."[310] Zuma thus ascended to power less because he was loved and more because Mbeki was hated.

Even though excited about Zuma's ascendancy, I left room for doubt:

> The question at the end of the day is whether the new leadership under Jacob Zuma has the emotional temperament, the ethical-moral commitment, the political willingness and the

---

310   Ernesto Laclau (2005). *On Populist Reason* (London: Verso), 123.

institutional resources needed for the revival of democracy. If they do not, then we will be in no better position than we were under Mbeki. In fact, we might even be in worse shape. In the end Mbeki's autocratic behaviour might simply be replaced by anarchy under Zuma. The democratic moment would have been just that – a passing moment.[311]

It was indeed only a matter of time before allegations of corruption against Zuma's administration began to surface, and before the president himself started to behave in pretty much the same way as his predecessor. Zuma would come to define yet another type of Max Weber's three types of leadership – traditional or "prebendal" authority.

Under this kind of leadership there is no distinction between public authority and private interests. However, unlike charismatic authority – where leader and led are bound by a higher moral cause – the leader-led relationship is based on patrimonialism. The followers are dispensable and are totally at the mercy of the "chief". This is not the place to go into detail about some of the problems that have beset the Zuma administration, other than to note that it has prebendalism written all over it. According to Plaut and Holden, "the president's wives, children and other persons closely associated with him are reported to have developed 220 businesses between them, many established since Zuma became president".[312] Plaut and Holden write that the president's family

---

311 Xolela Mangcu (2009). *The Democratic Moment: South Africa's Prospects under Jacob Zuma* (Johannesburg: Jacana Press), 3.
312 Martin Plaut and Paul Holden (2012). *Who Rules South Africa?* (Cape Town: Jonathan Ball Publishers) 284.

businesses extend beyond South Africa to places such as Mozambique and the Democratic Republic of Congo, and that some Zuma family members have received construction projects without going through proper tender processes. The most highly publicised relationship has been that between the president, his family and the politically well-connected Gupta family – to the extent that some cabinet ministers have said they knew about their fate in cabinet reshuffles from members of the Gupta family. One cabinet minister informed me that he has refused summonses from the Guptas to come to their house. Some of these relationships have blown up in the president's face – a mining deal in which his son stood to gain millions was overturned by the courts and his nephew ran into the ground another mining company, Aurora, leading to its liquidation and losses of jobs for employees.

Zuma did not cover himself in glory by making a series of high-level decisions that were overturned by the courts. The Supreme Court of Appeal ruled that the president had not exercised his mind when he appointed Menzi Simelane as head of the National Prosecuting Authority – even after he was deemed to have lied to the Ginwala Commission of Inquiry into the firing of Vusi Pikoli by former president Thabo Mbeki. The Public Service Commission had even recommended that disciplinary action be taken against Simelane, and yet the president saw fit to appoint him as head of the National Prosecuting Authority.

The Constitutional Court reversed the president's extension of Judge Sandile Ngcobo's term on the Constitutional Court by ruling that the legislation on which the president relied – section 8A of the Judges' Remuneration and Conditions of Employment Act – was unconstitutional. The president is reported to have sat on a report by controversial former director of crime intelligence, Richard Mdluli, stating that there was a plot by Tokyo Sexwale and other senior members of the ANC to oust him. Mdluli – who has been dogged by a combination of murder and corruption charges – has been accused of tapping the phones of those perceived to be Zuma's enemies within the ANC. It took the acting national commissioner of police, Nhlanhla Mkhwanazi, to suspend Mdluli against the will of the minister of police, Nathi Mthethwa.

At the time of writing the Democratic Alliance had won a major victory against the president himself – by obtaining a Supreme Court of Appeal ruling to have a judicial review of the dropping of corruption charges against him. It is in the light of all these reversals that the president calls for the powers of the Constitutional Court to be reviewed.

And then there have been the attacks on the media through a combination of proposed pieces of legislation – one called the Protection of State Information Bill. If passed, this bill would have had a chilling effect on anti-corruption activities, as it carried a potential jail sentence of 25 years for whistle-blowers who revealed state secrets. The bill was so controversial and met with such public opposition that the ANC was forced to introduce a public interest clause – which would protect those individuals who revealed information in the public interest, particularly corrupt activities.

In a nutshell, Zuma brings to mind the emperor Napoleon's frustration at the checks imposed on him by the institutions of the French Revolution. "A constitution must not interfere with the process of government, nor be written in a way that would force the government to violate it," thundered the French emperor.[313] Archbishop Desmond Tutu captured the spirit of our times – the essence of our public philosophy – when he responded to the government's refusal to grant the Dalai Lama a visa to attend his birthday party: "You do not represent me, Mr Zuma, you represent yourself and your interests."

Tutu's response captured the essence of our current malaise: that interests instead of values have taken over in our political culture. This is a far cry from Steve Biko's approach to politics.

---

313 Lefebvre, *Napoleon*, 114.

Epilogue: Coming Full Circle

Outside my own family, no single individual shaped my life in the way that Steve Biko did. My earliest memories swirl with the imagery of Black Consciousness activists in Ginsberg in the 1970s. As Aelred Stubbs notes, confirming what Fikile Mlinda said earlier: "King [William's Town] became a centre for all those committed to the Black Consciousness Movement. The BPC (the Black People's Convention) was growing in strength and the branch at King was one of the strongest in the country." And as Steve's childhood friends and adult-life comrades, Fikile Mlinda and Sonwabo Yengo remarked, everyone in Ginsberg belonged to the BPC – "even a dog was BPC here". No wonder, then, that my political and intellectual trajectory has had Steve Biko as its pivot.

However, to think of my obsession with Biko as purely political and intellectual would be to underplay the personal dimension. I am no psychologist, but I cannot help thinking that Steve Biko's death must have been a deeply traumatic experience for both adults and children in our community. On more than one occasion I found myself choking up – 35 years after the fact – when writing about the circumstances of his death.

One of the most painful moments for me was learning that Steve had offered to kiss one of his killers for giving him water and *mageu* (a non-alcoholic drink made from fermented mealie pap) – and this was after he had already suffered a brain injury.

A writing career has given me the opportunity to spend more time thinking about Steve's death than most in our little community. It is in these moments that I realise that I am indeed still in mourning. In his book *Something Torn and New*, Ngugi wa Thiong'o observes that "the political and cultural struggles of Africans since the great dismemberment wrought by European slavery and colonialism have been driven by the vision of wholeness. These struggles, taken as a whole, have been instrumental as strategies and tactics for remembering the fragmented. Indeed, they have comprised a quest for wholeness."[314] If the artist Paul Stopforth sought, through his artwork, to restore Steve's dismembered body to wholeness, my own life as an artist has been to restore Steve in our public consciousness, and in the process perhaps regain my own wholeness.

I remember receiving Steve's wife, Ntsiki, and their son, Nkosinathi, in New York in 1998 as I was getting ready to come back home after a decade of studying in the United States. I was working for the Rockefeller Foundation in New York City when the Bikos visited, and was trying to get the Foundation interested in funding a Steve Biko Memorial Heritage Centre in our township. As it turned out, the Bikos had not only been thinking along similar lines but they had also already regis-

---

314 wa Thiong'o, *Something New and Torn*, 29.

tered the Steve Biko Foundation. Even though I had studied city planning, I found myself attracted to a public role. I did not see myself fitting in government and given my political history had no reason to believe that I would be welcome in an ANC government. I also simply could not relate to the corporate world. The thought of joining a university as a junior lecturer just petrified me.

Luckily enough, Steven Friedman, who was then running the Centre for Policy Studies in Johannesburg, visited me at the Rockefeller Foundation and convinced me that his Centre was the place to be. It was indeed the leading think tank in South Africa at the time – with prominent thinkers such as Khehla Shubane, Chris Landsberg, Claude Kabemba, Mcebisi Ndletyana and Shaun MacKay. Friedman was gracious enough to allow me and Nkosinathi Biko to use the Centre to further the idea behind the formation of the Biko Foundation. We approached the Ford Foundation for funding. (The Rockefeller Foundation did not provide any funding in South Africa.) I tried my hand at moral blackmail, reminding the Ford Foundation that back in the 1970s, Steve had unsuccessfully approached them for funding, and that they had instead chosen to fund the South African Institute of Race Relations. But blackmail was not necessary: We received the grant because of the strength of our argument. Steve Biko's name had been erased from public memory and something needed to be done to correct this injustice. As it turned out, Black Consciousness stalwart Ishmael Mkhabela had already been allocated funding from the Ford Foundation for a research project on family-based economic development and was persuaded to work with us in Ginsberg.

In Ginsberg we identified youths – Thabisa Bata and Lindani Ntenteni – to work as researchers for Mkhabela. These two have their own interesting histories: Thabisa was sitting around in Ginsberg unemployed, even though she had a BSc Honours in Medical Microbiology with distinction from the University of the Western Cape. Lindani had dropped out of his legal studies at the University of Fort Hare when he could no longer pay the fees. In his interaction with the young people, Mkhabela suggested that they form a youth umbrella body that would address the problems of youth in Ginsberg. I had been meeting with some of these youth leaders at my mother's house about what could be done to overcome the divisions among their youth formations. Youth leaders from the different groups then eventually formed the Ginsberg Youth Council under the leadership of Andile Big Joe Jack – son of the legendary Doctor Pringle Jack of Steve Biko's youth described in Chapter 3. The Foundation gave the new organisation a small grant of R3 000 for their launch in the local community hall. That meeting, which was attended by government representatives, elected their first executive committee with several sub-committees to deal with issues such as health, education, entertainment and economic development.

The Foundation also helped the youth raise funding from the Anglo American Corporation for the Ginsberg Social History Project. Partnerships were formed with both government and academic institutions: for example, the provincial department of forestry offered outdoor excursions and two historians from the University of Fort Hare, Sean Morrow and Brown Maaba, were commissioned to run history workshops with the young people.

Epilogue: Coming Full Circle

The highlight of the Ginsberg Social History Project was that two of the youths travelled to Australia as guests of the Fred Hollows Foundation to share their experiences of the history project with indigenous communities of Australia. This was the first time that they had travelled outside the country.

The University of Fort Hare became increasingly interested in the work with the young people. The dean of the Faculty of Management Sciences at Fort Hare, Nhlanganiso Dladla, offered the university campus as a venue for an Annual Youth Conference. The conference brought together hundreds of activists from around the Eastern Cape, and sometimes had international guests such as the Clinton Democracy Initiative, and Mel King from the Massachusetts Institute of Technology. Prominent guest speakers included the likes of Steve's contemporaries – Malusi Mpumlwana and Bishop Mvume Dandala.

The important thing about these initiatives is that they gave young people a sense of identity and self-confidence, enabling them to pursue their interests. Thus, Thabisa Bata obtained a Ford Foundation scholarship and obtained a Master's degree in Public Health at Boston University; Big Joe Jack is a prominent community leader and active member of the Ginsberg Civic Association; Lala Aplom and Mfundo Ngele are assistant directors in the department of traditional and local government; Lindani Ntenteni is at the Steve Biko Foundation and Xola Moni is an entrepreneur.

The Foundation also worked closely with a women's organisation, Sosebenza Sonke. This was a group of women entrepreneurs and community activists – Sybree Keke, Sibongile Qaba, Busi Mneno and Steve's widow, Ntsiki. They worked closely with people living with HIV/AIDS and initiated community economic development projects in rural areas surrounding King William's Town. Another community group, known as Nomzamo, was a group of elderly women, mostly pensioners, some of them former professionals. These women ran community gardens and worked closely with the youth council, especially around issues of violence against older women.

While the community work proceeded, mainly in the Eastern Cape under the leadership of the late Mncedi Ngoloyi, the question in my mind was how Steve Biko's teachings and the Biko Foundation could gain greater visibility. Then came a "eureka moment": How about an annual Steve Biko Memorial Lecture to be given by a distinguished intellectual? This would be consistent with Steve's own ideas. In 1972 he edited *Black Viewpoint* with essays by Njabulo Ndebele, Gatsha Buthelezi, CMC Ndamse and Ben Khoapa. In the preface Steve spoke about the importance of developing an intellectual culture in the black community:

> We have felt and observed in the past the existence of a great vacuum in our literary world and newspapers. So many things are said so often to us, about us and for us, but seldom by us. This has created a dependency mood amongst us which has given rise to the present tendency to look at ourselves in terms of how we are interpreted by the white press.

He continued in a vein that has relevance to the media debates in South Africa today:

Epilogue: Coming Full Circle

> One must quickly add that the moral of the story is not that we must therefore castigate the white society and its newspapers. Any group of people who identify as a unit through shared interests and aspirations need to protect those interests they share. The white press is therefore regarded by whites as doing a good service when it sensitises its own community to the "dangers" of Black Power . . . the real moral of the story can only be that we blacks must on our own develop those agencies that we need, and not look up to unsympathetic and often hostile quarters to offer these to us.[315]

Sadly, this is a challenge that still remains for the black community, forty years after Steve uttered those prophetic words.

As I toyed with the idea of an annual lecture, Njabulo Ndebele immediately came to mind. In the late 1990s Ndebele and I had stayed in the same apartment building in New York's Roosevelt Island. On occasion I would ask him to baby-sit my little girls, Thando and Ranji, a task to which he took with great relish. I was thus sufficiently familiar with him to pick up the phone and ask if he would deliver the inaugural Steve Biko Memorial Lecture at the University of Cape Town, where he had just been appointed vice-chancellor. He accepted immediately and without hesitation.

Ndebele's lecture in September 2000, titled *"Iph' indlela?"* – Where is the way? – was a tour de force. He highlighted the inhumanity of apartheid, while asking searing questions about our own readiness to lead. Did we possess the social imagination to create a new society?

---

315 Steve Biko (1972). *Black Viewpoint* (Durban: Spro-Cas Black community Programmes), 7-8.

The second lecture, titled "Biko's Children", was delivered by the celebrated South African writer Zakes Mda in 2001. "In Sesotho there is a saying: *motjheka sidiba ha a se nwe* – he who digs a well does not drink from it. Only those who come after him will quench their thirst from its cool water. When the forebears formulated this adage, they had Steve Bantu Biko in mind," Mda said. He held up the community development programmes of the Black Consciousness Movement as an example of self-reliant development, something that needed to be nurtured among South African youth growing up in today's entitlement culture.

The third lecture, by the doyen of African literature, Chinua Achebe, was the biggest event yet. The story behind Achebe's visit is itself worth re-telling.

I visited Achebe at his home at Bard College in upstate New York where he was teaching. "Steve Biko," he murmured and remained silent for a while, while his wife served a delicious lunch. And then: "You know, Steve Biko always reminded me of Christopher Okigbo – both men died very young. They seemed to be in a rush to finish their missions here on earth." He mentioned that he had never been invited to South Africa, which made my heart sink a little. If neither the government nor our universities had invited this man, who were we to think we would be successful? I made every promise I could about how wonderful the trip would be. I even promised I would persuade the University of Cape Town (UCT) to award him an honorary doctorate. He agreed to come . . . on one condition. My heart sank again. He wanted to bring his family with him. Where were we going to get the money? But I could not let my thoughts show. "No problem, oh, no problem at all, Prof," I said, my mind racing with ideas for raising the money.

Achebe's visit in 2002 was as exciting as it was nerve-racking. Achebe was in a wheelchair – he had been in a car accident, and had lost the use of his legs. We had to take extra care that there were no glitches or potential embarrassment to him or ourselves. All transport and accommodation had to be wheelchair friendly. One of my best memories was when I ran into Abdullah Ibrahim at the foyer of the Hyatt Hotel, where Achebe was staying. I walked up to Ibrahim and said, "Guess who we have as a guest in the hotel?"

"Who?"

As he said this, he was sizing me up in his intimidating manner.

"Chinua Achebe," I said.

I don't know what made me approach Ibrahim – after all, I hardly knew the man, but he was as excited as a teenager and asked if I could arrange for them to meet. It turned out that Achebe was a great fan of Ibrahim, and asked if we could come up to his room. It was just one of those remarkable moments when two icons meet. They were falling over each other, taking photographs and bantering like little kids as if they had known each other for ages.

We also arranged for Achebe to meet with Nelson Mandela at his house in Cape Town. Again, Achebe was as curious about Mandela as Mandela was excited about having him in his house. And off we went to UCT. The university had agreed to give Achebe an honorary doctorate. Seeing the UCT staff and professoriate march into Jameson Hall in honour of Achebe, and seeing him being hoisted on the stage was deeply moving.

Achebe invoked the writers Alex La Guma and Peter Abrahams, aware of their roots in the Western Cape – in yet another symbolic statement of the hybridity of the South African journey towards freedom.

"Don't worry about Biko," he would later say, at a dinner the Foundation organised in his honour at the Sandton Convention Centre, "he is fine. What about you?"

In that room was Es'kia Mphahlele, whom Achebe cited as his great teacher, someone who never received the honour that he deserved in his own country.

For the next year's lecture we had Ngugi wa Thiong'o in our sights. And of course it helped that Achebe had given the previous lecture. "If Achebe saw fit to accept, who am I to turn down such an honour?" Ngugi said in his characteristically humorous style.

The Foundation organised a series of activities for him in the Eastern Cape, including Ginsberg. He wanted to interact with local writers and we organised a workshop with African language writers. Ngugi had been introduced to African intellectual history by Ntongela Masilela, whose digital archive on African intellectuals is simply unparalleled. Ngugi was particularly interested in the work of the great Xhosa writer SEK Mqhayi, and devoted a great deal of his 2003 lecture to the need to re-imagine ourselves in African ways, particularly through our languages.

However, the biggest fish for us was Nelson Mandela. There were a number of reasons for this, including the fact that it would be a gesture of reconciliation, given the long history of antagonism between the BCM and the ANC in the 1980s. The first opportunity presented itself in 2002 when a rather incredible thing happened. I was sitting at my office at the Foundation, minding my own business, when a call came through from the Nelson Mandela Foundation. Our secretary Pam Mbuli put her hand on the mouthpiece and said it was Mr Mandela's secretary, Zelda la Grange, on the line. Zelda is an incredible Afrikaner woman who has been on Nelson Mandela's staff since 1994 and became Mandela's personal assistant after he left office in 1999. She is an effective, if sometimes fierce, gatekeeper, and I sympathise with her tough job of managing the hordes of people who want to see the greatest leader in the world. I remember Reverend Jesse Jackson, frustrated at the Nelson Mandela Foundation offices in Houghton because he could not see Mr Mandela. He was made even more furious by the fact that a white woman would not let him see an African brother.

Zelda told Pam that Mr Mandela wanted to talk to me. Pam in turn asked if she should put him through. Yeah right, I said to myself. As if I could have said: "Please ask Mr Mandela to call back, I am busy at the moment." I told Pam I would take the call from where she was sitting. I was not about to leave to chance the opportunity to speak to Mandela – what if the connection was lost and he never called again? "Hello, Tata, *ninjani?*" I asked. "*Siphilile, ninjani nina?*" – We are well and how are you? – the old man enquired. He then told me he needed my help. He was writing a book about his years as president and needed to confirm something. There was a certain Mr Skhosana of the BCM who had visited him soon after his release from Robben Island. This gentleman had asked him to be "the president of all South Africans, not just the ANC". He wanted to include this in his book, but he first wanted to meet the man. I told him that the man in question was most likely Mahlomola Skhosana, who was my comrade in AZAPO but was more involved with the National Council of Trade Unions (NACTU). I traced Skhosana to the NACTU offices in Johannesburg, and he confirmed that he, together with Cyril Ramaphosa and other community leaders from Soweto, had visited Mandela at his home with that specific message of unity. I reported back to Mandela but before I rang off, I asked if he would write a tribute to Steve Biko for a newspaper supplement we were producing for the 25th anniversary of Steve's death. That tribute became the Prologue to this book.

But we still wanted Mandela for the Steve Biko Memorial Lecture and the opportunity came after a visit to his house in 2003. As we walked out of that meeting, he put his arm around me and said jokingly: "You see, Xolela, if Steve Biko were alive he would have joined the ANC. You know why? This is because in Africa, liberation movements rule for a long, long time." I then asked if he would consider giving the upcoming Steve Biko Memorial Lecture. "Oh yes," he thundered. "Just speak to Zelda, she controls my life." I drove back at break-neck speed to break the news to my colleagues.

In September 2004, the University of Cape Town's Jameson Hall was filled to capacity, with endless lines forming outside. And then the man's grand entrance, accompanied by his wife, Graça Machel, who also was the chancellor of the university. It was my duty to introduce Mandela to the crowd. I told myself I would not say a word more than was necessary, and made a perfunctory remark about how my little daughter had refused to believe me when I told her I would be introducing Mr Mandela that evening. And without any further ado, I

Epilogue: Coming Full Circle

invited him to deliver the fifth annual Steve Biko Memorial Lecture. The crowd greeted him with deafening applause.

Mandela started in his characteristically humorous manner: "You see, in my younger days I would never have shared the stage with this young man here, Xolela."

The applause was thunderous! For me, that statement was enough. He needed to go no further. Our mission of sending a message of reconciliation was accomplished, and I suspect he too knew the significance of his statement.

By linking Biko to the Khoi and the San, Nelson Mandela had brought full circle the history of what he has called "the long walk to freedom". An even more appropriate characterisation may indeed be that of "a long gallop to freedom". It is a gallop that begins with the Khoi and the San chased out of the northern Cape frontier; continuing with the Xhosa chief Hintsa chased to his death by his colonial tormentors; and the people of Sharpeville shot in their backs while responding to Sobukwe's call to defy apartheid's pass laws; and Nelson Mandela being tracked down by the apartheid security police; and the children of Soweto being chased down the streets of Soweto; Allan Boesak running with the horses in the 1980s; and Chris Hani being shot galloping through his own neighbourhood at the dawn of freedom.

Steve Biko was one of those who said black people were tired of running. He stood his ground and prophetically staked his claim – our claim – to the future of our country. With the following words he issued his challenge to the apartheid regime and gave us the courage and the language to finally take our freedom: "Gentlemen, this is what we want. This is where you are and this is where we are, and this is what we want."[316]

316 Biko, *I Write What I Like*, 150.

Select Bibliography

Arnold, Millard (ed.). 1979. *The Testimony of Steve Biko*. London: Maurice Temple Smith Publishers.

Attwell, David. 2005. *Rewriting Modernity: Studies in Black South African Literary History*. Scottsville: University of KwaZulu-Natal Press.

Badat, Saleem. 2009. *Black Man, You Are On Your Own*. Johannesburg: Steve Biko Foundation and STE Publishers.

Berlin, Isaiah (edited by Henry Hardy). 1990. *The Crooked Timber of Humanity: Chapters in the History of Ideas*. London: John Murray.

Biko, Steve. 2004 [1978]. *I Write What I Like*. Johannesburg: Picador Africa.

Burns, James MacGregor. 1978. *Leadership*. New York: Harper Row Publishers.

Calland, Richard. 2006. *Anatomy of South Africa: Who Holds the Power?*. Cape Town: Zebra Press.

Chabal, Patrick. 2003. *Amilcar Cabral: Revolutionary Leadership and People's War*. Trenton, NJ: Africa World Press.

Chalmers, John. 1877. *Tiyo Soga: A Page of South African Mission Work*. Edinburgh: Andrew Elliott.

Fanon, Frantz. 1963. *The Wretched of the Earth*. New York: Grove Press.

Fanon, Frantz. 1963. *Black Skin, White Masks*. 2008 [1967]. London: Pluto Press.

Gates Jr., Henry Louis and Cornel West (eds). 1996. *The Future of the Race*. New York: Vintage Books.

Gerhart, Gail. 1978. *Black Power in South Africa: The Evolution of an Ideology*. Berkeley: University of California at Berkeley.

Gibson, Nigel. 2011. *Fanonian Practices in South Africa: From Steve Biko to Abahlali baseMjondolo*. Scottsville: University of KwaZulu-Natal Press.

Heifetz, Ronald. 1994. *Leadership Without Easy Answers*. Cambridge, MA: The Belknap Press of Harvard University Press.

Hitchens, Christopher. 2011. *Arguably*. London: Atlantic Books.
Hughes, H Stuart. 1976. *Consciousness and Society*. New York: Octagon Books.
Jordan, AC. 1973. *Towards an African Literature: The Emergence of Literary Form in South Africa*. Los Angeles: University of California Press.
Kundera, Milan. 1996. *The Book of Laughter and Forgetting*. London: Harper Collins.
Laclau, Ernesto. 2005. *On Populist Reason*. London: Verso.
Lefebvre, Georges. 2011. *Napoleon*. New York: Routledge.
Legassick, Martin. 2010. *The Struggle for the Eastern Cape 1800-1854: Subjugation and the Roots of South African Democracy*. Johannesburg: KMM Review Publishers.
Levine, Roger. 2011. *A Living Man From Africa: Jan Tzatzoe, Chief and Missionary, and the Making of Nineteenth-Century South Africa*. New Haven: Yale University Press.
Lodge, Tom. 2011. *Sharpeville: An Apartheid Massacre and Its Consequences*. Oxford: Oxford University Press.
Macqueen, Ian. 2011. *Re-imagining South Africa: Black Consciousness, Radical Christianity and the New Left, 1967-1977*. PhD Thesis, University of Sussex.
Magaziner, Daniel. 2010. *The Law and the Prophets: Black Consciousness in South Africa, 1968-1977*. Athens, Ohio: Ohio University Press.
Mandela, Nelson. 1994. *Long Walk To Freedom*. New York: Little, Brown and Company.
Mangcu, Xolela. 1993. *Social Movements and City Planning*. Cornell Working Papers in Planning. Ithaca, New York: Cornell University, Department of City and Regional Planning.
   2007. *The Meaning of Mandela*. Cape Town: HSRC Press.
   2008. *To the Brink: The State of Democracy in South Africa*. Scottsville: University of KwaZulu-Natal Press.
   2009. *The Democratic Moment: South Africa's Prospects Under Jacob Zuma*. Johannesburg: Jacana Media.
   2011. *Becoming Worthy Ancestors*. Johannesburg: Wits University Press.
Mills, C Wright. 1959. *The Sociological Imagination*. New York: Oxford University Press.
Mostert, Noel. 1992. *Frontiers: The Epic of South Africa's Creation and the Tragedy of the Xhosa People*. London: Cape Publishers.
Mngxitama, Andile, Amanda Alexander & Nigel Gibson. 2008. *Biko Lives*. New York: Palgrave MacMillan.
Mqhayi, SEK (edited by Jeff Opland). 2009. *Abantu Besizwe: Historical and Biographical Writings, 1902-1944*. Johannesburg: Wits University Press.

Select Bibliography

Murray, Bruce. 1979. *Wits: The Open Years, A History of the University of the Witwatersrand, 1939-1959*. Johannesburg: Wits University Press.

Ndletyana, Mcebisi. 2008. *African Intellectuals in 19th and Early 20th Century South Africa*. Cape Town: HSRC Press.

Nolutshungu, Sam. 1982. *Changing South Africa: Political Considerations*. Manchester: Manchester University Press.

Nyerere, Julius K. 1973. *Freedom and Development*. New York: Oxford University Press.

Odendaal, André. 1984. *Vukani Bantu!: The Beginnings of Black Protest Politics in South Africa to 1912*. Cape Town: David Philip.

O'Meara, Dan. 1996. *Forty Lost Years: The Apartheid State and the Politics of the National Party 1948-1994*. Johannesburg: Ravan Press.

Papenfus, Theresa. 2011. *Pik Botha and His Times*. Pretoria: Litera.

Peires, Jeff. 1981. *The House of Phalo: A History of the Xhosa People In the Days of their Independence*. Cape Town: Jonathan Ball.,

Peires, Jeff. 1989. *The Dead Will Arise: Nongqause and the Great Xhosa Cattle-Killing Movement of 1856-7*. Cape Town: Jonathan Ball.

Penn, Nigel. 2005. *The Forgotten Frontier*. Ohio University Press.

Peterson, Bhekizizwe. 2000. *Monarchs, Missionaries and African Intellectuals: African Theatre and the Unmaking of Colonial Marginality*. Johannesburg: Wits University Press.

Pityana, N Barney, Mamphela Ramphele, Malusi Mpumlwana & Lindy Wilson. 1992. *Bounds of Possibility: The Legacy of Steve Biko and Black Consciousness*. New York: Zed Press.

Plaatje, Sol. 2007 [1916]. *Native Life in South Africa*. Johannesburg: Picador Africa.

Plaut, Martin and Paul Holden. 2012. *Who Rules South Africa?* Cape Town: Jonathan Ball Publishers.

Rubusana, Benson Walter and SC Satyo. 2002 [1906]. *Zemk'Inkomo Magwalandini*. Cape Town: New Africa Books.

Sandel, Michael. 1996. *Democracy's Discontent: America in Search of a Public Philosophy*. Cambridge, MA: The Belknap Press of Harvard University.

Soga, John Henderson. 1930. *The South-Eastern Bantu*. Johannesburg: Wits University Press.

Stiebel, Lindy and Liz Gunner (eds). 2006. *Still Beating the Drum: Critical Perspectives On Lewis Nkosi*. Johannesburg: Wits University Press.

West, Cornel. 1993. *Race Matters*. New York: Vintage Books.

1999. *The Cornel West Reader*. New York: Basic Civitas Books.

Williams, Donovan. 1983. *The Journal and Selected Writings of Reverend Tiyo Soga*. Cape Town: AA Balkema.

1978. *Umfundisi: A Biography of Tiyo Soga, 1829-1871*. Alice: Lovedale Press.

Van der Merwe, Hendrik and David Welsh. 1972. *Student Perspectives on South Africa*. Cape Town: David Philip.

Van Wyk, Chris. 2007. *We Write What We Like*. Johannesburg: Wits University Press.

wa Thiong'o, Ngugi. 2009. *Something Torn and New: An African Renaissance*. New York: Basic Civitas Books.

Williams, Raymond. 1966. *Modern Tragedy*. Stanford: Stanford University Press.

Wilson, Francis and Dominique Perrot. 1973. *Outlook on a Century, 1870-1970*. Alice: Lovedale and Spro-Cas.

Woods, Donald. 1978. *Biko*. New York: Penguin.

Acknowledgements

The idea for this book – the first full-length biography of Bantu Stephen Biko – came to me while I was a graduate student in the United States in the early 1990s, and I would like to acknowledge the people who helped me along in my early conceptualisations, especially Martin Bernal (author of *Black Athena*) and Isaac Kramnick, who wrote the British socialist Harold Laski's biography. I tried to smuggle Biko's work into my city planning dissertation but my advisor and I ultimately agreed that I should be content with a paper on Biko's developmental legacy. I am grateful to many people who helped with different aspects of the research after I returned to South Africa to work at the Centre for Policy Studies and subsequently at the Steve Biko Foundation – Steve Biko's family (Ntsiki Biko, Nkosinathi and Samora Biko, Hlumelo Biko), Brown Maaba, Sean Morrow and the young men and women of the Ginsberg Youth Council (Andile "Big Joe" Jack, Thabisa Bata, Lindani Ntenteni, Mfundo Ngele, Lala Aplom, Noshumi and Mncedi Ngoloyi). I would also like to acknowledge the generosity of funders – the Ford Foundation and the Kellogg Foundation at various points provided funding for the early research.

Over several years I interviewed scores of people and I have not included specific references to each interview. Among those interviewed were Khaya Biko, Peter Jones, Barney Pityana, Malusi Mpumlwana, Harry Nengwekhulu, Jeff Baqwa, Olaf Baloyi, Mandla Tshabalala, Goolam Abram, Aubrey Mokoape, Ben Khoapa, the late Strini Moodley, the late Stanley Ntwasa, Hlaku Rachidi, Rams Ramokgopa, Neville Alexander, Njabulo Ndebele, the late Fikile Bam, Justice Moloto, Chris Mokoditoa, Colin Collins, Saths Cooper, Pandelani Nefolovhodwe, Mamphela Ramphele, Nobandile Biko, Larry Bekwa, Sonwabo and Beth Yengo, Fikile Mlinda, Zolani Mtshotshisa, Eugenia Nyathi, Nozipho Bhisholo, Zinzo Gulwa, Sithethi Keke, Fumbathile Mbilini, Promotia Mangcu, Aunt Mbeki Tyamzashe, Aunt Damsie Monaheng, Forbes Nyathi, Nonezile Nondalana, Mam'u No-Fence waseNjwaxa, MaPolisa Duna, Nonesi Duna, Lunga Lefume, Bhabha Gcweni, David Russell, Francis Wilson, the late Cosmas Desmond, Neville Curtis, Duncan Innes, John Kane-Berman, Mark Orkin, Paula Ensor, Geoff Budlender, Robert Schrire, Horst Kleinschmidt, Paul Pretorius, Sheila Lapinsky, Renfrew Christie and many other NUSAS activists that the late Barry Streek ensured I could talk to, and, of course, my greatest teacher, my mother, the late Olive Nonji Mangcu.

I am also grateful to my unofficial editor, my most beautiful and lovely wife, Siphokazi – who read each and every page of the manuscript. "The things that love makes us do," she says. "The love you've put in my heart," I say.

I want to acknowledge the support of friends and family over the past few years – Mthobi and Queeneth Tyamzashe, Mzwandile and Nowonga Mangcu, Pumeza Mangcu, Zukisa Nyamakazi, Pam Nyamakazi, Hale Qangule, Mcebisi Ndletyana, Baker Ngubane, Lamla Mapukata, Connie Molusi, Siphiwo and Thandi Lucas, and my dear brother at Princeton, Cornel West.

My drinking buddies at my favourite haunt in Joburg would kill me if I did not mention them: Themba Vundla, Thabo Morena,

Acknowledgements

Sibayeni Kunene, Malope Mojapelo, Tshepo Mohapi, Lawrence Modise, Zola Tsotsi, Moso Bholofo, Bhutana Jali, Wiseman Madinane, Maki Nogaga, Pat Banda, Sifiso Pretorius and Tito Ndibongo.

My biggest thanks, though, go to Erika Oosthuysen who first approached me about publishing this book more than five years ago. I did not pay attention to her then but she persisted and resurfaced a few years ago to ask a mutual friend, Mcebisi Ndletyana, whether I was still writing the book. Mce connected us and the rest is . . . this book. Since then she has been on my case about deadlines – without this harassment we might have had to wait another ten years. As it turns out, she is my homie from King Willliam's Town. Because of the crazy coincidence of skin colour we grew up on different sides of the railway tracks, but here we are. Keep the faith, Erika.

I would also like to thank the respective heads of the Department of Sociology at the University of Cape Town, David Cooper and David Lincoln, for allowing me the space and time to finish this book, and of course the university for research funding to finish this project.

Anyone I have not mentioned will surely surface in the second edition of this book. I say so deliberately because I intend to use this book to facilitate public engagement based on academic research and study – quite like my dear brother Henry Louis Gates Jr. has done with the legacy of WEB Du Bois at Harvard University. Black people cannot continue to celebrate their leaders without institutionalising their legacies through sustained scholarship. As Paula Backscheider[317] puts it, "history is centre stage in black biography . . . the intersection of little-known history and unknown, forgotten, or habitually misrepresented people confronts the biographer at every

---

317 Paula Backscheider (1999). *Reflections on Biography*, (London: Oxford University Press), 210-227.

turn. These are invisible lineages. Rosa Parks' predecessor Ida B Wells defended herself from ouster from a white train car by among other things biting the conductor who laid violent hands on her."

Tracing these "invisible lineages" is a great hazard for the biographer because it takes one into the lives of others who are themselves worthy of biography. The presence of these others and the disparate events they are associated with, Backscheider observes, "threatens to bring narrative to a halt while the biographer has to review their lives and importance". This has also meant moving in and out of studies about modernity, revolution, religion, race, gender, class, leadership, cultural and development studies, social capital, sociology, and very reluctantly into psychology with its ever-present danger of psychobiography. Writing this book has meant confronting difficult questions about what to include without sanitising history and falling into the lure of hagiography. My compass in navigating the cross-currents of these multiple vantage points has been that this is, simply put, a story about leaders and their people, over time.

If Steve Biko stood squarely within the "invisible lineages" of the struggle for freedom, the question is: where does our generation stand in that history? For if truth be told, the biography is as much about the past as it is about what Backscheider calls "its presentness . . . the life is, not just was important". And "the reasons for choosing a particular person as the subject for a biography can be deep, even unreachably in the psyche . . . carried from childhood, born in a chance encounter – the range is infinite".

I therefore write this book acutely aware that "just as biographers bring themselves to biography, so do readers". And so I invite you to bring yourself, dear reader. However, if arrows are shot in my direction, I asked for it.

XOLELA MANGCU is an internationally respected political analyst and commentator, and is currently Associate Professor of Sociology at the University of Cape Town. He was most recently a non-resident Senior Fellow at the Brookings Institution in Washington DC, and was Distinguished Fellow and Executive Director at the Human Sciences Research Council. In addition, he has held fellowships at Harvard University, the Massachusetts Institute of Technology (MIT), and the Rockefeller Foundation. He holds a PhD from Cornell University.

Mangcu, who was a regular columnist for *Business Day*, the *Weekender* and the *Sunday Independent*, has authored and co-authored six books, including *The Meaning of Mandela* (2007), *To the Brink* (2008), *The Democratic Moment* (2009) and *Becoming Worthy Ancestors* (2011). He was the founding Executive Director of the Steve Biko Foundation and grew up in Steve Biko's hometown of Ginsberg, King William's Town.

The *Sunday Times* has described Mangcu as "possibly the most prolific public intellectual in South Africa".

Index

Abrahams, Peter, 320
Abrams, Armien, 252
Abram, Goolam, 113, 115, 128, 135
Achebe, Chinua, 20, 318-320
Action, Theory of, 240-241
African Melodies, 86
African National Congress (ANC), 8, 12, 15, 27, 32, 41, 73, 71, 78, 88, 93-94, 97, 113, 117, 127, 140, 186, 196, 216, 225, 239, 243-249, 257, 266, 270, 280, 287-289, 292-293, 295, 309, 313, 320-322
African Renaissance, 276, 304-305
African Students Association (ASA), 117
African Students Union of South Africa (ASUSA), 117
African Theology, 173-174
Africans, 12-13, 15, 35, 37, 41, 43, 53, 72, 74-75, 81, 86, 147-148, 152, 158, 234-235, 281, 316
Afrikaner Bond, 72, 75
Alexander, Neville, 228, 248, 252-256, 289, 292, 332
ama-Kabasa, 294
amaGqunukhwebe, 45, 53, 267
amakholwa, 40
Amalinde, Battle of, 54, 268
amaMpondomise, 52
amaNtinde, 41, 44, 53, 267
amaqaba, 40
amaRharhabe, 52, 267
amaRhudulu, 52
ANC (see African National Congress)
ANC Youth League, 78, 186
Anderson, Benedict, 265
Andrew Smith Bursary, 101, 107
Anglican Church, 31, 218, 230
Anglo American Corporation, 136, 138-139, 314
Annual Youth Conference, 315
apartheid, 8, 16, 25-26, 94, 113, 119-120, 126, 129, 131-132, 137, 140, 151-152, 155-156, 158, 163-164, 168, 179, 190, 201-202, 215, 234, 239, 256, 262, 264, 266-267, 278, 281, 288-290, 296-297, 317, 323
Aplom, Lala, 315, 329
Appiah, Kwame Anthony, 285-286

Index

Arnold, Millard, 24, 78, 164, 272
Association for the Educational and Cultural Advancement of African People (ASSECA), 185
Attwell, David, 38-39, 70
Axe, War of the, 80
Azanian National Liberation Army (AZANLA), 246
Azanian People's Liberation Army (APLA), 107
Azanian People's Organisation (AZAPO), 266, 291-296, 322
Azanian Student Movement (AZASM), 293-294
Azanian Student Organisation (AZASO), 291-294

Badat, Saleem, 232-233, 241-242, 266
Baird, sir David, 50
Baloyi, Olaf, 109, 330
Bam, Fikile, 30, 114, 248, 252-254
Bambatha, 270
Bambatha Rebellion, 41
Bantu World, 71
Baqwa, Jeffrey, 109, 111
Bard College, 318

Bata, Thabisa, 314-315, 329
Bekwa, Larry, 101-102, 105-106
Bekwa, Ntombomzi, 101
Bekwa, Thozama, 101
Bentham, Jeremy, 275
Benyon, John, 107
Beresford, William, 50
Berlin, Isaiah, 273-274, 284
Bernal, Martin, 236, 297, 329
Bernstein, Rusty, 127
Bethelsdorp, 41, 44, 57, 59
Bhisholo, Nisopho, 227
Bhotomane, 53
Big Chief Syndrome, 299-310
Biko, Alice (MamCethe), 16-17, 22, 81, 88-89, 103-104, 204, 237
Biko, Bukelwa, 87, 89
Biko, Hlumelo, 205, 329
Biko, Khaya, 14-16, 78, 89, 92-97, 99, 105-108, 239, 330
Biko, Lerato, 205
Biko, Motlatsi, 205
Biko, Mzingaye, 23, 88-89
Biko, Nkosinathi, 205, 312-313, 329
Biko, Nobandile, 31, 89, 330
Biko, Ntsiki, 19, 190,
204-206, 208, 210-211, 226, 255, 301-302, 312, 315, 329
Biko, OB, 112
Biko, Samora, 329
Biko, Sipho, 89, 112
Biko, Stephen Bantu:
  Xhosa prophet, 11;
  response to modernity, 12, 14;
  expelled from Lovedale College, 15, 16;
  at St Francis College, 15;
  and Christianity, 16-17, 40;
  and NUSAS congress, 124-125, 129, 134;
  and SASO, 18;
  and BPC 18;
  personal relationships 19;
  trip to Cape Town, 20, 221, 249-250;
  death of, 8, 20, 23, 25-26, 199, 203, 205, 215, 225, 231-232, 242-265;
  and freedom songs, 22, 232;
  funeral of, 28-30;
  and Black Consciousness Movement, 23, 35, 39;
  at Lovedale College, 40, 103-110;
  and white liberalism, 62;

335

and study of history, 76;
lives with relatives in Cathcart, 89, 97;
death of father, 89;
and rugby, 93;
organises bursary for Mthobi Mangcu, 94;
at St Andrews, Primary School, 98;
at Charles Morgan Primary School, 98-100;
identified as leader, 99;
helps Major Sihunu with schoolwork, 99-101;
friendship with Larry Bekwa, 101-102, 105;
delivers valedictorian address at Forbes Grant Secondary School, 102;
prank played on Mantyoyi, 103;
runs away from Lovedale College, 107;
admitted to St Francis College, 108;
at St Francis College, 108-111;
and initiation, 110-111;
attends Durban Medical School 113-115;
elected to Student Representative Council, 117;
visits Robert Sobukwe, 118-119;
and NUSAS Conference at Rhodes University, 15, 123-125;
and NUSAS Conference at the University of the Witwatersrand, 134-137;
and Duncan Innes, 129-131, 133-134;
and NUSAS Conference in Eston, 139, 146;
and Paula Ensor, 139-141, 144;
and Paul Pretorius vs. Steve Biko XV rugby match, 143;
Geoff Budlender's thoughts on 146-148;
and UCM Conference, 152-154;
and Stutterheim Meeting of UCM 157-158, 160-162, 167;
and partnership with Barney Pityana, 178-180;
and takeover of UCM 167;
elected president of SASO, 168-170;
and African Theology, 173-174;
lecture on Black Consciousness, 177-179;
paper at Abe Bailey conference, 178-179, 184;
declines leadership position in BPC, 187;
excluded from University of Natal, 189;
works full time for Black Community Programmes 190;
banning order served on 190;
restricted to King William's Town, 190-191;
opposed to Frelimo Rallies 191, 299;
defends SASO/BPC trialists, 193-194;
and armed struggle, 196;
"On Death" essay, 202-203;
marriage to Ntsiki Mashalaba, 204-205, 207-208;
birth of Nkosinathi, 205;
birth and death, of Lerato, 205;
birth of Hlumelo, 205;
birth of Motlatsi, 205;
and Mamphela Ramphele, 205-206;
registered at UNISA, 213;

336

Index

and BPC, branch in Ginsberg, 214-217;
and Aelred Stubbs, 217-218;
and Ginsberg Education Fund, 224-225;
and life in Ginsberg, 237-238;
Theory of Action, 240-241;
desire for unity among, black liberation movements, 242-249;
and Mangosuthu Buthelezi, 244-245;
and Dick Clark, 249-250;
criticism of the United States, 250;
and police road block near King William's Town 256-258;
arrest of, 259-260;
inquest into death of, 261-264;
and quest for Higher Consciousness, 272-280;
and Nation Building, 280-287;
leadership qualities of, 301-303
Bisholo, Nozipho, 227
Bishop's College, 130
Black Community Programmes, 19, 31, 160, 188, 190, 205, 217, 219-220, 241, 252, 299, 317
Black Consciousness Movement (and concept), 5, 9, 11, 13, 16, 30-31, 37, 76, 107, 109, 138, 140, 172-173, 223, 237, 242, 246-247, 264, 286-287, 293, 296-297, 309, 318-319;
decline of, 287-289
Black Consciousness Movement of Azania, 246
Black Local Authorities, 288
Black Messiah, 174
Black People's Convention (BPC), 18, 31, 44, 176, 184, 186-194, 196-197, 199-200, 215, 217, 223, 243, 291-292, 296, 311
Black Students Society, 292
Black Theology, 39, 152, 172-174, 184, 292
Black Viewpoint, 316-317
Black Wednesday, 265
Boesak, Allan, 174, 292, 323
Bonaparte, Napoleon, 49
Border Council of Churches, 222
Botha, PW, 288
Bozzoli, Belinda, 235-239

BPC (see Black People's Convention)
Breidbach, 21
Brereton, Lieutenant-General, 54
British Colonial Rule, 49-63
British Kaffraria, 62, 78
Broederbond 135, 153
Brownlee (location), 85-92
Brownlee Mission, 83
Brownlee, Charles, 82
Brownlee, FH de J, 83
Brownlee, John, 81, 84
Budlender, Geoff, 146-147
Burns, James Mac-Gregor, 90, 183
Burnside, Janet, 67
Buthelezi, Gatsha (Mangosuthu), 185, 244-245, 316
Buthelezi, Sipho 187-188, 190

Cabral, Amilcar, 240-242, 305
Calata, Fort, 30
Calderwood, Henry, 61, 63
Calland, Richard, 304
Cape African Teachers Association, 235
Cape Legislative Assembly, 75
Cape Parliament, 74
Carlyle, Thomas, 300

337

Carneson, Fred, 127
Cathcart, George, 81
Catholic Students Association, 165
Cekisani, Moki, 246
Ceko, Siphiwo, 98
Centre for Policy Studies, 313, 329
Chabal, Patrick, 241-242, 305
Chalmers, John, 67, 69
Chalmers, William, 66
Charles Morgan Primary School, 98
Chikane, Frank, 292
Christian Institute 155-156
Christianity, 16, 39-41, 43, 54, 57-58, 68, 156, 174-175, 274
Christie, Renfrew, 138, 330
Cindi, Zithulele, 193
Cirha, 52, 66
Ciskei, 29, 52, 178, 219, 234
Clark, Dick, 249-250
Clinton Democracy Initiative, 315
Collins, Colin, 18, 153-157, 171-172
Coloureds, 13, 15, 21, 44, 49, 152, 174, 235, 281, 288
commando system, 44, 47
Community of the Resurrection, 13, 89, 217

Cone, James, 173
Congregational Church, 152, 177
Congress of Democrats, 117
Congress of South African Trade Unions (COSATU), 287, 295
Constitutional Court, 117, 308-309
Cooper, Saths, 18, 187-188, 190-193, 199, 265, 292-293, 330
Cornell University, 297
Costa, Ken, 144-145
Cottesloe Conference, 155
Cradock Four, 30
Crenshaw, Kimberlé, 178
Crewe, CP, 75
Cronin, Jeremy, 132
Crotz, Ronnie, 252
Cubans, 32, 229, 231
Curry, David, 146
Curtis, Jack, 136
Curtis, Jeanette, 137
Curtis, Neville, 136-138, 142, 144-145, 154, 330

D'Urban, Benjamin, 79-80, 269
Daily Dispatch, 16, 30, 190
Dalai Lama, 310
Dale College, 153
Dandala, Mvume, 315
Dange, 52
Davis, John, 152

De Wet, Johannes Marthinus, 163
Degenaar, Johannes, 132
Democratic Alliance, 309
Dimbaza, 218, 233
Direko, Winkie, 172
Dladla, Nhlanganiso, 315
Dlamini, A, 188
Dolomba, Jack, 94
Donaldson Community Centre, 186
Driver, Jonty, 136
du Bois, WEB, 71, 331
Dube, John, 38, 41, 71, 166
Duna, Thembile, 213, 294
Durban Medical School, 113-115
Durkheim, Emile, 16
Dutch East India Company, 45, 49
Dutch Reformed Church, 151
Dwane, Sigqibo, 226
Dwanya, Daniel, 75
Dwesi, Feya, 162
Dyani, Malcolm, 97

Eastern Cape, history of, 43
Enlightenment, 273-275
Ensor, Paula, 17, 138, 139-142, 144
Espey, Don, 113, 135
European modernity, 12, 14-15, 33-41, 241
Extension of University

Index

Education Act (1959), 116
Eye of the Needle, The, 132

Fanon, Frantz, 14, 15, 21, 34-36, 38, 43, 74, 182, 200, 232, 236, 240, 283-287
Federal Seminary, 13, 217, 224, 303
Forbes Grant Secondary School 87-88, 93-95, 97, 100-102, 108, 213, 244, 294
Ford Foundation, 313, 315, 329
Fort Cox Agricultural College, 88
Fort Hare College, 39
Fourie, GA, 256
Fred Hollows Foundation, 315
free burghers, 45-47
Freedom Charter, 95
freedom songs, 26-28, 230
Freire, Paulo, 15, 285
Frere Hospital, 230
Friedman, Steven, 313
Frontier Wars, 34, 42, 50, 58, 63, 66, 79, 269

Garvey, Marcus, 71
Gates, Henry Louis, 29, 331
Gawe, James, 219
Gcabashe, Thulani, 114

Gcaleka 52-53, 267
Gcilishe, Gordon, 85
Gcilishe, Nomalungelo, 225
Gcweni, Bhabha 98, 102, 330
George, Mluleki, 94
Gerhart, Gail, 37, 187
Getty's Place, 228-229
Gibson, Nigel, 21, 182, 200-201, 242
Ginsberg (location), 14-15, 18-19, 21, 25-26, 28, 32, 34, 78, 79-85, 91-92, 95-96, 99, 103-104, 106-107, 161, 190, 203-205, 212-215, 217-218, 223, 226-231, 235, 237-238, 244, 247-248, 250, 291, 294-295, 301, 311, 313-315, 320, 329, 333
Ginsberg Bursary Fund, 104
Ginsberg Civic Association, 315
Ginsberg Crèche, 218, 227
Ginsberg Education Fund, 218, 224-225
Ginsberg Native Advisory Board, 85
Ginsberg Social History Project, 314-315
Ginsberg Village Women's Unity Club, 88
Ginsberg Youth Council, 314, 329

Ginsberg, Franz, 82
Ginwala Commission of Enquiry, 308
Goniwe, Matthew, 30
Goosen, Piet, 264
Gqabi, Joe 248
Gqaliwe, Baldwin, 85, 92
Gqola, Pumla, 140
Grahamstown, Battle of, 57, 79
Great House, 51, 52, 66, 267
Grey Hospital, 73, 81, 89, 94
Grey, George, 81
Gulwa, Zinzo, 98, 330
Gumbi, Mojanku, 304
Gupta family, 308
Gushman, Richard, 85, 86
Gwala, Harry, 244
Gwali, 52

Hani, Chris 38, 107, 323
Hathaway, Donny, 230
Hattingh, Warrant Officer, 260
Haya, Lulama, 97
Head of Lion (rugby team), 93-94
Healdtown, 38
Healdtown College, 76, 86, 108
Heifetz, Ronald, 188, 303-304
Hendrickse, Allan, 146
Hersch, Colin, 261
Hintsa, 267-271, 323

339

Hirson, Baruch, 232
Hitchens, Christopher, 19-20, 40
Hleke, 52
Hodgson, Jack, 127
Hofmeyr, GS, 81
Hofmeyr, JH, 72
Hughes, H Stuart, 275
Hurley, Denis, 151

Ibrahim, Abdullah, 319
Imbongi Yesozwe Jikelele, 75
imiDange, 267
Imvo Zabantsundu, 72, 75
Indians 13, 15, 43, 49, 152, 174, 235, 281, 288
Industrial Revolution, 275
Initiation, 111-112
Inkatha Freedom Party, 289
Inkatha Movement, 41
Innes, Duncan, 129-133, 136, 139, 145, 330
Interdenominational African Ministers' Association of South Africa (IDAMASA), 184
Irish, Deon 144-145
Isigidimi SamaXhosa, 67
Issel, Johnny, 249, 252
Ityala Lamawele, 75
iXhanti Choral Society, 86

izibonda, 85-86
Izwi Labantu, 74-75, 77

Jabavu, Don Davidson Tengu, 37, 71
Jabavu, John Tengu, 71-74, 75, 233-234
Jabavu, Noni, 40
Jack, Andile Big Joe, 314-315
Jack, Doctor Pringle, 91, 92, 106, 314
Jackson, Jesse, 321
Jaffer, Zubeida, 11
James, Ntombomhlaba, 223
Janssens, Jan Willem, 50
Jeppe Boys High School, 136-137
Jojozi family, 101
Jones, Peter 31-32, 209, 216, 252-254, 256, 258-260, 262, 293, 330
Jooste, Steve, 145
Jordan, AC, 55-56, 76-77, 139
Jose, Eric, 110
Judaism, 274
Jwara, 52

ka Shezi, Mthuli, 188-189, 199
Kabemba, Claude, 313
kaDinizulu, Solomon, 41
Kajee Hall, Durban, 198
Kane-Berman, John, 125-128, 137-138, 330

Kane-Berman, Louis, 127
Kant, Emmanuel, 27
Kaplinsky, Raphael, 131
kaSeme, Pixley, 38, 41
Kat River settlement, 45
Kathrada, Ahmed, 119
kaTyamzashe, Benjamin (B ka-T), 28-29
Kay, Stephen, 268
Keiskammahoek, 66, 88
Keke, Monde, 225
Keke, Sthethi, 231, 330
Keke, Sybree, 315
Kennedy, Edward, 295-296
Kennedy, Robert, 130
Kente, Gibson, 230
Kentridge, Sydney 262
Keyisi, Ndoda, 294
Kgware, Manana, 169, 171
Kgware, William, 186
Kgware, Winnifred, 186, 188
Khama, Seretse, 87
Khawuta, 267
Khoapa, Ben, 186, 194, 257, 316, 330
Khoi-Khoi, 11-14, 35, 43, 45-47, 49, 60, 267, 270, 323
Khoisan, 12, 43-45, 47, 51, 59-61, 63-64, 341
Kila, Sipho, 112
Kimbo, Bra, 87
King Edward Hospital, 204

340

Index

King William's Town, 19, 20, 28, 68, 73, 79-82, 86, 88=98, 92, 101, 106, 108, 153, 157, 190, 199, 204-205, 212, 217-219, 227, 231, 238, 246, 250-252, 254, 256, 258-260, 316, 333
King, Mel 315
Klaas, Thami, 216
Klaaste, Aggrey, 290-291
Kleinschmidt, Horst, 134-135, 137, 139, 144, 330
Kobe, 53
Kobus, Kwezi, 291-292
Koka, Drake, 188
Koranta Ea Becoana, 73
Kruger, Jimmy, 24, 262
Krune, Tyumphrie, 94

La Grange, Zelda, 321-322
La Guma, Alex, 320
Labour Party, 146
Laclau, Ernesto, 306
Laing, James, 51
Land Claims Court, 30, 117
Landingwe, Danile, 251
Land Act (1913), 72-73
Landsberg, Chris, 313
Lang, Ivor, 261
Langa, 96
Lapinsky, Sheila, 133, 138, 139, 144, 330
Laurence, Patrick, 137
Leballo, Potlako, 120, 166

Lefebvre, Georges, 49-50
Lefebvre, Henri, 132
Lefume, Lunga, 213, 229, 294, 330
Lefume, Zanemvula, 94
Legal Resources Centre, 146
Legassick, Martin, 45, 59, 61-64, 136, 145
Lehtonen, Risto, 150
Leightonville, 21, 26, 212
Lekota, Patrick (Terror), 193, 293, 295
Lembede, Anton, 78
Lengane, Kabelo, 293-294
Levine, Roger, 12, 14, 41-42, 44-45, 50, 61, 66, 79, 83
Liberal Party, 127
Lily White (rugby club), 89
Lipset, Seymour Martin, 151
Lodge, Tom, 95-96, 121
London Missionary Society, 60, 80
Lovedale College, 15, 16, 38-39, 41, 66, 75, 78, 87, 101, 104, 105-108
Lumnkwana, Ace, 294

M-Afrika, Andile, 295
Maaba, Brown, 314, 329
Mabandla, Lindelwe, 184, 217
Mabasa, Lybon, 291, 293, 296

MacCrone, Ian, 126-128
Machaka, PM, 169
Machel, Graça, 322
Machel, Samora, 205
MacKay, Shaun, 313
Maclean, Sindisile, 94, 225
Macqueen, Ian, 38-39, 151
Mafeje, Archie, 114, 131-132, 166
Mafumadi, Sydney, 293
Mafuna, Bokwe, 19, 190, 207-208, 302
Magaziner, Daniel, 34-35, 44, 155-156, 174, 199-200
Magida, Ray, 216
Maharaj, Mac, 256-257, 289
Mahlangu, Solomon, 270
Mahomed, Ishmail, 252
Makanda, Welsh, 114
Makhubalo, Sam, 88
Makwedini, Sipho, 98
MamCethe (see Biko, Alice)
Mandela, Nelson, 7, 9, 21, 38, 76-78, 87, 116, 119, 194, 215, 225, 250, 257, 277-278, 280, 292, 295, 297-298, 303-304, 319-323
Mandela, Winnie, 248, 292
Maneli, PV, 94
Mangcu, George Mayile, 86-88, 213

341

Mangcu, Mthetho, 87
Mangcu, Mthobi, 94, 224-225
Mangcu, Mzwandile, 87, 204-205, 224, 330
Mangcu, Pumeza, 224, 330
Mangcu, Ranji, 317
Mangcu, Thando, 317
Mangena, Mosibudi, 188, 246, 296
Manthatha, Tom, 215
Mantyoyi, 103
Manyelo, Zola, 98
Mapikela, Thomas, 75
Maqhina, Reverend, 294
Maqoma 42, 44-45, 51, 62-64, 66, 81, 268-270
Marais, Dr, 231
Margo, Cecil, 128
Margo, Robin, 125
Mariannhill, 15, 104, 108, 112
Marshall, Margaret, 124-125, 137
Mashalaba, Nontsikelelo (Ntsiki), 19, 204-206, 208, 210-211, 226, 255, 301, 305, 312, 315, 329
Mashalaba, Vuyelwa, 115, 117, 169, 185, 204
Mashinini, Tsietsi, 28, 164, 265
Masilela, Ntongela, 15, 70-71, 320
Masizakhe, 86-87, 104
Massachusetts Institute of Technology, 315, 333

Matanzima, Kaizer, 245
Matanzima, Mthetho, 162
Mathabatha, Legau, 164
Mathanda, Dorrington, 109
Matsepe-Casaburri, Ivy, 109
Matsipa, Joel, 192
Mattera, Don, 164
Mayatula, A, 188
Mazibuko, Fanyana, 164
Mazibuko, Sizo, 109-110
Mbalu, 52
Mbembe, Achille, 305
Mbeki, Epainette, 140
Mbeki, Govan, 27, 119, 139, 249
Mbeki, Michael, 93
Mbeki, Moeletsi, 11, 289
Mbeki, Thabo, 94, 101, 107, 226, 246, 250, 296, 304-308
Mbhele, Boardman, 109
Mbilini, Fumbathile, 231, 330
Mbilini, Kholeka, 229
Mbilini, Mzwandile, 31-32, 216
Mbilini shebeen, 32, 229
Mbilini, Shkweyi, 32
Mbiti, John, 173-174
Mboni, Xolela, 79, 98-99
Mbuli, Pam, 321
McNamee, Anne, 94
McNamee, Margaret, 94
McNamee, Michael, 94
McNamee, Peter, 94

Mda, AP, 78
Mda, Zakes, 80, 318
Mdalidiphu, 57
Mdange, 52
Mdluli, Richard, 309
Medupe Writers Association, 164
Methodist Church, 152
Mgubelo, Boy, 99
Mhlawuli, Sicelo, 30
Mini, Vuyisile, 27
missionaries, 12, 41, 45, 55-56, 58-63, 84
Mjamba, Harry, 87-88, 94-95, 97, 101
Mkhabela, Ishmael, 291, 313-314
Mkhencele, Toyo, 89
Mkhonto, Sparrow, 30
Mkhwanazi, Nhlanhla, 309
Mlawu, 53
Mlinda, Fikile, 99, 213-217, 221, 311, 330
Mlonyeni, Siphetho, 225
Mmabane, Dick, 206
Mneno, Busi, 315
Mngxitama, Andile, 182
Mnqayi, 84
Moerane, MT, 185-187
Moffat, Robert, 61
Mogoba, Stanley, 97, 224
Mohapi, Mapetla, 31, 190, 193, 216, 224, 226, 246-247
Mohapi, Nohle, 178, 220
Mokoape, Aubrey Ncaupe, 115-116, 118,

Index

120-123, 125-126, 184, 191, 193, 239, 330
Mokoape, Keith, 189-190, 198, 239
Mokoditoa, Chris, 166-167, 188, 330
Mokoena, Aubrey, 293
Molala, Nkosi, 296
Moletsane, Nontobeko, 220
Moletsane, Sidney, 220
Moloto, Justice,117, 157, 162-163, 165-167, 170-171
Monaheng, Damsie, 98, 330
Moodley, Samantha, 134
Moodley, Strini, 128, 134, 193, 265, 330
Moore, Basil, 18, 153, 157, 162, 173
More, Percy, 182
Moreilane, Moreilane, 291
Morgan, Charles, 86
Morobe, Murphy, 164, 293
Morphet, Tony, 113
Morrison Isaacson High School, 163
Morrow, Sean, 314, 329
Moseneke, Dikgang, 212
Moseneke, Tiego, 291, 293
Mosime, Kenny, 294
Moss, Ndikho, 98
Moss, Nkosomzi, 94
Mostert, Noel, 34, 42-43, 49, 54, 56-57, 80, 212, 268-271
Mothopeng, Zephania, 247
Motlana, Nthatho, 30
Motlanthe, Kgalema, 280, 306
Mphahlele, Es'kia, 320
Mpumlwana, Malusi, 31, 116, 183, 191-193, 216, 223, 243, 246-247, 263, 315
Mpumlwana, Thoko, 31, 226
Mpungutyane, 92
Mpupha, Esther, 223
Mpupha, Nolulamile, 223
Mqhayi, SEK, 52-55, 75-77, 80, 320
Msauli, Dubs, 220
Masilela, Ntongela, 15, 70, 320
Msumza, Luyanda, 82
Mthethwa, Nathi, 309
Mthintso, Thenjiwe, 31, 216
Mtshizana, Linda, 291-292
Mtshotshisa, Zolani, 32, 330
Mugabe, Robert, 88
Murray, Bruce, 115
Mvovo, Mxolisi, 31
Mvovo, Nobandile, 31
Mxenge, Griffiths, 30, 94-95, 244
Mxenge, Victoria, 30, 94, 244
Myeza, Muntu, 18, 191-193, 265, 293

Naidoo, DV, 167
Nano, Themba, 98
National Catholic Student Federation, 153, 165
National Council of Trade unions (NACTY), 322
National Forum, 292
National Party, 114, 116, 127, 136-137, 163, 180, 243
National Planning Commission, 298
National Prosecuting Authority, 308
National Union of South African Students (NUSAS), 17, 113, 117-118, 122-130, 132-133-148, 152, 154-155, 161, 165, 168-170, 172-173, 177, 180, 292, 330
Native Educational Association, 234
Native Hospital, 81
Native Reserves Act (1902), 81
Native Vigilance Association, 234
Naudé, Beyers, 155
Ndamse, CMC, 316
Ndebele, Njabulo,15, 262, 271-272, 316-317, 330

343

Ndlambe, 14, 35, 51, 53-54, 56-57, 70, 267-268
Ndletyana, Mcebisi, 66, 312, 330-331
Ndwalaza, Sigqobo, 91, 93
Nefholovhodwe, Pandelani, 189, 131, 265
Negritude movement, 276
Neku, My-Boy, 98
Nelson Mandela Foundation, 7, 277, 321
Nengwekhulu, Harry, 18, 186, 189-190, 198, 245, 330
Ngcelwane, Mzwandile, 102, 105
Ngcobo, Sandile, 308
Ngele, Mfundo, 315, 329
Ngesi, Mrs, 86, 87
Ngesi, Peter, 85, 88
Ngoloyi, Mncedi, 295, 316, 329
Ngonyama, Smuts, 94
Ngqika, 14, 35, 51, 53, 54, 57, 60, 64, 70, 266-268
Ngqongqo, SJ, 234
Ngubane, Ben, 109, 115-116, 132-133, 135, 143
Njwaxa Home Industries, 218, 222
Nkomo, Nkwendkwe, 193
Nkomo, William 186
Nkosi Sikelel' iAfrika, 129

Nkosi, Lewis, 36, 276
Nkosiyamntu, 51
Nofenisi, 222-223, 230
Nolutshungu, Sam, 107, 126, 191, 232
Nolutshungu, Winnifred, 87
Nompumezo, 24
Nomzamo, 316
Nondalana, Nonezile, 220, 330
Nongqause, 80, 81
Nqakula, Charles, 101, 226
Ntantala, Phyllis, 139-140
Ntenteni, Lindani, 314-315, 329
Ntenteni, Vusumzi, 295
Ntinde, 52
Ntloko, Mbulelo, 162
Ntshongwana, Liston, 94
Ntsikana, 14, 35, 43, 51, 54-58, 64-66, 70
Ntwasa, Stanley, 119, 207, 217, 246
NUSAS (see National Union of South African Students)
Nxele, 14, 35, 43, 51, 54, 56-58, 70, 268
Nyakathi, Linda, 295
Nyakathi, Mveleli, 94
Nyathi, Forbes, 23
Nyengane (see Van der Kemp, Johannes)
Nyerere, Julius, 15, 232, 298

O'Meara, Dan, 113-114
Oberlin College, 71
Odendaal, André, 72, 75
Ohio State University, 224
Okigbo, Christopher, 20, 318
Old Boys Association of St Peter's Seminary, 185
Omar, M, 135
Oosthuizen, Alf, 258-259
Orkin, Mark, 137
Orlando High School, 120

Paarl Boys High School, 134
Palweni, Chippy, 115
Pan Africanist Congress (PAC), 12, 14, 15, 58, 78, 94-97, 105, 107, 113-114, 117-118, 142, 166, 186, 196, 222, 224, 239, 243-244, 246-247, 249, 288, 296
Parliamentary Voters Registration Act, 72
Paterson, Mr (Oom Pat), 105-106
Pather, S, 135
Peddie, 101, 107
Peelton Missionary School, 234
Peires, Jeff, 13, 27, 51, 57, 58, 80, 270
Penn, Nigel, 46-48

Index

Peteni, Lester, 163, 226
Peteni, Nomsa, 92
Peterson, Bheki, 37-38
Pfanner, Francis, 109
Phalo, 52
Philip, John, 60-62
Pikoli, Vusi, 308
Piliso, Vuyisani, 225
Pityana, Barney, 13, 15, 17, 26-28, 39, 107-108, 116, 146, 152-153, 159-163, 178, 181-185, 187, 190, 207-208, 210-211, 217, 239, 250, 257, 263, 287, 299-300
Pityana, Dimza, 190
Plaatje, Sol, 73-74, 77
Popham, Sir Home, 50
POQO, 107, 120
Fort Glamorgan jail, 107
Presbyterian Church, 152
Pretorius, Paul, 138-139, 143-146, 330
Progressive Party, 75, 136
Protection of State Information Bill, 309
Public Service Commission, 308
Pule, Retsi, 103

Qaba, Sibongile, 315
Qaba, Sidney, 101
Qambatha, Thamsanqa, 216
Queen Adelaide, Province of, 80

Rachidi, Hlaku, 31, 190, 330
Rachidi, Kenny, 31, 199
Radical Students Society, 131
Ramaphosa, Cyril, 322
Ramokgopa, Rams, 162, 251, 258
Ramphele, Mamphela, 19, 31, 115-116, 134, 177, 205-206, 213, 220-221, 263, 330
Read, James, (Ngcolongolo), 41, 59, 61-62
Reconstruction and Development Programme, 297
Red People, 40
Rharhabe, 52-53, 64, 268-269
Rhodes University, 17, 123, 125, 127, 153, 161
Rhodes, Cecil John, 72, 75
Right Hand House, 51-52
Rivonia Trial, 18, 194
Robben Island, 30, 57, 110, 116, 118, 213, 226, 248, 265, 268, 280, 291-293, 295, 321
Rockefeller Foundation, 312-313, 333
Roman Catholic Church, 152
Roman law, 214, 274
Romantic movement, 275-276
Ross, Johan Jurgens, 163

Rubusana, Walter Benjamin, 65, 74-75, 77, 233-235, 238
rugby, 89, 91, 93, 94, 97, 130, 143
Russell, David, 16, 30, 209, 215, 330

San, 11-14, 35, 43-44, 46-49, 61, 267, 323
Sandel, Michael, 287
Sandile, 63-64, 269
Sangotsha, Pumla, 220
SASO (see South African Students Organisation)
Schlebusch Commission, 146
Schoon, Katryn, 137
Schoon, Marius, 137
Schornville, 21
Schrire, Robert, 124, 135, 330
Sea Lions (rugby club), 93
Seathlolo, Khotso, 265
Sebe, Lennox, 29
Sedibe, Kaborane, 193
Taylor, Robert Selby, 152
Sharpeville, 26, 95, 96, 121, 142, 193, 195, 323
Shubane, Khehla, 293, 313
Sibisi, Charles, 115-116
Sibisi, Sibusiso, 109
Siebert, Daniel, 260

Sihunu, Major, 99-100, 213, 294
Simelane, Menzi, 308
Simons, Jack, 133
Simons, Ray, 131
Sisulu, Albertina, 140, 292
Sisulu, Walter, 78, 140
Skhosana, Mahlomola, 321-322
Skweyiya, Louis, 117
Skweyiya, Mzukisi, 225
Skweyiya, Zola, 108
Slovo, Joe, 127
Smith, Ian, 111
Smith, Harry, 79, 270
Sosebenza Sonke, 315
Sobukwe, Dinilesizwe, 118
Sobukwe, Robert, 19, 38, 58, 78, 88, 97, 118-120, 206-207, 209-210, 246-247, 250, 323
Sobukwe, Victoria, 118
Socialist Party of Azania, 296
Soga, Allan Kirkland, 74, 75
Soga, Tiyo, 26, 33, 41-43, 45, 63-71, 77, 238
Sogo, Jotelo, 41, 64, 65
Soka, Chris, 227
Solempilo, 221
Solombela, ACS, 216, 220
Somerset, Lord Charles, 53-54, 60
South Africa Act (1910), 75

South African Communist Party (SACP), 117, 132
South African Council of Churches (SACC), 155
South African Council on Sport, 292
South African Institute of Race Relations (SAIRR), 37, 154, 313
South African National Convention (SANC), 75
South African Native National Congress (SANNC), 71, 73, 75
South African National Student Press Association (SANSPA), 138
South African Students Organisation (SASO), 13, 17-18, 85, 109, 113, 116, 119, 122, 128, 133, 135, 138-145, 157, 160, 162, 165, 167, 169-172, 176-177, 184-187, 189, 193-194, 197, 200, 233, 239, 292, 299, 301
South West Africa National Union (SWANU), 30
South West Africa People's Organisation (SWAPO), 30
Southey, George, 270
Sprack, John, 129, 133
Springbok Legion, 127

Squire, Smith and Laurie, 108
St Andrew's Church, 215
St Andrew's Primary School, 98
St Francis College, 15-16, 104-105, 108-110, 112
St John's College 127, 224
St Peter's College, 13, 153, 303
St Peter's Seminary, 169, 185
Staffrider, 231
Star of Hope (rugby team), 93-94, 97, 106
Stem, Die, 129
Steve Biko Foundation, 7, 313, 315, 329, 333
Steve Biko Garden of Remembrance, 30
Steve Biko Memorial Heritage Centre, 312
Steve Biko Memorial Lecture, 28, 262, 271, 316-317, 322-323
Stopforth, Paul, 263, 312
Stubbs, Aelred, 13, 16-17, 19-20, 89-90, 160-161, 178, 194, 207-213, 215, 217, 272, 278, 299-301, 303, 306, 311
Student Christian Association (SCA), 151
Student Representative Council, 117, 162-163, 292

Study Project on Christianity in Apartheid Society (Spro-Cas), 156
Supreme Court of Appeal, 308-309
Suzman, Helen, 114
SWANU (see South West African People's National Union)
SWAPO (see South West African People's Organisation)

Tabane, Lorrain, 205
Tambo, Oliver, 8, 78, 88, 245, 256-257, 266, 289
Teachers League of South Africa, 235
Tembeni, Master, 162
Temperance Boarding House, 88
Terrorism Act, 193, 195
Thema, RV Selope, 71
Timol, Ahmed, 198
Tiro, Abraham Onkgopotso, 163-164
Tloubatla, Sam, 291
Transvaal Teachers Association, 235
trekboere 46-49, 52
Tricameral Parliament, 288
Trumbull, Howard, 177
Truth and Reconciliation Commission, 256-258, 264
Tshatshu, Dyani, 41-42, 50, 53, 79-80

Tshatshu, Kote, 41
Tshawe, 51-52, 231
Tshiwo, 52
Tshwete, Steve, 88, 93, 95
Tsolo, 82, 85-87, 91-93, 228
tsotsis, 91-92, 295
Tucker, Benjamin, 261
Turner, Rick, 132
Tuskegee Institute, 71
Tutu, Desmond, 30, 174, 282, 296, 310
Twain, Mark, 19
Tyamzashe, B ka T, 28-29, 219
Tyamzashe, James, 219
Tyamzashe, Mthobi, 93
Tyamzashe, Nganga, 219
Tyamzashe, Wonga, 219

UCM (see University Christian Movement)
uDon Jadu, 75
ukwaluka, 111
Umkhonto we Sizwe, 127
Umteteli wa Bantu, 75
Union Seminary, 174
Uniondale, 66
United Democratic Front (UDF), 140, 266, 287, 291-295
United Party, 136
Unity Movement, 12, 78, 226, 244, 247-248
University Academic Freedom Award, 132

University Christian Movement (UCM), 18, 152-158, 160, 162, 165, 167, 170-173
Stutterheim, meeting, 150, 157, 160
University of Natal meeting, 167-171
University Exchange Fund, 257
University of Cape Town, 114, 116, 130, 132-135, 144, 166, 178, 248, 317-318, 322, 331, 333
University of Durban-Westville, 192
University of Fort Hare, 27, 37, 72, 86-87, 116, 153, 162, 224, 314
University of Natal, 17, 19, 113-118, 121, 128, 134, 139, 167, 169-171, 188-189, 206, 294
University of Natal Non-European Section, 113, 115, 169, 170
University of South Africa, 88, 169, 190, 213-214, 305
University of Stellenbosch, 132, 179
University of the North, 116-117, 134, 162-163, 169, 293
University of the Western Cape, 179, 314
University of the Witwatersrand, 114, 115,

125-128, 130, 134, 136-138, 140-141, 144, 153, 246, 291-293
University of Zululand, 117, 169, 191

Van der Horst, Frank, 292
Van der Kemp, Johannes (Nyengane), 41, 50, 55-56, 59, 60-61
Van der Stel, Simon, 46
Versfeld, Martin, 132
Verwoerd, Hendrik, 113, 151
Victoria Stadium, 28-29, 219
Vilakazi, BW, 109
Viva Frelimo Rallies, 18, 191
von Holdt, Karl, 34
Vorster, BJ, 113-114, 119, 138, 197

wa Thiong'o, Ngugi, 28, 276, 312, 320
War Veterans' Torch Commandos, 126
Washington, Booker T, 71

Wauchope, George, 294
Weber, Max, 303, 307
Wellington, Dr, 76-77
Welsh High School, 93
West, Cornel, 35, 201
Westcott, Nicki, 248
Williams, Donovan, 41, 45, 64, 70
Williams, Raymond, 201
Williamson, Craig, 137, 256
Wilson, Frances, 226, 248
Wits Student, 138
Woods, Donald, 21, 30, 212, 243, 303
World, The, 183
World Catholic Student Federation, 153
World Council of Churches, 151, 155
World Student Christian Federation (WSCF), 150-151, 153

Xaphe, Mncedisi, 223
Xhosa, 11, 12, 60, 61, 62, 63, 64, 267-270;
click consonants, 12-13;
resistance to British colonial rule, 49-59
Xoxo, 42
Xundu, Mcebisi, 228

Yengo, Beth, 230-231
Yengo, Sonwabo, 99, 229-231, 260, 311
Young Women's Christian Association (YCWA), 88
Young, Andrew, 250

Zanempilo Health Clinic, 19, 31, 178, 205, 218-221, 230, 251, 258
Zani, Thami, 31, 216
Zaula Street, 89, 91, 93, 97, 99, 101, 229
Zaula, Wycliffe, 85
Zingisa, 226
Zinyoka village, 219-220
Zuma, Jacob, 100, 131, 226, 257, 306-310
Zwelitsha (township), 25, 92
Zwelitsha Community Hall, 92